SOCIAL PSYCHOLOGY

Rob McIlveen and Richard Gross

Hodder & Stoughton

A MEMBER OF THE HODDER HEADLINE GROUP

DEDICATION

To the players, manager and assistant manager of Grimsby Town Football Club. William McIlveen would like to give a big hug to Kevin Donovan and Aidan Davison.   R.M.

To all victims of prejudice and discrimination, hatred and intolerance, and other forms of inhumanity.   R.G.

ACKNOWLEDGEMENTS

Many thanks to Tim Gregson-Williams and Marie Jones at Hodder and Stoughton for their (usual) patience, help and guidance. Marie, let's hope this is the first of many!

Orders: please contact Bookpoint Ltd, 39 Milton Park, Abingdon, Oxon OX14 4TD. Telephone: (44) 01235 400414, Fax: (44) 01235 400454. Lines are open from 9.00–6.00, Monday to Saturday, with a 24 hour message answering service. Email address: orders@bookpoint.co.uk

British Library Cataloguing in Publication Data
A catalogue record for this title is available from The British Library

ISBN 0 340 69125 5

First published 1998
Impression number   10   9   8   7   6   5   4   3   2   1
Year   2004   2003   2002   2001   2000   1999   1998

Typeset by Wearset, Boldon, Tyne and Wear.
Printed in Great Britain for Hodder & Stoughton Educational, a division of Hodder Headline Plc, 338 Euston Road, London NW1 3BH by Redwood Books, Trowbridge, Wilts.

ii

CONTENTS

Part 3: Social Influence

Part 4: Pro- and anti-social behaviour

Contents

PREFACE

Our aim in this book is to provide an introduction to the area of social psychology. In order to do this, we have divided the book into four parts. The first, *Social Cognition*, comprises four chapters. In Chapter 1, we look at theories of attribution and biases in the attribution process. In Chapter 2, we discuss social and cultural influences on perception, namely stereotypes and social representations. Chapter 3 considers theories of prejudice and discrimination, whilst Chapter 4 examines attempts at their reduction.

Part 2, *Social Relationships*, comprises three chapters. Chapter 5 is devoted to theory and research relating to the formation of adult relationships, whilst Chapters 6 and 7 discuss their maintenance and dissolution respectively.

The third part of the book, *Social Influence*, consists of four chapters. Chapter 8 discusses conformity, Chapter 9 obedience, and Chapter 10 leadership. Chapter 11 is concerned with collective behaviour.

Part 4, *Pro- and Anti-Social Behaviour*, comprises three chapters. Chapter 12 looks at altruism and bystander behaviour. Chapter 13 discusses the causes, reduction and control of aggressive behaviour, and Chapter 14 considers the media as influences on both pro- and anti-social behaviour.

We believe that this book covers the major aspects of social psychology as it would be taught on most courses, including A level and undergraduate courses. Whilst the sequence of chapters and much of the content is based on the revised AEB A level syllabus, the general issues and major theories that are discussed represent the core of this important area of psychology. For the purposes of revision, we have included detailed summaries of the material that is presented in each chapter. Although we have not included a separate glossary, the *Index* contains page numbers in **bold** which refer to definitions and main explanations of particular concepts for easy reference.

PART 1
Social Cognition

THEORIES OF ATTRIBUTION AND BIASES IN THE ATTRIBUTION PROCESS

Introduction and overview

A fundamental aspect of social behaviour concerns how we arrive at explanations for people's behaviour in social situations. *Attribution theory* deals with the general principles that govern how we select and use information to arrive at *causal explanations* for behaviour in a *wide variety of situations* (or domains). *Theories of attribution* draw on the principles of attribution theory and make predictions about how people respond in *particular situations* (or *life domains*: Fiske and Taylor, 1991).

Rather than being a single body of ideas and research, attribution theory is actually a collection of diverse theoretical and empirical contributions that share several common concerns. According to Fiske and Taylor (1991), six different theoretical traditions form the backbone of attribution theory. These are: (1) Heider's (1958) *commonsense psychology*, (2) Jones and Davis's (1965) *correspondent inference theory*, (3) Kelley's (1967, 1972, 1983) *covariation and configuration models*, (4) Schachter's (1964) *cognitive labelling theory*, (5) Bem's (1967, 1972) *self-perception theory*, and (6) Weiner's (1986, 1992) *motivational theory of attribution*.

Our first aim in this chapter is to critically consider some of these theories and models of attribution. Limitations of space prevent us from considering all in

detail, so we will confine ourselves to examining the contribution to this area made by Heider and the theories and models advanced by Jones and Davis, and Kelley. As we will see, these theories and models view people as being logical and systematic when they explain behaviour. In practice, however, people tend to make attributions quickly, use much less information than the theories and models suggest, and show clear tendencies to offer certain sorts of explanations for particular behaviours (Hewstone and Fincham, 1996). Our second aim in this chapter is to examine some of the *biases* that occur in the attribution process and consider why they occur.

Fritz Heider and 'commonsense' psychology

In his 1958 book *The Psychology of Interpersonal Relations*, Heider argued that the starting point for studying how we understand our social world is the 'ordinary' person. Heider wanted to know the answer to questions like 'How do people usually think about and infer meaning from what goes on around them?' and 'How do they make sense of their own and other people's behaviour?' These questions relate to what he called *commonsense* psychology. In Heider's view, the 'ordinary' person is a *naive scientist* who links observable behaviour to unobservable *causes*, and it is these causes (rather than behaviour itself) that provide the meaning of what people do.

According to Bennett (1993), what interested Heider was the fact that within our culture all of us share certain basic assumptions about behaviour, and that these are an element of the belief system which forms part of the culture as a whole and distinguishes one culture from another. As Bennett has observed:

> 'it is important that we *do* subscribe to a common psychology, since doing this provides an orienting context in which we can understand, and be understood by, others. Imagine a world in which your version of everyday psychology was fundamentally at odds with that of your friends – without a shared 'code' for making sense of behaviour, social life would hardly be possible.'

Heider pointed out that, in our culture at least, commonsense psychology does not involve the belief that internal and unobservable factors are the only causes of behaviour. As well as explaining people's behaviour in terms of *personal* (or *dispositional/internal*) *factors* (such as ability or effort), we also use *situational* (or *environmental/external*) *factors* (such as circumstances or luck) to explain why a behaviour occurred. In Heider's view, when we observe somebody's behaviour we are inclined to attribute its cause to one or other of these two general sources.

Although Heider did not formulate his own theory of attribution, he did inspire other psychologists to follow up his original ideas. As well as the insight relating to personal and situational factors as causes of behaviour, three other ideas of Heider's have been particularly influential in shaping the development of theory in this area (Ross and Fletcher, 1985). First, he suggested that when we observe others we tend to search for enduring, unchanging, and dispositional characteristics. Second, we distinguish between intentional and unintentional behaviours. Third, we are inclined to attribute behaviours to events (causes) that are present when the outcome is present and absent when the outcome is absent.

Jones and Davis's correspondent inference theory

Suppose you are on a bus and see someone give up his or her seat so that an elderly person can sit down. If, from this behaviour, you think 'what a kind and unselfish person', you are making what Jones and Davis (1965) call a *correspondent inference*. This is because the disposition you attributed to the person ('kind and unselfish') corresponds to the behaviour itself (giving up a seat for another person is 'kind and unselfish'). As we know, though, we do not always attribute behaviour to people's dispositions, and we sometimes explain it by reference to the circumstances or situation in which it occurred. So why do we make correspondent inferences in some cases but not in others?

Jones and Davis argue that a precondition for a correspondent inference is the attribution of *intentionality*, that is, the behaviour is deliberate rather than accidental. Two criteria (or conditions) are seen as being necessary for the attribution of intentionality. First, we have to be confident that the person *knew* the behaviour would have the effects it did, and second that the person had the *ability* to perform that behaviour. Only if we are confident that a behaviour was not accidental can we proceed to try to explain why it occurred in dispositional terms.

When a behaviour has been judged to be intentional, we then look for a disposition that could have caused it. One way we do this is through the *analysis of non-common effects*. Suppose there are several places you could visit for your holiday. All of them will be hot and have bars and discos, and all of them *except one* has hotels offering full board. If you were to choose the place that offers self-catering, we could infer that you had a strong preference for being independent and did not wish to be tied to regular meal times.

According to Jones and Davis, the smaller the number of differences between the course of action that is chosen and those that are not, the more confidently we can make a dispositional attribution. We can be even more confident about the importance of a behaviour's distinctive consequence the more *negative* elements there are involved in the chosen action. For example, if self-catering means that you will have to walk to restaurants, and the price of a meal is more expensive than if it was taken at a hotel, your desire for independence would assume even greater importance to someone explaining your chosen course of action.

As well as the analysis of non-common effects, Jones and Davis saw a number of factors influencing the likelihood of a dispositional attribution being made. These are described in Box 1.1.

Box 1.1   Factors influencing the likelihood of a dispositional attribution

Free choice: If we know that a person freely chose to behave in a particular way, we usually assume that the behaviour reflects an underlying disposition. However, if we know that a person was pressed to act in a particular way, behaviour is more likely to be attributed to external causes.

Expectedness and social desirability: Some behaviours are so expected and socially acceptable that they tell us little about a person's dispositions, and we are unlikely to draw correspondent inferences about them when the behaviour is performed (such as when a politician shakes hands with people and kisses babies). However, unexpected and socially undesirable behaviour is much more informative about a person's dispositions (Jones *et al.*, 1961). This is largely because when we behave unexpectedly or in a socially undesirable way (such as making jokes and laughing at a funeral), we are more likely to be shunned, ostracised or disapproved of.

Prior expectations: The better we know somebody, the better placed we are to decide whether his or her behaviour on a particular occasion is 'typical'. If it is 'atypical' (such as 'she doesn't normally react like that'), we are more likely to dismiss it, play down its significance, or explain it in terms of situational factors.

Whilst there are data consistent with Jones and Davis's theory, several weaknesses in it have been identified. For example, Eiser (1983) has argued that intentions are *not* a precondition for correspondent inferences. For example, when someone is called 'clumsy', that dispositional attribution does not imply that the behaviour was intentional. In Eiser's view, behaviours which

are unintended or accidental are beyond the scope of Jones and Davis's theory. Also, and as Hewstone and Fincham (1996) have pointed out, whilst behaviour which disconfirms expectations is informative, so sometimes is behaviour which confirms expectations (a good example being behaviour that confirms a stereotype).

Kelley's covariation and configuration models

Whilst Jones and Davis's theory continues to attract much interest, most of the studies supporting it did not measure *causal* attributions (Gilbert, 1995). Inferring a disposition is not the same as inferring a cause, and each appears to reflect different underlying processes (Hewstone and Fincham, 1996). Both of Kelley's (1967, 1972, 1983) models are concerned with the processes that determine whether an *internal* or *external* attribution is made for the cause of behaviour.

THE COVARIATION MODEL

The covariation model tries to account for the attributions we make when we have some degree of knowledge about how a person whose behaviour we want to explain usually behaves in various situations, and how other people behave in the same situation. According to the *principle of covariation* (Kelley, 1967):

'an effect is attributed to one of its possible causes with which, over time, it covaries'.

This means that if two events repeatedly co-occur, we are more likely to infer that they are causally related than if they rarely co-occur. According to Kelley, attributions about some effect (or behaviour) depend on the extent to which it covaries with each of three different kinds of information. These are called *consensus*, *consistency*, and *distinctiveness*, and are described in Box 1.2.

Box 1.2   Consensus, consistency and distinctiveness

Consensus refers to the extent to which other people behave in the same way towards the same stimulus. For example, if one person is laughing at a particular comedian and other people are as well, consensus is *high*. However, if nobody else is laughing at the comedian, then consensus is *low*.

Consistency refers to the stability of behaviour, that is, the extent to which a person has reacted in the same way to the same stimulus on other occasions. For example, if a person is laughing at a comedian now, and has laughed at this comedian in the past, then consistency is *high*. However, if the person has not laughed at this comedian in the past, then consistency is *low*.

Distinctiveness refers to the extent to which a person reacts in the same way towards other stimuli or entities. For example, if a person is laughing at a comedian and laughs at other comedians, then distinctiveness is *low* (there is nothing distinctive about the behaviour). However, if the person does not find other comedians funny, then distinctiveness is *high* (laughing at this comedian *is* a distinctive behaviour).

Kelley proposed that the ways in which these three types of information covary determines the type of attribution we make. Consider, for example, explaining the behaviour of Peter, who is late for a psychology tutorial. As can be seen in Figure 1.1 (see page 5), Kelley's model predicts that Peter's behaviour will be explained differently when the information about him and other students covaries in certain ways.

Several studies have shown that when people are asked to explain a behaviour (such as Peter being late for his tutorial) and are given information which covaries in the ways shown in Figure 1.1 (see page 5), attributions tend to be made in the ways suggested by Kelley (McArthur, 1972; Harvey and Weary, 1984). However, and as Hewstone and Fincham (1996) have remarked, just because people make attributions as if they are using covariation 'rules', does not *necessarily* mean that those 'rules' are being used. Several researchers have attempted to look at exactly how people make causal attributions, the most promising of these being Hilton and Slugoski's (1986) *abnormal conditions focus model*.

In this model, the three types of information are useful to the extent that the behaviour which needs to be explained contrasts with the information given. Thus, with low consensus information, it is the person who is abnormal, whereas with low consistency information it is the circumstances that are abnormal. With high distinctiveness information, the stimulus is abnormal. The model proposes that we attribute as a cause the necessary condition that is abnormal when compared with

the background of the target event (Hewstone and Fincham, 1996). This model may be able to explain certain findings that Kelley's model has difficulty accounting for, one of these being that the three types of information do not appear to be used to the same extent (Nisbett and Borgida, 1975; Wells and Harvey, 1977; Major, 1980).

THE CONFIGURATION MODEL

Kelley recognised that in many situations (most notably when we do not know the person whose behaviour we are trying to explain), we will not have access to any, and perhaps all, of the three types of information identified in the covariation model. Yet we are still able to offer explanations for behaviour. The configuration model was Kelley's attempt to account for how we make attributions about behaviour given a single occurrence of it by a particular individual. Kelley (1972) says that when we make 'single event attributions' we do so using *causal schemata*. These are general ideas (or ready-made beliefs, preconceptions, and even theories: Hewstone and Fincham, 1996) about how certain kinds of causes interact to produce a specific kind of effect. Put another way, causal schemata are a 'causal shorthand' (Fiske and Taylor, 1991) for explaining behaviour quickly and easily.

We develop causal schemata through our experiences, and two of the most extensively researched are *multiple sufficient causes* and *multiple necessary causes*. These are described in Box 1.3.

Box 1.3   Two types of causal schemata

Multiple sufficient causes: With some behaviours, any number of causes might be *sufficient* to explain their occurrence. For example, a footballer who advertises aftershave may do so because he genuinely believes it is a good product, or because he is being paid a large sum of money to advertise it. Either of these is a sufficient cause. In these circumstances, we follow what Kelley (1983) calls the *discounting principle*, according to which:

'given that different causes can produce the same effect, the role of a given cause is discounted if other plausible causes are present'.

In the case of the footballer advertising aftershave, it is more reasonable to assume that money explains the behaviour and so we discount the other possible cause.

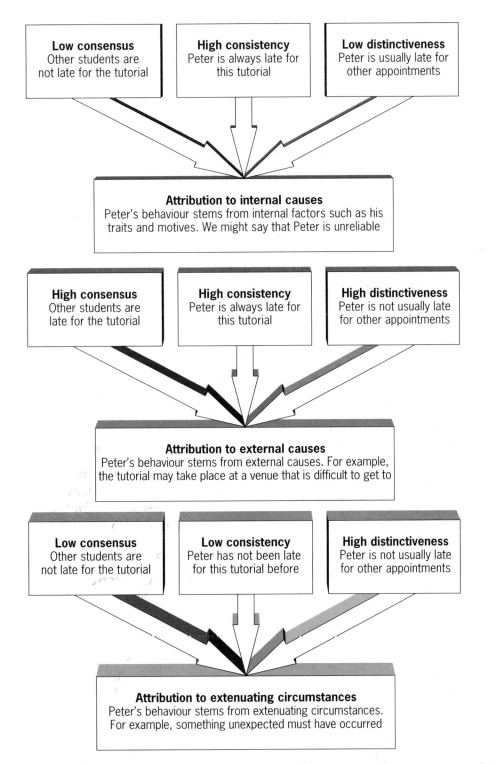

Figure 1.1 **Predictions made by Kelley's covariation model given different types of consensus, consistency and distinctiveness information**

The concept of multiple sufficient causes is also associated with the *augmenting principle*. According to this:

'the role of a given cause is augmented or increased if the effect occurs in the presence of an *inhibitory* factor' (Kelley, 1983).

So, we are more likely to make an internal attribution (to effort and ability) when a student passes an exam after (say) suffering the death of a family member, than would be the case for a student who had passed the exam without having suffered such a loss.

Multiple necessary causes: Experience tells us that, for example, to stand any chance of winning a marathon a person must be fit, highly motivated, have trained hard for several months, wear the right sort of running shoes, and so on. Even if all these conditions are met, success is not guaranteed. However, the absence of any one of them is likely to produce failure. Thus, there are many causes needed to produce certain behaviours (typically those which are unusual or extreme).

Biases in the attribution process

Kelley's is a *normative model* of the attribution process, that is, it tells us how people *should* make causal attributions. As we have seen, however, people are far less logical and systematic (they are 'less scientific') than the model requires. A more accurate account of how we make causal attributions may be to look at the systematic errors and biases that occur in the attribution process. According to Zebrowitz (1990), a bias is:

'the tendency to favour one cause over another when explaining some effect. Such favouritism may result in causal attributions that deviate from predictions derived from rational attributional principles like covariation'.

Although almost all behaviour is the product of *both* the person and the situation, we tend to emphasise one or other of these when making attributions about behaviour. As Jones and Nisbett (1971) have remarked, perhaps this is because we want to be seen as competent interpreters of behaviour, and so we naively assume that simple explanations are better than com-

plex ones. Our tendency to act as 'cognitive misers' means that we do not analyse the interactions between personal and situational factors even if lots of information is available to us. Three attributional biases that have received much research interest are the *fundamental attribution error*, the *actor–observer effect*, and the *self–serving bias*.

THE FUNDAMENTAL ATTRIBUTION ERROR

The fundamental attribution error (FAE) – also known as the *correspondence bias* (Gilbert, 1995) – is the tendency to overestimate the importance of personal or dispositional factors and underestimate the importance of external or situational factors as explanations for other people's behaviours (Ross, 1977). The FAE, then, is a failure to use the discounting principle (see page 4) and it has been demonstrated in numerous studies. One of these is described in Box 1.4.

Box 1.4   An experimental demonstration of the FAE

Napolitan and Goethals (1979) had students talk, one at a time, with a young woman who acted in either an aloof and critical manner or a warm and friendly one. Before the experiment began, half the students were told that the woman's behaviour would be spontaneous. The other half were told that, for the purposes of the experiment, she had been *instructed* to act in an unfriendly (or friendly) way.

The researchers found that even though the students had been told the woman was behaving in a particular way for the purposes of the experiment, they disregarded that information. So, if she acted in a friendly way towards them, they inferred that she really was a warm person. However, if she acted in an unfriendly way, they inferred that she really was a cold woman. Only if the students interacted with the woman twice and saw her act in a friendly way on one occasion and in an unfriendly way on the other, did they begin to consider the situational reasons for her behaviour.

Jones and Nisbett (1971) have proposed two explanations for the FAE. First, we have a different *focus of attention* when we view ourselves, and when we behave we see the world around us more clearly than we see our own behaviour. However, when we observe somebody else behaving, we focus our attention on what is most salient and relevant, namely their behaviour, and not on the situation the person is in. Second, *different types of information* are available to us about our own and other people's behaviour. For example, we have more consistency information available because we are likely to be able to remember how we have acted on previous occasions in the same circumstances, and we also have a better notion of the stimuli to which we are attending.

Ross (1977) has argued that by explaining behaviour in terms of personal or dispositional factors, other people seem to be more predictable to us, and this enhances our sense of control over the environment. Gilbert (1995) sees the FAE as an efficient and automatic process of inferring dispositions from behaviour which, on average, produces accurate perceptions by perceivers who are too 'cognitively busy' to make conscious corrections based on situational causes.

We should note, however, that in some circumstances we *overestimate* the importance of situational factors as causes for other people's behaviour. For example, Quattrone (1982) showed that when people are alerted to the possibility that behaviour may be influenced by environmental constraints, there is a tendency to perceive these as causing behaviour. This occurs even though such behaviour can be explained in terms of the dispositions of the person carrying it out. For this reason, Zebrowitz (1990) prefers the term 'bias' to 'error' in this respect (see above). In Zebrowitz's view,

> 'this bias may be limited to adults in Western societies and it is most pronounced when they are constrained to attribute behaviour to a single cause'.

Certainly, the FAE is by no means universal (Fletcher and Ward, 1988). In our society, we tend to believe that people are responsible for their actions. In India, however, people are more embedded in their family and caste networks, and are more likely to recognise these situational constraints on behaviour. As a result, situational attributions are more likely for other people's behaviour (Miller, 1984).

Research has also shown that the likelihood of the FAE being made in our culture depends on the *importance of the consequences* (Walster, 1966). The more serious the consequences of a behaviour, the more likely the actor is to be judged responsible for it. Walster, for example,

gave participants an account of a car accident in which a young man's car had been left at the top of a hill and had rolled down backwards. Those told that the car had crashed into a shop, and injured the shopkeeper and a small child, rated the young man as more 'guilty' than those told that the car had crashed into, and damaged, another vehicle. Those told that very little damage was done to the young man's car, and that no other vehicle was involved, rated him least 'guilty' of all. Similarly, Chaikin and Darley (1973) found that the FAE is more likely to be made when a person is described as having spilt ink over a large and expensive book than over a newspaper. Two additional factors influencing the likelihood of the FAE being made are described in Box 1.5

Box 1.5 Two other factors influencing the occurrence of the FAE

Intentionality: In an extension of Walster's research, Darley and Huff (1990) found that participants' judgements of the damage caused by an action depended on intentionality. Three groups of participants read the same description of some damage that had been done. However, one group was told that the damage had been done intentionally, one that it had been done as a result of negligence, and one that it had occurred naturally. Estimations of the damage were inflated by those told that it had been done intentionally.

Personal relevance: The way in which a behaviour affects us personally also influences the likelihood of the FAE being made. The greater the personal (or *hedonic*) relevance an action has, the more likely the FAE is. So, if the large and expensive book used as stimulus material in Chaikin and Darley's study (see text) had been described as belonging to us, the FAE would be more likely than if it was described as belonging to someone else.

THE ACTOR–OBSERVER EFFECT

The actor–observer effect (AOE) refers to our tendency to make a different attribution about a behaviour depending on whether we are performing (or 'acting') it or observing it. Actors usually see behaviour as being a response to the situation, whereas observers attribute

Figure 1.2   Actors tend to look for situational causes of their behaviour (Copyright House of Viz/John Brown Publishing Ltd)

the same behaviour to the actor's intentions and dispositions (that is, observers make the FAE).

Several explanations for the AOE have been proposed. One of these claims that because we do not like to be pigeon-holed, we tend not to explain our own behaviour in terms of trait labels. However, we have no such reservations about pigeon-holing others. Because we like to see ourselves as flexible and adaptive, and others as understandable and predictable, we explain the same behaviour differently depending on whether we are doing it or seeing it being done (Sande *et al.*, 1988). Another explanation concerns the amount of information actors and observers have at their disposal. Actors know they have behaved differently in other situations and would behave differently in this situation if conditions were changed. Unless they know the actor well, observers have no such information and assume that this person has behaved similarly in the past, consequently making a dispositional attribution.

A third possible explanation is perceptual, and suggests that we do not usually look at or perceive ourselves (unless in a mirror). When explaining our own behaviour, we attend to things we can see or are most conspicuous, namely the external situation or environment. As observers, though, we attend to other people because they are the most interesting thing in the environment, and a dispositional attribution becomes more likely. Storms (1973), for example, found that when people are induced to view *themselves* as observers (by means of a videotape of themselves from the per-

spective of an observer: see Figure 1.3), they do make internal attributions about themselves. Conversely, Regan and Totten (1975) have shown that when people are induced to view others from the same perspective they view themselves (by, for example, empathising with them), external attributions for the behaviour of others tend to be made.

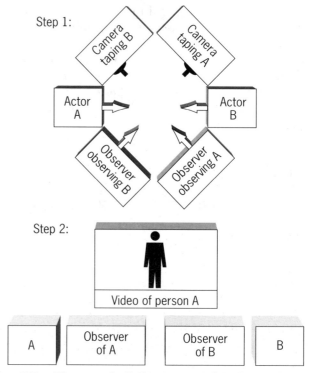

Figure 1.3   Diagram depicting Storm's (1973) experiment

THE SELF-SERVING BIAS

From what we have just said about the AOE, we might think that actors *always* explain their own behaviour in external terms. Everyday experience, though, indicates that this is not the case. If we fail an examination, we typically offer an explanation in terms of poor teaching or a very hard paper, rather than our lack of intelligence. If we pass an examination, however, we typically do not explain our success in terms of 'an easy examination paper' or 'soft marking'. Most of us explain our success in terms of 'effort', 'ability', 'high intelligence' and so on (dispositional factors).

The tendency for us to 'take credit' when things go right and 'deny responsibility' when they go wrong is called the self–serving bias (SSB: Miller and Ross, 1975) and, as Box 1.6 shows, it has been demonstrated in a variety of settings.

Box 1.6   Some illustrations of the self-serving bias

- Lau and Russell (1980) found that American football players and coaches tend to credit their wins to internal causes, such as determination, but blame their defeats on external causes, such as bad luck or injuries.
- Gilovich (1983) found that gamblers attribute winning bets to the greater ability of the winning team, whereas losing bets are explained in terms of 'flukes', such as refereeing errors or unforeseen factors.
- Students who taught boys whose performance in maths was rigged to 'improve', explained the improvement in terms of their teaching skills. Those who taught boys whose performance did not 'improve' explained the poor performance in terms of the boys' poor motivation or intelligence (Johnson *et al.*, 1964)
- Students tend to regard exams in which they do well as good indicators of their abilities and exams in which they do badly as poor indicators. When students do well, teachers are more likely to assume responsibility for their performance than when they do badly (Arkin *et al.*, 1980)
- When politicians are victorious in elections, they tend to attribute their success to internal factors, such as their personal service to constituents. When they are defeated, their loss tends to be attributed to external factors, such as national trends (Kingdon, 1967).

Several explanations for the SSB have been advanced and two broad positions can be identified. One proposes that the bias can best be explained in *motivational* or '*need-serving*' terms. According to Greenberg *et al.* (1982), one such motive is the need to enhance or protect self-esteem. If a person explains success in terms of dispositional factors, self-esteem is enhanced (a *self-enhancing bias*). If failure is explained in terms of external factors, self-esteem is protected (a *self-protecting bias*). Alternatively, the SSB could reflect a motivation to appear in a favourable light to other people (Weary and Arkin, 1981).

The second position proposes that the SSB can best be explained in *cognitive* or *information–processing* terms. Miller and Ross (1975) and Feather and Simon (1971) argue that we typically intend and expect to succeed at a task although there are, of course, occasions on which we expect to be unsuccessful. Intended and expected successful outcomes would tend to be attributed internally to factors such as trying hard. Unintended and unexpected outcomes would tend to be attributed to external factors such as bad luck. Disentangling the role played by motivational and cognitive factors in the SSB is difficult, but there is evidence to suggest that both play a role (Tetlock and Levi, 1982).

An interesting exception to the SSB comes from observations of the attributions made by clinically depressed people. Abramson *et al.* (1978) reported that depressed people tend to explain their failures in terms of their own inadequacies, and their successes in terms of external factors such as luck or chance. The *attributional style* employed by depressed people has also been observed in non-depressed women. According to Davison and Neale (1994), evidence suggests that, as compared with men, women are more likely to cope with stress by blaming themselves for their plight and more likely to attribute their achievements to external factors. Although these differences in attributional style can help explain why married people differ in their degree of happiness (see Chapter 7), the exact reasons as to why different attributional styles are used remain the subject of much research.

Conclusions

This chapter has looked at some of the theories of attribution and biases in the attribution process that have attracted social psychological interest. As we have seen, theories of attribution are helpful in understanding how we arrive at explanations for people's behaviours but, because of the various biases that have been shown to exist, they cannot tell the whole story. As normative theories of the attribution process, theories of attribution tell us how we *should* make causal attributions for behaviour. How we actually do make them continues to be the subject of much research.

SUMMARY

- **Attribution theory** deals with the general principles governing how we arrive at **causal explanations** of behaviour in a wide variety of situations. **Theories of attribution** draw on these principles to make predictions about how people respond in **particular situations/ life domains**.

- Attribution theory is a collection of diverse theoretical and empirical contributions. Its backbone consists of Heider's **'commonsense' psychology**, Jones and Davis's **correspondent inference theory** and Kelley's **covariation and configuration models**.

- According to Heider's **'commonsense'** psychology, the starting point for studying how we understand our social world is the 'ordinary' person, who is a **naive scientist**, inferring the unobservable **causes** (meaning) of observable behaviour.

- Members of a culture share certain basic assumptions about behaviour, without which social life would hardly be possible. This commonsense psychology, in our culture at least, explains people's behaviour in terms of both **personal/dispositional/internal** and **situational/environmental/external** factors.

- Other insights provided by Heider include the suggestion that when we observe others, we tend to search for enduring dispositions, the distinction between intentional and unintentional behaviour, and the tendency to attribute behaviours to causes that are correlated with the outcome.

- Jones and Davis were concerned with explaining why we make **correspondent inferences** about people's dispositions. A precondition for this is the attribution of **intentionality,** which depends on the belief that the person **knew** the behaviour would have the effects it did, and that he or she had the **ability** to perform it.

- One way of looking for a disposition that could have caused behaviour is through the **analysis of non-common effects**. The smaller the number of differences between the chosen and non-chosen courses of action, the more confidently we can make a dispositional attribution, especially if **negative** elements are involved.

- In addition to the analysis of non-common effects, the likelihood of a dispositional attribution being made is influenced by **free choice, expectedness and social desirability** and **prior expectations**. Unexpected and socially undesirable behaviour is much more informative about a person's dispositions, and the better we know someone, the better placed we are to decide whether their behaviour is typical or the result of situational factors.

- According to Eiser, intentions are **not** a precondition for a correspondent inference, and unintended/accidental behaviours are outside the scope of Jones and Davis's theory. Also, behaviour that confirms expectations can be informative (as in stereotypical behaviour).

- Whilst inferring a disposition does not constitute a **causal** attribution, Kelley was concerned with the processes by which an **internal** or **external** attribution is made for the cause of behaviour.

- Kelley's **covariation model** tries to account for the attributions we make when we know something about how the actor usually behaves in a situation and how other people behave in the same situation. Based on the **principle of covariation**, we are more likely to infer that two events are causally related if they repeatedly co-occur.

- Our attributions about some effect/behaviour depend on the extent of its covariation with information regarding **consensus** (other people's behaviour towards the same stimulus), **consistency** (the stability of behaviour) and **distinctiveness** (the actor's reaction towards other stimuli/entities). Each can be **high** or **low**.

- The ways in which these three types of information covary determines the type of attribution we make. A combination of **low/high/low** results in an attribution to **internal** causes with a **high/high/high** combination we make an attribution to **external** causes, and a **low/low/high** combination results in an attribution to **extenuating circumstances**.

- Although several studies have found support for Kelley's covariation model, this does not necessarily mean that people are using covariation 'rules'. According to Hilton and Slugoski's **abnormal conditions focus model**, the three types of information are useful to the extent that they contrast with the behaviour being explained, that is, low consensus (the person is abnormal), low consistency (the circumstances are abnormal) and high distinctiveness (the stimulus is abnormal).

- Based on his recognition that we often do not have access to any or all of these three types of information, Kelley's **configuration model** tries to account for 'single event attributions' in terms of **causal schemata**. These represent a 'causal shorthand' for explaining behaviour quickly and easily.

- The two most widely researched causal schemata are **multiple sufficient** and **multiple necessary causes**. The former are associated with the **augmenting principle,** and we choose between two or more possible causes by using the **discounting principle**.

- People are far less rational and scientific than is required by Kelley's **normative model,** and a more accurate account of the attribution process involves looking at systematic **biases** in it. Although most behaviour is the product of **both** the person and the situation, we tend to emphasise one or other, reflecting our tendency to act as 'cognitive misers'.

- According to the **fundamental attribution error/FAE** (or **correspondence bias**), we exaggerate the importance of internal/dispositional factors relative to external/situational factors. This can occur even when we have been told that someone has been **instructed** to act in a particular way.

- According to Jones and Nisbett, the FAE may occur either because of the different **focus of attention** that we have as an actor and observer of another's behaviour, or because of the **different types of information** available to us, such as consistency information.

- Ross believes that the FAE helps to make other people seem more predictable, thus enhancing our sense of control over the environment. According to Gilbert, it generally produces accurate perceptions by 'cognitively busy' perceivers.

- According to Zebrowitz, the FAE (which she prefers to call a bias) may be limited to adults in Western culture, where people are seen as responsible for their actions. By contrast, people in India are more likely to recognise situational constraints on behaviour, such as family and caste networks.

- The likelihood of the FAE occurring depends on the **importance of the consequences**: the more serious they are, the more likely the actor is to be judged responsible. It is also made more likely by **personal/hedonic relevance**.

- According to the **actor–observer effect (AOE)**, actors usually see behaviour as being a response to the situation, whilst observers attribute the same behaviour to the actor (observers make the FAE).

- The AOE may arise because we do not wish to be pigeon-holed in terms of trait labels, although we are willing to do this to others, whom we like to see as predictable. Alternatively, actors have more information about their own behaviour than observers do, unless they know the actor well.

- A perceptual explanation relates to differences in what actors and observers attend to, namely the situation/environment and other people respectively. If people's perspectives are deliberately altered, the AOE can be reversed.

- Contrary to what the AOE implies, actors do not always explain their own behaviour in external terms. Whilst we do tend to blame our failures on external factors, we also like to take credit for our successes (the **self–serving bias/SSB**). This has been demonstrated in a variety of settings.

- One explanation of the SSB involves **motivational/'need-serving'** factors, such as the need to enhance (**self-enhancing bias**) or protect (**self-protecting bias**) self-esteem. Alternatively, a **cognitive/information–processing** explanation proposes that we attribute intended/expected successful outcomes internally, whilst unintended/unexpected negative outcomes are attributed externally.

- Abramson *et al.* have found that the **attributional style** of clinically depressed people, also displayed by non-depressed women, represents an exception to the SSB. The exact reasons for these differences are still being investigated.

2

SOCIAL AND CULTURAL INFLUENCES ON PERCEPTION: STEREOTYPES AND SOCIAL REPRESENTATIONS

Introduction and overview

The concept of a 'stereotype' was introduced to psychology by Lippmann (1922). The word derives from its use in printing, where it refers to a printing mould or plate which, when cast, is difficult to change (Reber, 1985). Research into stereotyping has a long history in social psychology, and our first aim in this chapter is to examine theories and studies relating to the origins and maintenance of cultural and social stereotypes.

Related to stereotypes are social representations. Social representations are shared beliefs and expectations held by the society in which we live or the group to which we belong (Moscovici, 1961, 1976). Our second aim in this chapter is to review some of the research relating to social representations, and to examine the contribution made by such research to our knowledge of the ways in which we share, transmit, and reflect upon our understanding of the world.

Implicit personality theory and illusory correlations

In a study of the processes involved in interpersonal perception, Asch (1946) showed that when people are presented with characteristics describing a person, they tend to go beyond the information given and assume that the person also possesses certain other characteristics. For example, Asch found that when people were presented with a list containing the words 'intelligent', 'skilful', 'industrious', 'warm', 'determined', 'practical' and 'cautious', they also inferred that the person was 'serious' rather than 'frivolous', 'persistent' rather than

'unstable', and so on. Asch also showed that certain words had much more impact on the inferences that were made than others. Thus, 'warm' and 'cold' had a greater effect than 'polite' and 'blunt'. Asch used the term *central trait* to describe words that had an impact, and *peripheral trait* to describe those that played a less influential role.

> **Box 2.1   The halo effect**
>
> Asch's finding that the inclusion of the word 'warm' in a list of traits produces a more positive impression of a person compared with the same list including the word 'cold' demonstrates the *halo effect*. If we are told that a person has a particularly favourable characteristic (such as being 'warm'), we tend to attribute other favourable characteristics to them (a *positive* halo). If we are told that a person has a particularly unfavourable characteristic (such as being 'cold'), then we attribute other unfavourable characteristics to them (a *negative* halo).

According to Bruner and Tagiuri (1954), our perception of others is not based on what those others are 'really' like, but on our own general 'theory' or expectations about them. Put another way, everyone has ideas about which personality traits go with, or are consistent with, other personality traits, and use these to 'fill in the gaps' in their representations of other people. Bruner and Tagiuri coined the term *implicit personality theory* (IPT) to describe the unconscious inference processes that enable us to form impressions of others on the basis of very little evidence.

Bruner and Tagiuri proposed that IPTs are shared by everyone and are consistent within a culture. This explains why, for example, many people think that bulging eyes are a sign of extroversion, that intellectuals have larger than average skulls, and that thick lips mean gluttony (Leyens and Codol, 1988). Indeed, so entrenched are these beliefs, despite evidence to the contrary, that the term *illusory correlation* (see also page 15) has been used to describe them (Chapman and Chapman, 1969).

Although our implicit personality theory is at least partly derived from our background culture, individual experiences of interacting with, and making judgements about, people also provide us with a set of assumptions and inferences. These may not be shared with other people. For example, one student in a class who hears that a new member is 'vivacious' might feel differently from another student, depending on their personal experiences.

Moreover, since certain languages such as Eskimo and Maori embody very different theories about people from those embodied in English (Harré, 1983), the resulting perception of others is likely to be very different since they begin with a very different set of basic categorisations. As Abrahams and Stanley (1992) note, we share a basic theory of others through our language, but we develop personal variations through our particular social experience.

Stereotypes and stereotyping

Implicit personality theory has been demonstrated using various experimental techniques, and has been shown to manifest itself in a number of different ways (Gahagan, 1980). One of these is the phenomenon of *stereotyping*. In IPT, a single item of information about a person will generate inferences about other aspects of that person's character. In stereotyping, information is limited to some highly visible aspect of a person such as his or her sex, race, nationality, and so on. This information generates judgements about what any person belonging to a given group is like (an *individual stereotype*) and that all people belonging to a given group possess the same characteristics (a *group stereotype*). Social stereotypes, then, can be defined as grossly over-simplified and generalised abstractions that people share about their own group or another group (Oakes *et al.,* 1994; Hogg and Vaughan, 1995).

Figure 2.1   Millie Tant is the embodiment of the stereotype of feminists as held by non-feminists (Copyright House of Viz/John Brown Publishing Ltd)

Early research examined the ways in which different ethnic groups were stereotyped, and whether people actually held the traditional social stereotypes portrayed in newspapers and magazines. Some of the findings from this research are summarised in Box 2.2.

Box 2.2   Some findings from early research into stereotyping

Katz and Braly (1933) asked Princeton University students to indicate which five or six of a list of 84 words describing personality were most closely associated with each of 10 ethnic groups (including Germans, Negroes, Jews and Turks). Katz and Braly used agreement across students as the criterion for the existence of a stereotype. Thus, if 75 per cent or more of students assigned the trait of, say, 'obedience' to a given ethnic group, that was taken as evidence for the existence of a stereotype.

The results showed a high degree of agreement amongst the students and with traditional social stereotypes, especially derogatory traits. For example, Negroes were stereotyped as 'lazy' and 'ignorant', whilst Jews were stereotyped as 'shrewd', 'mercenary' and 'grasping'. Disturbingly, these stereotypes were held despite the fact that few students had had any personal contact with members of most of the ethnic groups. Presumably, the images of these groups as portrayed by the media had been 'absorbed' by the students. The results were also used to compare different ethnic groups in terms of their favourability. In 1933, Americans had the best stereotype, being described as 'industrious', 'intelligent' and 'ambitious', and Turks the worst.

Using Katz and Braly's methodology, other researchers examined the ways in which stereotypes change over time. For example, Gilbert's (1951) study of Princeton students showed that the stereotypes reported by Katz and Braly had become significantly weaker. Thus, only 41 per cent thought Negroes were 'superstitious' (as compared with 84 per cent reported by Katz and Braly), 47 per cent thought Jews were 'shrewd' (70 per cent), and 62 per cent thought Germans were 'scientifically minded' (78 per cent).

Later research (Karlins *et al.*, 1969) showed that whilst Americans were seen as 'industrious', 'intelligent', but not particularly 'materialistic' in 1933, by 1967 they were seen as 'materialistic' but not particularly 'industrious' or 'intelligent'. This research also revealed changes in the favourability of ethnic groups. By 1969, for example, Turks had improved quite markedly in terms of their favourability, whilst Americans had lost their position slightly. Interestingly, in both Gilbert's and Karlins *et al.*'s study, the student participants expressed great irritation at being asked to make generalisations at all.

As interesting as the findings described in Box 2.2 may be, one criticism of research in this area is that it forces judgements and is subject to the artefacts of *social desirability responding* (Gahagan, 1991). As mentioned in Box 2.2, in studies that followed Katz and Braly's, students were markedly less willing to engage in the exercise. Since negative stereotypes have become less acceptable, people would be less likely to offer a negative stereotype even if they held such a stereotype.

One way of overcoming the possibility of social desirability responding was devised by Razran (1950). Participants were led to believe they would be rating pictures of girls according to various psychological qualities. Later, the participants were shown the same pictures, but this time each girl was identified with an Irish, Italian or Jewish-sounding name. Razran used changes in the ratings previously given as evidence of ethnic stereotyping. Amongst other things, he reported that girls with Jewish-sounding names were rated higher in terms of 'intelligence' and 'ambition', but lower on 'niceness'. Razran argued that since his participants did not know they were involved in a study on stereotyping, their responses were free from social desirability responding.

EXPLAINING STEREOTYPING: THE 'GRAIN OF TRUTH' HYPOTHESIS

One question of central importance in this area of research is where stereotypes about others come from. According to Campbell (1967), stereotypes originate from two major sources – a person's experience with another person or group of people, and the communication of those experiences to others. For example, if the stereotypical view of the Scots is that they are extremely thrifty, someone at some time must have experienced a thrifty Scot. Equally, if Germans are stereotyped as 'getting up at dawn to reserve a sunbed', somebody at some time must have observed this.

At one time, then, the stereotypical characteristic attributed to a given group must have been an attribute of at least one member of that group. Later on, the process of communication would establish the stereotype as a truism in many people's minds. Stereotypes therefore originate in someone's experience and, consequently, must contain at least a 'grain of truth' (Allport, 1954). The fact that people do make inferences corresponding with their experiences was shown by Wegner *et al.* (1976). Their study is described in Box 2.3.

Box 2.3   Inferences and experiences

Wegner *et al.* (1976) gave one group of participants a series of personality traits designed to cultivate the inference that the traits of 'persuasiveness' and 'realism' were positively correlated. A second group was read similar descriptions, but the descriptions were designed to cultivate the inference that 'persuasiveness' and 'realism' were negatively correlated.

Afterwards, both groups were asked to read other descriptions that made no reference to 'persuasiveness' or 'realism'. However, each participant was asked to rate how 'persuasive' and 'realistic' the individual described appeared to be. Those participants given experience suggesting a positive correlation between the traits perceived a more positive correlation than those given experience suggesting a negative correlation. Thus, experiences can change expectations about behaviour.

One criticism of the 'grain of truth' hypothesis is that it assumes that a person, who was at one time in a particular situation, made a perfectly logical inference, that is, the person's expectancies and inferences matched his or her experiences *exactly*. As noted on page 13, however, people sometimes see two variables as being related when in fact they are not (the *illusory correlation*).

In connection with stereotypes, people perceive differences between two or more social groups in terms of the strength of correlation between membership in one of the groups and certain characteristics, even when such differences do not exist (Baron, 1989). For example, Sanbonmatsu *et al.* (1987) found that their participants saw people of Cuban descent as being more violent than people of European descent, even though being Cuban or European is equally unrelated to this characteristic.

EXPLAINING ILLUSORY CORRELATIONS

It has been suggested that illusory correlations occur because expectations about certain events distort the ways in which we process information. An example of this is shown in Box 2.4.

Box 2.4   The distorting effects of expectations on the processing of information

Hamilton and Gifford (1976) asked participants to read two short statements about various people. Two-thirds of the people they read about were identified as members of 'Group A'. The other one-third were identified as members of 'Group B'. Statements about the people were either 'desirable' ('John, a member of Group A [Group B] visited a sick friend in hospital') or 'undesirable' ('Roy, a member of Group B [Group A] always talks about himself and his problems').

Within each group, the majority (that is, two-thirds) were described by 'desirable' qualities. However, even though there were twice as many Group A members as Group B members, neither group had a higher *proportion* of 'desirable' or 'undesirable' members. The results indicated that although there was no relationship between membership of either group and 'desirability', participants thought that there was, since when they read about all the people and then reported their impressions of the 'typical' member of each group, the ('minority') Group B member was rated as less desirable than the Group A member.

Wegner and Vallacher (1976) have argued that the illusory correlation is similar to the fundamental attribution error (see Chapter 1, page 6). In the same way that other people's behaviour tends to be explained in terms of personal rather than situational factors, 'odd' behaviour can be explained by attributing it to a person's membership in an unusual group of people. When two distinctive events occur together one or more times, we tend to conclude that they must be causally related (Mullen and Johnson, 1990). According to Wegner and Vallacher, although a person's inference system is built from his or her transactions with reality, in some instances our perceptions go awry, and we make inferences about relationships that were never there at all.

Moreover, once an illusory correlation is made, we tend to seek out, notice, and remember information that supports a belief. This is called the *confirmation bias*. As a result, the belief in non-existent correlations grows stronger. Such illusory correlations can give rise to serious inferential errors (Gahagan, 1991). For example, an employer who believes that being blonde and having fun are causally linked may conclude that blondes are a poor choice for responsible jobs since they are too busy having fun (Baron and Byrne, 1984).

STEREOTYPING: A NORMAL OR ABNORMAL COGNITIVE PROCESS?

Many North American psychologists (e.g. Katz and Braly, 1933) have condemned stereotypes for being both false and illogical, and people who use stereotypes have been seen as prejudiced and even pathological. According to Taylor and Porter (1994), there are compelling reasons why Americans should condemn stereotyping and wish to rid society of this evil. One of these is the political ideology, according to which everyone who lives in America is first and foremost 'American', regardless of their country of origin or their ethnic/cultural origins. This has been called the 'melting pot' idea, in which differences between people are 'boiled away', leaving just one culture.

Some notable European social psychologists, however, were brought up in contexts in which it was normal to categorise people into groups, where they expected society to be culturally diverse, and where people are proud of their identity. A good example is Henri Tajfel (whose work is considered elsewhere in this book). Drawing on his own experiences, Tajfel (1969) challenged the American view of stereotyping. According to him, stereotyping can be reconceptualised as the product of quite normal cognitive processes common to all (non-prejudiced) people.

As we saw earlier on, though, stereotypes have been defined as oversimplified and generalised abstractions (or *exceptionless generalisations*) so that, for example, *every* skinhead is assumed to be aggressive and *every* American is assumed to be materialistic. However, it is extremely doubtful that stereotypes are factually true, because no group is completely homogeneous and individual differences are the norm. Yet in the study conducted by Katz and Braly (see Box 2.2), the instruction to list traits typical of each ethnic/national group was thought to have been understood by the participants as an instruction to list the traits *true of all members* of each group (Brown, 1986).

Early studies like Katz and Braly's, though, never actually found out exactly what was understood by the word 'typical'. However, and as noted in Box 2.2, in the follow-up studies, some students objected to doing what was asked of them. In fact, a substantial number actually refused to take part in the study, sensing that characterising ethnic groups at all would be interpreted as ignorant or even morally wrong.

That 'typical' does *not* appear to mean an exceptionless generalisation was shown by McCauley and Stitt (1978). They had students answer questions that required them to estimate things like the percentage of American cars that are Chevrolets. Interspersed with questions like this were 'critical' questions about the percentage of Germans that are efficient, extremely nationalistic, scientifically minded, pleasure-loving, and superstitious. There were also questions about the percentage of people in the world who possessed these characteristics. McCauley and Stitt found that none of the estimates given about Germans was close to 100 per cent, so clearly 'typical' is not an exceptionless generalisation, and does not seem to mean 'true of all'. What 'typical' does seem to mean is 'true of a higher percentage of the group in question than people in general', or *characteristic* (Brown, 1986)

The view of stereotyping as a normal cognitive process has led to interesting developments in research, particularly with respect to prejudice and discrimination (Taylor and Porter, 1994). Some of the findings that have emerged are considered in the following chapter. What can be said here is that relying on stereotypes to form impressions of strangers (*category-driven processing*) is

'the least effortful "cognitive route" we can take, whereas relying on the unique characteristics of the target person [*attribute-driven processing*] is the most effortful route' (Fiske and Neuberg, 1990).

Perhaps stereotypes are so resistant to change because they represent a way of simplifying the complex social world in which we live.

Social representations

Whilst stereotypes illustrate the shared nature of cognition, we do not all share the same knowledge constructs or form precisely the same opinions about other people. However, as Leyens and Dardenne (1996) have noted:

'It is apparent ... that a great deal of information, and hence meaning, is collectively shared by sets of individuals, groups or societies. This is a natural consequence of the social life we lead, which involves a plethora of communication and sources of information. As many studies have shown, our perception is determined by the ecological context in which we exist. Our religious beliefs, political and social ideologies, ideas about right and wrong, and even scientific theories are for the most part defined by the social contexts in which they occur'.

As mentioned at the beginning of this chapter, Moscovici (1961, 1976) coined the term *social representations* to refer to the shared beliefs and explanations held by the society in which we live or the group to which we belong. Specifically, Moscovici (1981) defines social representations as

'a set of concepts, statements and explanations originating in daily life in the course of inter-individual communications'.

In his view, social representations in our society are equivalent to the myths and belief systems that exist in traditional societies and are 'the contemporary version of common sense'. Such representations 'explain how the strange and the unfamiliar become, in time, the familiar' (Farr and Moscovici, 1984).

The social representations held by a group or society provide the framework within which its members can share, transmit, and reflect upon their understanding of the world. To that extent, social representations are 'the essence of *social* cognition' (Moscovici, 1981), because they help us to master and make sense of the world, and enhance our communication about it with others. Two main processes that are used to realise the functions of social representations are *anchoring* and *objectifying*. *Anchors* are established concepts within a pre-existing system to which new experiences can be related. The process of *objectifying* involves making abstract things concrete in a way that most people can understand, so that they become generally accepted as 'knowledge'.

Objectification can be achieved by means of *personification* and *figuration*. For example, Moscovici (1961) showed that people have simplified (and often mistaken) ideas about psychoanalytic theory, but that they know the name Sigmund Freud. In the same way, there are few of us who have much of an understanding about the origins of the universe or evolutionary theory, but most of us have heard the names Stephen Hawking and Charles Darwin. These are all examples of the *personification* of complex ideas, that is, linking an idea with a particular person's name that represents those ideas.

Complex ideas can also be converted into images and metaphors that represent the concept in question. This is *figuration*. When British general elections occur, for example, the concept of a 'swing' to one political party, as a result of people's voting behaviour, is depicted in the form of a pendulum that shows the effect such behaviour would produce on the national balance of power. In the case of Freud's psychoanalytic theory, the impulsive (or id) side of a person's nature is often portrayed as a devil, whilst the moralistic (or superego) side is portrayed as an angel. Both of these images stand on the shoulders of the person him or herself (the ego).

Figure 2.2   A representation of Freud's concepts of the Id, ego and superego, using figuration

Perhaps the best example of figuration is the formula $E = mc^2$ where E = energy, m = mass, and c^2 = the speed of light squared, a formula derived from the theory of relativity personified by Albert Einstein. As Leyens and Dardenne (1996) have observed:

'even this trivial amount of knowledge is sufficient to maintain conversation at a party, which is good evidence that cognitions can be socially shared'.

A good example of a social representation deriving from psychological research is shown in Box 2.6.

Box 2.6   Social representations of 'split-brain' research

In the so-called 'split-brain' operation, the nerve fibres connecting the two cerebral hemispheres are severed. The purpose of this operation is to attempt to control the severity of epileptic seizures by confining abnormally amplified brain activity to one cerebral hemisphere.

As a result of studying patients who had undergone this surgical procedure, Robert Sperry and his colleagues discovered that, as a *broad generalisation*, the two cerebral hemispheres are specialised for different kinds of mental activity, with the left hemisphere showing superior linguistic and mathematical skills, and the right hemisphere showing superior skills on spatial tasks (see Gross and McIlveen, 1998).

Moscovici and Hewstone (1983) have argued that the findings obtained by Sperry and his colleagues have been transformed in the public mind to the belief that people are 'logically left-brained' or 'intuitively right-brained', depending on how they behave. As Sperry (1982) has noted, 'the left–right dichotomy is an idea with which it is very easy to run wild', but what was a tentative description of how the brain is organised *has* become a general statement about the social and economic differences between people and societies (Hayes, 1994).

Box 2.7   Social representations in childhood

Teachers in an Italian nursery prohibited the children from bringing personal objects to school. From the perspective of a 4-year-old, this presumptuous constraint makes little sense (the whole point of having personal objects is that they are fun to play with), but the children know that grown-ups set the rules. So, the sensible thing to do is smuggle small playthings in, concealed in one's pockets. Of course, having got around the system it is essential to share the achievement with one's peers, who can appreciate the risks undertaken and the delights of the illicit goods. This calls for discretion, and all disclosures have to be made out of sight of the agents of repression. But through these defiant arrangements, the rules themselves are given meaning and are transformed into a basis for social organisation.

According to Corsaro, the children are trying to make sense of the adult rule by anchoring it in the collective security of their own culture. As they begin to incorporate the rule, and find ways of working around it, so they themselves lend it a form of objectivity: it influences how they organise their shared activities. By avoiding someone's authority and persuading your peers to avoid his or her authority, you confirm the authority. In this way, through working jointly within the rules that adults impose, children begin to reconstruct jointly a social representation of how the world (or their fragment of it) is regulated.

(From Durkin, 1995.)

SOCIAL REPRESENTATIONS IN CHILDHOOD

Durkin (1995) has reviewed the evidence relating to social representations in childhood and social representations of development itself. Drawing on research conducted by Emler *et al.* (1990) and Corsaro (1993), Durkin argues that children attempt to transform the puzzling and ambiguous features of the adult world (such as the rules that adults impose on them) by incorporating them into their own collective practices, so making 'the unfamiliar familiar'. The findings obtained by Corsaro are described in Box 2.7.

With respect to development, Durkin argues that it is something about which any society has social representations. As he says:

'a society has a belief system, a set of expectations and explanations, concerning what children should be like and what should be done with them. These social representations influence the context in which the young are raised'.

An example of a relevant social representation in this regard is *intelligence*, a construct that eludes a definition with which everyone agrees, but is widely believed in our society to be a useful 'thing' to have. Our beliefs about what determines intelligence will influence the way we behave towards others. For example, teachers who believe that intelligence is a genetically determined and inherited 'thing' are likely to teach children differently from teachers who see intelligence as something that is acquired through experience (Selleri *et al.,* 1995; Hayes, 1997).

OTHER RESEARCH INTO SOCIAL REPRESENTATIONS

Although we have discussed social representations as shared beliefs, we should acknowledge that different groups within a single society may have different social representations, and that this can lead to differences between them. A good example of this was provided by Di Giacomo (1980), who studied Belgian university students staging a protest movement about changes to their grants. Di Giacomo found that the representations held by the student leaders and those held by the main student body were different. Principally, the 'concept of student–worker solidarity', which was held by the student leaders, was not held by the main body. As a result, when the leaders called for action there was very little student support for it.

The stability of social representations has also attracted research interest. Whilst particular social representations may be held by individuals and societies, they are not completely unchanging and may be altered by a variety of sources, one influential source being the mass media. Moscovici (1984) explains the durable but open-to-change nature of social representations in terms of what he calls a *central figurative nucleus*. This is linked to a number of peripheral elements that pro-

vide additional detail about something. Changes in social representations occur when major changes in the peripheral elements break the link between them and the central core.

The major weakness of social representation theory concerns its abstract or 'fuzzy' nature (Jahoda, 1988). As a result, its critics argue that it does not suggest many hypotheses that can be experimentally investigated and that it is non-falsifiable: any data obtained can be interpreted in a way that is consistent with the theory. The first criticism is refuted by the various studies we have described in this section. However, the second criticism is more difficult to defend, and a major task of social representation theorists is to address the theory's 'fuzziness'.

Conclusions

This chapter has reviewed some of the theory and research relating to stereotyping and social representations. Amongst other things, we have seen that stereotypes are not exceptionless generalisations, and may even be an example of a normal rather than abnormal cognitive process. Research into social representations has told us something about the ways in which we share, transmit, and reflect upon our understanding of the world, although its critics have challenged the 'fuzzy' nature and non-falsifiability of social representation theory.

SUMMARY

- Asch found that people tend to go beyond the information they have been given about another person by assuming that he or she also possesses other characteristics. Also, **central traits** (e.g. 'warm' and 'cold') had much more impact on the inferences that were made than **peripheral traits** (e.g. 'polite' and 'blunt').
- Inferring other favourable characteristics from a list of traits that includes 'warm' is called a **positive halo effect**. Inferring other unfavourable characteristics from a list that includes 'cold' is a **negative halo effect**.
- According to Bruner and Tagiuri, our perception of

others is not based on what they are 'really' like, but reflects our beliefs about which personality traits belong together. We use these **implicit personality theories/IPTs** to 'fill in the gaps' when we have very little information about a person.
- IPTs are shared by everyone within a culture and are so entrenched that, despite evidence to the contrary, they illustrate **illusory correlation**. However, individuals' social experiences also contribute to the impressions they form of others, and different languages embody very different theories about people and provide a different set of categorisations.

- One way in which IPT manifests itself is in the form of **stereotyping**, in which information about someone is limited to something highly visible, such as sex or race. This information generates judgements about what anyone belonging to a particular group is like (**individual stereotype**), and that everyone belonging to this group possesses the same characteristics (**group stereotype**).

- Katz and Braly's early research found a high degree of agreement among Princeton University students regarding their perception of various ethnic groups, especially derogatory traits. These stereotypes were held despite most of the students having had no actual contact with anyone from most of the ethnic groups.

- Gilbert's follow-up study showed that Princeton students' stereotypes had become significantly weaker, and Karlins *et al.* found changes in the overall favourability of ethnic groups.

- A criticism of this type of research is that it is subject to **social desirability responding**. In both the later Princeton studies, students were much less willing to do what was asked of them, which might reflect the greater unacceptability of negative stereotypes. Razran attempted to overcome this problem by concealing from his participants the true nature of the study.

- According to Campbell, stereotypes originate from a person's experience with another person or group, so that at some time the stereotypical characteristic attributed must have been displayed by at least one member of that group. These experiences are later communicated to others, thus establishing the stereotype as a truism in many people's minds. This is the '**grain of truth**' **hypothesis**.

- People do make inferences corresponding with their experiences. However, the 'grain of truth' hypothesis assumes that there is an **exact** match between a person's expectancies/inferences and his or her experiences, and this is contradicted by **illusory correlations**.

- One explanation of illusory correlations relates to distortions in information processing. Wegner and Vallacher argue that it is similar to the FAE, whereby 'odd' behaviour can be explained by attributing it to the actor's membership of an unusual group.

- The tendency to believe that two distinctive events which co-occur must be causally related can sometimes lead us to make inferences that do not match reality. Once an illusory correlation has been made, the **confirmation bias** tends to fol-

low, reinforcing the belief in non-existent correlations.

- According to Taylor and Porter, there are compelling reasons why American psychologists should condemn stereotyping, including the 'melting pot' idea. By contrast, many European psychologists see group categorisation and cultural diversity as the norm.

- Tajfel sees stereotyping as the product of normal cognitive processes and a special case of **categorisation**, which involves the **accentuation principle**. His ideas helped to change the research emphasis **away** from the **content** of stereotypes and **towards** the **process** of stereotyping itself.

- Like Tajfel and Allport, Brislin sees stereotypes as 'categories about people', mental shortcuts that are both universal and inevitable. However, they have also been defined as oversimplified and generalised abstractions (or **exceptionless generalisations**).

- Whilst it is extremely unlikely that any stereotype is factually true, the instructions in Katz and Braly's study were assumed to have been understood by the Princeton students to mean **true of all members** of each ethnic group. However, not only did many of the students in the follow-up studies refuse to participate, but McCauley and Stitt have shown that 'typical' does not appear to mean 'true of all members'. Rather, it seems to mean **characteristic** of the group in question.

- In relation to prejudice and discrimination, **category-driven processing** is the least demanding cognitive route we can take, whilst **attribute-driven processing** is the most demanding. Stereotypes may be so resistant to change because they help to simplify our complex social world.

- Although we clearly do not all share the same knowledge or form exactly the same impressions of others, many of our religious beliefs, political and social ideologies, moral codes and scientific theories are defined by their social contexts. Moscovici calls these shared beliefs **social representations.**

- Social representations originate in everyday life in the course of communication between individuals, and are equivalent to the myths and belief systems of traditional societies. Because they help us master and make sense of the world, and enhance our communication about it with others, they are the essence of **social** cognition

- Two major processes involved in social representations are **anchoring** and **objectifying**. Objectifying can be achieved through **personification**, whereby complex ideas are linked with a particular person's name, and **figuration**, in which complex ideas are converted into images and metaphors.

- A good example of a social representation deriving from psychological research is how Sperry's studies of 'split-brain' patients have been transformed in the public mind to beliefs about left- and right-brained people and societies.
- According to Durkin, children attempt to transform the puzzling and ambiguous features of the adult world by incorporating them into their own collective practices, thus making 'the unfamiliar familiar'. An example of this is Corsaro's study of Italian nursery children.
- All societies also have social representations about development itself, a set of expectations and explanations concerning what children should be like and how they should be treated. An example is the construct **intelligence,** and teachers' beliefs about its origins are likely to affect how they teach children.
- Different groups within a particular society may have different social representations, which may lead to differences between them.
- Social representations are subject to change, one major source of change being the mass media. The **central figurative nucleus** is linked to several peripheral elements; when this link is broken, the social representation changes.
- The major weakness of social representation theory is its abstract or 'fuzzy' nature, making it non-falsifiable and difficult to test experimentally, although some relevant studies have been conducted.

3

SOME THEORIES OF PREJUDICE AND DISCRIMINATION

Introduction and overview

Literally, 'prejudice' means to pre-judge, and all of us are prejudiced towards and against certain things. In everyday language, we typically use the words 'prejudice' and 'discrimination' synonymously. For social psychologists, however, the two words have subtly different meanings. Prejudice is held to be a special type of *attitude*, an attitude being a psychological tendency that is expressed by evaluation of a particular entity with some degree of favour (Hewstone *et al.*, 1996). As an example of an extreme type of attitude, prejudice comprises the three components of all attitudes, these being the *cognitive*, *affective* and *behavioural components*.

The cognitive component refers to the beliefs and preconceived expectations (or the *stereotypes* discussed in the previous chapter) a person has about a particular group or its individual members. These may be positive, but are generally negative. The affective component refers to the feelings or emotions (which may be positive, but are mostly negative) that a particular group or its members engender in us. The behavioural component refers to the way in which a person acts towards a group or its members. This component constitutes *discrimination* and can range from anti-locution (telling racist jokes) to the genocide (or extermination) of an entire group (Allport, 1954; Hirsch, 1995). Discrimination, then, is *not* the same thing as prejudice. Rather, it is the behavioural component of it.

Much psychological research has been undertaken into understanding the causes of prejudice and discrimination based on age (e.g. Levy and Langer, 1994), sex (e.g. Tavris, 1993), sexuality (e.g. Rose and Platzer, 1993) and race (Coolican, 1997). The aim in this chapter is to look at some of the ways in which psychologists have tried to explain the occurrence and maintenance of *racial* prejudice (and hence discrimination). Some of these explanations focus on the role of *individual* factors, others on the role of *external* factors, and yet others emphasise the impact of *group membership*.

The prejudiced personality

In his book *Anti-Semite and Jew*, the philosopher Jean-Paul Sartre (1948) asked whether:

'a man may be a good father and a good husband, a conscientious citizen, highly cultured, philanthropic, *and* in addition detest the Jews'.

Sartre did not think so. In his view, anti-semitism, and hostility to other groups, was a symptom of the 'fear of the human condition'. Sartre believed that ethnic prejudice was not a personality characteristic that resided in an otherwise normal personality, but a 'symptom' of a broader style or type of personality (Brigham, 1986).

There have been a number of attempts to establish a link between personality and prejudice, one of the most famous being that of Adorno *et al.* (1950). Funded by the American Jewish League, they reported the results of a research programme aimed at understanding the anti-semitism and *ethnocentrism* (or 'general prejudice') that had emerged in Nazi Germany in the 1930s. Adorno's team hypothesised that a person's political and social attitudes formed a coherent pattern that was 'an expression of deep-lying trends in personality'.

Adopting a Freudian perspective, they argued that personality development was shaped by a child's parents. In normal development, parents strike a balance between disciplining the child and its self-expression. If, however, parents adopted an excessively harsh disciplinary regime which did not allow self-expression, the child would *displace* aggression against the parents on to some alternative target (the reason for this being that the consequences of displacing aggression towards the parents would elicit too much fear).

Adorno *et al.* reasoned that likely targets for displaced aggression would be those who were perceived as being weaker or inferior, such as members of ethnic or deviant groups who could not fight back, and who possessed the hostility towards authority that was repressed in the child itself. The researchers devised a number of personality inventories which measured anti-semitism (*AS scale*), ethnocentrism (*E scale*), political–economic conservatism (*PEC scale*) and potentiality for fascism (*F scale*).

The AS scale was designed to measure

'stereotyped negative opinions describing the Jews as threatening, immoral, and categorically different from non-Jews, and . . . hostile attitudes urging various forms of restriction, exclusion, and suppression as a means of solving the "Jewish problem"' (Adorno *et al.*, 1950, cited in Brown, 1965).

The E scale was designed to measure what Sumner (1906) defined as

'a view of things in which one's own group is the centre of everything, and all others are scaled and rated with reference to it...Each group...boasts itself superior...and looks with contempt on outsiders. Each group thinks its own folkways the only right one...'

The PEC scale was designed to measure attachment to things as they are, and a resistance to social change. The F scale was intended to measure implicit authoritarian and antidemocratic trends in personality, which make someone with such a personality susceptible to explicit fascist propaganda. Some of the items appearing on the F scale are shown in Box 3.1.

Box 3.1   Some of the items appearing on the F scale

For each statement, respondents are asked to decide whether they strongly agree, moderately agree, slightly agree, slightly disagree, moderately disagree or strongly disagree. The scale is arranged so that higher scorers strongly agree with the statements and low scorers strongly disagree with them.

---

1 Obedience and respect for authority are the most important virtues children should learn.
2 Young people sometimes get rebellious ideas, but as they grow up they ought to get over them and settle down.
3 Sex crimes, such as rapes and attacks on children, deserve more than mere imprisonment. Such criminals ought to be publicly whipped or worse.
4 When a person has a problem or worry, it is best for him not to think about it, but to keep busy with more cheerful things.
5 Some day it will probably be shown that astrology can explain a lot of things.
6 People can be divided into two distinct classes: the weak and the strong.
7 Human nature being what it is, there will always be war and conflict.
8 Nowadays, when so many different kinds of people move around and mix together so much, a person has to protect himself especially carefully against catching an infection or disease from them.
9 The wild sex life of the old Greeks and Romans was tame compared to some of the goings-on in this country, even in places where people might least expect it.

Adorno *et al.* found that high scorers on the F scale (so-called *authoritarian personalities*) also tended to score highly on the other scales *and* were more likely to have had the sort of childhood described earlier. However, although it is tempting to conclude that experiences in childhood lead to the formation of a prejudiced personality, a number of criticisms have been made of Adorno *et al.'s* research. Some of these are shown in Box 3.2.

Box 3.2   Personality and prejudice: some important issues

• The F scale (and, indeed, the other scales) can be criticised on methodological grounds. The scale was constructed so that agreement with a statement *always* indicated authoritarianism (see Box 3.1). Constructing a scale in this way often leads to *acquiescent response sets*, that is, the tendency for a person who has agreed with the first few items on a questionnaire to agree with the rest, irrespective of their content. Other methodological criticisms include the biased nature of the original sample (white, middle class, non-Jewish, native Americans), the use of retrospective questions (about childhood) and experimenter effects (the interviewers *knew* the interviewee's scores on the F scale).

- Value-related biases may also have influenced the research. Jaensch (cited in Brown, 1965), for example, distinguished between weak, effeminate and indecisive 'A' types and strong, masculine and decisive 'J' types. Jaensch saw North Germans as 'J' types and Jews and other 'racially mixed groups' as 'A' types. As well as being a psychologist, Jaensch was German. He was also a Nazi.

- Notwithstanding the methodological concerns, predictions derived from the theory have sometimes failed to find support. For example, Pettigrew (1958) found that scores on the F scale were no higher among Southerners in the USA than among Northerners, even though anti-Black attitudes were more common in the south than the north of the USA when Pettigrew conducted his research.

- An approach based on personality is reductionist, simplistic and ignores sociocultural and demographic factors. Indeed, Maykovich (1975) has shown that personality factors are *weaker* predictors of prejudice than age, education, socioeconomic status, and the region of a country in which a person lives. For several researchers (e.g. Hogg and Abrams, 1988) the social nature of prejudice and discrimination requires a *social* explanation.

- If prejudice is due to personality *differences*, then it is hard to see why an entire society or subgroups of a society (in which there would be many differences between people) would be prejudiced. Such an approach also has difficulty in explaining why prejudice rises and declines within a society. The change from positive to negative attitudes towards the Japanese by Americans following the bombing of Pearl Harbour in 1940 cannot possibly be explained by reference to the factors proposed by Adorno *et al*.

    A much better explanation here is in terms of *conformity to social norms*. For example, Minard (1952) showed that whilst 80 per cent of a sample of white coalminers in the USA were friendly towards blacks *underground*, only 20 per cent of the sample were friendly *above ground*. This finding suggests that a different set of norms operated above and below

ground. However, it should be acknowledged that this approach to prejudice fails to explain why prejudice continues even if a social norm *changes* (as has been the case in South Africa). Perhaps more importantly, an approach based on conformity also fails to explain where the social norm to be prejudiced towards a particular group originated from (Reich and Adcock, 1976).

- The work of Adorno *et al*. only identified people on the political *right*. According to Rokeach (1948, 1960), *dogmatism* (a rigid outlook on life and intolerance of those with opposing beliefs *regardless* of one's own social and political position) is a major factor in explaining the origins of prejudice. Similarly, Eysenck (1954) has argued that prejudice arises from a personality dimension he calls *toughmindedness*. The toughminded individual is attracted to extreme left-wing *or* right-wing political ideologies.

The frustration–aggression approach

According to the *frustration–aggression hypothesis* proposed by Dollard *et al*. (1939), frustration always gives rise to aggression and aggression is always caused by frustration (see also Chapter 13). Frustration, or being blocked from achieving a desirable goal, has many sources. In some cases, *direct aggression* against the source of the frustration may be possible. In other cases, it may not. Drawing on Freudian theory, Dollard *et al*. proposed that when we are unable to be aggressive towards the source of our frustration, we *displace* it on to a substitute, or *'scapegoat'*.

The choice of a scapegoat is not usually random. In England during the 1930s and 1940s, the scapegoat was predominantly the Jews. In the 1950s and 1960s, West Indians became the scapegoats, and since the 1970s it has been Asians from Pakistan. In one retrospective correlational study, Hovland and Sears (1940) found that the number of lynchings of blacks in America from 1880 to 1930 was correlated with the price of cotton, such that as the price of cotton dropped, the number of lynchings increased. Presumably, the economic situation created frustration in the white cotton farmers who, unable to confront those responsible for that situation (the government), displaced their aggression on to blacks.

Although Hovland and Sears' interpretation of their data has been challenged (Hepworth and West, 1988), other research (e.g. Doty *et al.*, 1991) has confirmed that prejudice rises significantly in times of social and economic threat (a point that will be explored further in the following section). Whilst these findings are consistent with the concept of displaced aggression, the fact that some rather than other minority groups are chosen as scapegoats suggests that there are usually socially approved (or legitimised) groups that serve as targets for aggression induced by frustration. As the prominent Nazi Hermann Rausching once observed: 'If the Jew did not exist, we should have to invent him' (cited in Koltz, 1983).

Figure 3.1   According to the frustration–aggression hypothesis, prejudice is the displacement of frustration-induced aggression onto a socially approved scapegoat

In the laboratory, scapegoating has been demonstrated in several ways. In one study, for example, Weatherley (1961) had an experimenter insult students who were either low- or high-scorers on a measure of anti-semitism as they completed another questionnaire. After this, the students were asked to write short stories about pictures of men, two of which showed men with Jewish-sounding names. Low and high scorers did not differ in terms of the amount of aggression displayed in their stories about the pictures of men with non-Jewish

sounding names. However, high scorers displayed more aggression than low scorers towards the pictures of men with Jewish-sounding names. Similar effects have been found when frustration is induced in other ways, such as making people feel failures (Crocker *et al.*, 1987).

Conflict approaches

RELATIVE DEPRIVATION THEORY

According to relative deprivation theory, the discrepancy between our *expectations* (the things we feel entitled to) and our *actual attainments* produces frustration (Davis, 1959; Davies, 1969). When our attainments fall short of rising expectations, relative deprivation is particularly acute and results in collective unrest. A good example of such acute relative deprivation is the 1992 Los Angeles riots. The immediate cause of these riots was an all-white jury's acquittal of four police officers accused of beating a black motorist, Rodney King. Against a background of rising unemployment and deepening disadvantage, this was seen by blacks as symbolic of their low esteem in the eyes of the white majority (Hogg and Vaughan, 1995). The great sense of injustice at the acquittal seemed to demonstrate acutely the injustice, which is an inherent feature of both discrimination and relative deprivation.

Figure 3.2   The 1992 Los Angeles riots were triggered by an all-white jury's acquittal of four Los Angeles police officers accused of beating a black motorist, Rodney King

The Los Angeles riots are an example of what Runciman (1966) has called *fraternalistic relative deprivation*, which is based on a comparison either with dissimilar others or with other groups. A contrast to this is *egoistic relative deprivation*, which is based on comparison with other similar individuals. For example, Vanneman and Pettigrew (1972) found that whites who expressed the greatest anti-black attitudes were those who felt most strongly that whites *as a group* are badly off relative to blacks. Since, in objective terms, whites are actually better off, this shows the subjective nature of relative deprivation.

According to Vivian and Brown (1995), the most militant blacks appear to be those with higher socioeconomic and educational status. These individuals probably have higher expectations, both for themselves and for their group, than non-militant blacks. Consequently, they experience relative deprivation more acutely.

REALISTIC CONFLICT THEORY

Data obtained from many nations and historical periods show that the greater the competition for scarce resources, the greater the hostility between various ethnic groups. For example, competition for land between European settlers and native Americans during America's development led to prejudice and discrimination against the minority native Americans (Brigham and Weissbach, 1972).

Sherif's (1966) *realistic conflict theory* proposes that intergroup conflict arises as a result of a conflict of interests. When two distinct groups want to achieve the same goal but only one can, hostility is produced between them. Indeed, for Sherif, conflict of interest (or *competition*) is a *sufficient* condition for the occurrence of hostility or conflict. This claim is based on a field study conducted by Sherif *et al.* (1961), which is described in Box 3.3.

Box 3.3   Sherif *et al.*'s (1961) 'Robber's Cave' study

Sherif *et al.*'s experiment involved 22 eleven-year-old and twelve-year-old white, middle class, well-adjusted American boys who were attending a summer camp at Robber's Cave State Park in Oklahoma. The boys were divided in advance into two groups of 11 and were housed separately and out of sight of each other.

As a result of their shared activities, such as pitching tents and making meals, the two groups quickly developed strong feelings of attachment for their own members. Indeed, a distinct set of norms for each group emerged, which defined their identity. One group called themselves the 'Rattlers' and the other the 'Eagles'. A week later, the groups were brought together and a series of competitive events (for which trophies, medals and prizes would be awarded) was organised. The two groups quickly came to view one another in highly negative ways, which manifested itself in behaviours such as fighting, raids on dormitories, and refusing to eat together.

As Box 3.3 shows, the competition threatened an unfair distribution of rewards (the trophy, medals, and knives), and the losing group inevitably saw the winners as undeserving. The view that competition is a sufficient condition for intergroup conflict has, however, been challenged. For example, Tyerman and Spencer (1983) studied boy scouts at their annual camp. The boys already knew each other well, and much of what they did was similar to what Sherif's boys had done. The scouts were divided into four 'patrols', which competed in situations familiar to them from previous camps, but the friendship ties which existed between them prior to their arrival at the camp were maintained across the 'patrols'. The researchers found that under these conditions, competition remained friendly and there was no increase in ingroup solidarity.

In Tyerman and Spencer's view, the four groups continued to see themselves as part of the whole group (a view deliberately encouraged by the scout leader), and therefore Sherif *et al.*'s results reflect the *transitory* nature of the experimental groups. The fact that the scouts knew each other beforehand, had established friendships, were familiar with camp life, and had a leader who encouraged co-operation, were all important contextual and situational influences on their behaviour. So, whilst conflict *can* lead to hostility, it is not sufficient for it to do so and this weakens the explanatory power of this approach.

Social categorisation and social identity approaches

Whether conflict is a *necessary* condition for prejudice and discrimination, that is, whether hostility can arise in the absence of conflicting interests, has been addressed by a number of researchers. According to Tajfel *et al.*

(1971), even in the absence of competition, merely being in a group and being aware of the existence of another group are sufficient for the development of prejudice and discrimination.

Evidence for this claim comes from a study conducted by Tajfel *et al.* of 14-year-old and 15-year-old school-boys from Bristol. Each boy was told that he would be assigned to one of two groups, and that this would be decided according to some purely arbitrary criterion (such as the toss of a coin). The boys were also told that other boys would be assigned in the same way to either their group or the other group. However, none of the boys knew who these others were, and did not interact with them during the study.

Each boy worked alone in a cubicle on a task that required various matrices to be studied (an example of which is shown in Figure 3.3) and a decision to be made about how to allocate points to a member of the boy's own group (but not himself) and a member of the other group. The boys were also told that the points could be converted to money after the study. The top line in Figure 3.3 represents the points that can be allocated to the boy's own group, and the bottom line the points to the other group. For example, if 18 points are allocated to the boy's own group, then 5 are allocated to the other group. If 12 are allocated to the boy's own group, 11 are allocated to the other group.

MATRIX 4	18	17	16	15	14	13	12	11	10	9	8	7	6	5
	5	6	7	8	9	10	11	12	13	14	15	16	17	18

Figure 3.3   One of the matrices used by Tajfel *et al.* (1971)

At the end of the study, Tajfel *et al.* scored the choices made by the boys to see if they chose for fairness, maximum gain to their own group, or maximum difference in favour of their own group. Although the matrices were arranged so that both groups would benefit from a co-operative strategy, the boys allocated points to the advantage of their own group and to the disadvantage of the other group.

SOCIAL CATEGORISATION THEORY

A number of other studies using Tajfel *et al.'s* approach (which is known as the *minimal group paradigm*), have found that people favour their own group compared with other groups (Tajfel and Billig, 1974; Brewer and Kramer, 1985). According to *social categorisation theory* (Hewstone and Jaspars, 1982), this is because people tend to divide their social world into two categories, 'us' (or the *ingroup*) and 'them' (or the *outgroup*). In Tajfel's view, discrimination cannot occur until this division has been made (which makes categorisation a *necessary* condition for discrimination), but when it is made it produces conflict and discrimination (which makes categorisation a *sufficient* condition as well). Amongst the criteria that are used for categorisation are race, nationality, religion and gender.

Figure 3.4   How the 'ingroup' and 'outgroup' are defined can change depending on the circumstances. Here the ingroup (England supporters) incorporates a large number of what are usually outgroups (supporters of other clubs)

Research into ingroups and outgroups shows that ingroup members see themselves in highly favourable terms, as possessing desirable characteristics, and being strongly liked. Linville *et al.* (1989) call the ingroup's tendency to see all kinds of differences among them-selves the *ingroup differentiation hypothesis*. The oppo-site perceptions apply to outgroup members (Wilder, 1984). Additionally, outgroup members are evaluated less favourably, and the ingroup sees them as being more alike in attitudes, behaviour and even facial appearance (Judd and Park, 1988). The view that 'they all look the same to me' has been termed *the illusion of outgroup homogeneity* (Quattrone, 1986), and may be a natural cognitive process. The illusion-of-outgroup-homogeneity-effect has clear implications in society, especially as far as the legal justice system is concerned (Brigham and Malpass, 1985). Box 3.4 illustrates one such potential problem.

Box 3.4   The illusion of outgroup homogeneity

JUDGE DENIES 'ASIAN' REMARK WAS RACIST

A judge who told an all-white jury that Asians 'all look the same' to him refused to apologise last night. Judge Alexander Morrison made the comments during the trial at Derby Crown Court of a young Asian man accused of robbery. After viewing photographs of a dozen Asians, he told the jury: 'I have in front of me photographs of 12 Asian men, all of whom look exactly the same, which I'm sure you'll appreciate.'

He insisted his remark had been misinterpreted. 'I want to make it clear that [my] observation, far from being an accidental affront to any section of the community, was merely intended to indicate that on examination of the photographs, the appearance of those people depicted was similar. The comment – which perhaps should not have been made – was, if anything, directed by implication to warn the jury that there was nothing singularly striking about any of the persons depicted in the photographs, in so far as identification is an issue in this case. That comment has been taken as carrying with it some sort of insult. I'm appalled that anybody could suppose that such an inference was fairly to be drawn.'

(Adapted from *The Daily Telegraph*, 22nd February, 1995)

We should, however, note that there has been disagreement with the view that intergroup conflict is *inevitable* as a result of ingroup and outgroup formation. For example, Wetherell (1982) studied white and Polynesian children in New Zealand and found the latter to be much more generous towards the outgroup, reflecting cultural norms which emphasised co-operation. Also, the minimal group paradigm itself has been criticised on several grounds, most notably its artificiality (Schiffman and Wicklund, 1992; Gross, 1994).

SOCIAL IDENTITY THEORY

Exactly why people tend to divide the world into 'us' and 'them' is not completely clear. However, Tajfel (1978) and Tajfel and Turner (1986) have suggested that membership in a group provides people with a *positive self-image* and gives a sense of 'belonging' in the social world. According to this *social identity theory* (SIT) approach, people strive to achieve or maintain a positive self-image. There are two components of a positive self-image: *personal identity* (our personal characteristics and attributes which make us unique), and *social identity* (a sense of what we are like, derived from the groups to which we belong).

Each of us actually has several social identities corresponding to the number of different groups we identify with. In relation to each one, the more positive the image of the group, the more positive will be our social identity and hence our self-image. In order to enhance self-esteem, group members make *social comparisons* with other groups. To the extent that the group sees itself in favourable terms as compared with others, self-esteem is increased. However, since every group is similarly trying to enhance self-esteem, a clash of perceptions occurs, and prejudice and discrimination arise through what Tajfel calls *social competition*.

SIT has been applied beyond the laboratory setting (see Brown, 1988, for a review of applications to wage differentials, ethnolinguistic groups, and occupational groups). The theory also helps us understand how prejudice is *maintained*. Phenomena like the *confirmation bias* (the tendency to prefer evidence which confirms our beliefs: see page 15), *self-fulfilling prophecies* (in which our expectations about certain groups determine their behaviour) and the promotion of one's own group identity, can all be understood when viewed in terms of SIT.

Whilst there is considerable empirical support for SIT, much of this has come from the minimal group paradigm which, as we have noted, has been subject to criticism. More importantly, the evidence as it stands only shows a positive ingroup bias and not derogatory attitudes or behaviour towards the outgroup, which is what we normally understand by 'prejudice'. So, whilst there is abundant evidence of intergroup discrimination, this appears to stem from raising the evaluation of the ingroup rather than denigrating the outgroup (Vivian and Brown, 1995).

Conclusions

A number of theories of prejudice and discrimination have been advanced. Some of these see prejudice as stemming from individual factors, some concentrate on the role of external factors, and some emphasise the impact of group membership. Whilst evidence can be claimed in favour of all of these theories, none is completely supported by research.

SUMMARY

- For social psychologists, prejudice is an extreme **attitude**, comprising the three components shared by all attitudes, namely the **cognitive** (mainly negative **stereotyped** beliefs and preconceived expectations), **affective** (mostly negative feelings/emotions) and **behavioural** (**discrimination**, ranging from antilocution to extermination).
- According to Sartre, anti-semitism (and hostility to other groups) is a symptom of the 'fear of the human condition', indicative of a particular type of personality.
- Perhaps the most famous attempt to tie prejudice to personality was Adorno *et al.*'s study of anti-semitism in Nazi Germany. Based on Freudian theory, they argued that prejudiced individuals have been subjected to an excessively harsh disciplinary regime as children which prevents self-expression. Aggression towards the parents would be **displaced** on to targets seen as weaker or inferior, such as members of ethnic or deviant groups.
- Adorno *et al.* constructed several personality inventories which measured anti-semitism (**AS scale**), ethnocentrism (**E scale**), political–economic conservatism (**PEC scale**) and potentiality for fascism (**F scale**).
- The AS scale was designed to measure stereotyped negative images of the Jews and hostile attitudes favouring ways of solving the 'Jewish problem'. The E scale was based on Sumner's definition of ethnocentrism as judging all groups by reference to one's own and regarding one's own as superior. The PEC scale was intended to measure resistance to social change, and the F scale to measure implicit authoritarian/ anti-democratic tendencies (**authoritarian personalities**).
- Adorno *et al.* found that high F scale scorers also tended to score highly on the other scales, and were more likely to have had the sort of harsh upbringing that prevented direct expression of hostility towards the parents.
- However, all the scales were constructed such that agreement with a statement **always** indicated authoritarianism, anti-semitism, and so on. This could have produced **acquiescent response sets**. Also, the original sample was biased and there were likely to have been experimenter effects.
- Contrary to what Adorno *et al.*'s theory would predict, Pettigrew found that Southerners in the USA scored no higher than Northerners on the F scale, despite the more common anti-black attitudes in the south.
- Explaining prejudice in terms of personality is reductionist, simplistic, and ignores sociocultural and demographic factors, which may be **stronger** predictors of prejudice than personality. Social phenomena require social explanations.
- An approach in terms of personality **differences** cannot explain why an entire society or subgroups would be prejudiced, or why prejudice arises and declines in a society, as in the anti-Japanese attitudes that arose among Americans following the events at Pearl Harbor. These are better explained in terms of **conformity to social norms**. However, this in turn fails to explain both the origins of those norms and why prejudice continues following **changes** in social norms.
- According to Rokeach, **dogmatism** is a major factor involved in prejudice, regardless of the right- or left-wing political views of the individual. This corresponds to Eysenck's **toughmindedness** personality dimension.
- According to Dollard *et al.*'s **frustration–aggression hypothesis**, frustration always results in aggression, but it is not always possible to express this directly against the source of the frustration. An alternative course of action is to **displace** it on to a substitute or '**scapegoat**'.
- The choice of a scapegoat is not usually random and, in England, different ethnic groups have been the major scapegoat at different times during the 20th century. In the USA, lynchings of blacks between 1880 and 1930 was correlated with the price of cotton. Despite this and other evidence consistent with the concept of displaced aggression, there are usually socially approved targets for frustration-induced aggression.

- According to **relative deprivation theory**, the discrepancy between our **expectations** and **actual attainments** produces frustration, especially when the latter fall short of rising expectations. A good example of acute relative deprivation is the 1992 Los Angeles riots, which demonstrate what Runciman calls **fraternalistic relative deprivation**, as distinct from **egoistic relative deprivation**.
- The finding that the most anti-black whites were those who felt most strongly that whites **as a group** are badly off relative to blacks, shows the subjective nature of relative deprivation. The most militant blacks are those with higher expectations, both for themselves and their group, resulting in a more acute experience of relative deprivation.
- According to Sherif's **realistic conflict theory**, intergroup conflict is a result of a conflict of interests (or **competition**), which is a **sufficient** condition for hostility or conflict. This theory was based on the famous Robber's Cave field experiment, in which a distinct set of norms emerged for the 'Rattlers' and the 'Eagles', who came to view one another in very negative ways.
- Tyerman and Spencer's study of boy scouts strongly challenged Sherif's claim that competition inevitably produces intergroup conflict. Several contextual and situational factors influence the effects of competition, and the Robber's Cave findings reflect the **transitory** nature of the experimental groups.
- According to Tajfel *et al.*, conflict may not even be **necessary** for prejudice and discrimination. Merely belonging to one group and being aware of another group's existence are sufficient. This claim is based on a study involving Bristol schoolboys using the **minimal group paradigm**. Despite being allocated to their group on some arbitrary criterion and not knowing the identity of the other group members, they allocated points to the advantage of their own group and to the disadvantage of the other group.

- **Social categorisation theory** maintains that we favour our own group over other groups because we tend to divide the social world into 'us' (the **ingroup**) and 'them' (the **outgroup**). This division is both a **necessary and sufficient** condition for discrimination to occur.
- Not only are outgroup members evaluated less favourably, but the ingroup sees them as being more alike in attitudes, behaviour, and even facial appearance (the **illusion of outgroup homogeneity**). Whilst this may be a natural cognitive process, it has clear social implications, especially as far as the legal justice system is concerned.
- Wetherell's research in New Zealand casts doubt on the view that ingroup/outgroup formation **inevitably** results in intergroup conflict, and the minimal group paradigm itself has been criticised, mainly in terms of its artificiality.
- According to **social identity theory/SIT**, group membership provides people with a **positive self-image**. Self-image comprises **personal identity** and **social identity**. In relation to each of the several groups to which we belong, the more positive the group's identity, the more positive our social identity will be, and hence our self-image.
- The more favourable the **social comparisons** made with other groups, the higher members' self-esteem will be. This results in **social competition**, since every group is similarly trying to enhance self-esteem.
- SIT helps explain how prejudice is **maintained** through phenomena such as the **confirmation bias, self-fulfilling prophecies** and the promotion of one's own group identity.
- Much of the considerable evidence supporting SIT has come from studies using the minimal group paradigm. Also, the evidence tends to show a positive ingroup bias, rather than negative attitudes or behaviour towards the outgroup, which is what prejudice and discrimination normally imply.

THE REDUCTION OF PREJUDICE AND DISCRIMINATION

Introduction and overview

The previous chapter looked at some of the theories that have been advanced to explain the origins and maintenance of prejudice and discrimination. The aim of this chapter is to look at some of the approaches that have been proposed as ways of reducing them, and to examine the effectiveness of such approaches. As Hirsch (1995) has noted, 50 years after the Nazi extermination, and after the concentration camps were liberated, extreme discriminatory behaviour (in the form of genocide)

'. . . continues unabated, neither punished nor prevented. In what used to be . . . [Yugoslavia], torture, murder, rape and starvation are everyday occurrences . . .'

Given their continued existence, the reduction of prejudice and discrimination is a very important issue indeed.

Prejudice reduction based on theories of its causes

One way to approach the issue of how prejudice and discrimination can be reduced is to look at the implications of the theories of them that were discussed in the previous chapter. Box 4.1 considers these implications.

Box 4.1 Theories of prejudice and their implications for prejudice reduction

The prejudiced personality: There is evidence to suggest that the authoritarian personality is *self-perpetuating*, since authoritarian parents tend to produce authoritarian children, and positive correlations between high F-scale-scoring parents and their offspring have been reported (Cherry and Byrne, 1976). However, level of education is also correlated with authoritarianism. Presumably, then, the provision of, and access to, education, would go some way to reducing prejudice (Pennington, 1986). Additionally, changing patterns of child rearing (which, as discussed in the previous chapter, Adorno *et al.* saw as being crucially important) might reduce prejudice. By allowing children to express hostility, the need to displace it on to ethnic and other groups would not arise.

Frustration–aggression and relative deprivation: According to these theories, preventing frustration, lowering people's expectations, and providing them with less anti-social ways than discrimination of venting their frustration, should result in a reduction of prejudice and discrimination. However, the practical problems of putting the 'historical clock' back or changing social conditions in quite fundamental ways are immense.

Conflict approaches: Conflict approaches to prejudice make it very clear that removing competition and replacing it with goals requiring co-operation (*superordinate goals*) will remove or prevent hostility.

Social categorisation and social identity approaches: These approaches imply that if intergroup stereotypes can become less negative and automatic, and if the boundaries that exist between groups can be made less distinct or more flexible, then group membership may become a less central part of the self-concept. As a result, positive evaluation of the ingroup would no longer be inevitable.

Socialisation and the reduction of prejudice and discrimination

One theory of prejudice that was not explored in the previous chapter derives from *social learning theory*. According to this, children acquire negative attitudes towards various social groups as a result of 'significant others' (such as parents, peers and teachers) exposing them to such views or rewarding them for expressing such attitudes (Stephan and Rosenfield, 1978). For example, Ashmore and Del Boca (1976) have shown that children's racial attitudes are often closely aligned with those of their parents, and it may be that children internalise the prejudices they observe in their parents.

Another influential 'significant other' is the mass media. If some groups are portrayed by the mass media in demeaning or comic roles, then it is hardly surprising that children acquire the belief that some groups are inferior to others (Worchel *et al.,* 1988). Box 4.2 provides an illustration of this (see opposite).

If it is the case that children's attitudes are shaped by their observations of 'significant others', then, presumably, discouraging parents from expressing prejudiced views and discriminatory behaviour should help to prevent prejudice and discrimination from developing. Whilst psychologists cannot interfere in parent–child relationships, they can alert parents to the prejudiced views they are expressing and the important costs attached to them (Baron and Byrne, 1994).

Parents could also encourage *self-examination* in their children (Rathus, 1991). For example, some of the things we say or do reflect our prejudices without our being aware of this. Rathus gives the example of a Catholic referring to an individual as 'that damned Jew'. It is extremely unlikely that a Catholic would say 'that damned Catholic'. Parents could, therefore, stress to their children the importance of remembering to attribute behaviour to people as *individuals* rather than *group representatives* (Hogg and Vaughan, 1995).

There is evidence to suggest that low self-esteem is associated with prejudiced attitudes (Crocker *et al.,* 1987). Creating a home environment in which individual outcomes depend on group effort has been shown to reduce prejudice (Kelman and Cohen, 1979). As we

---

Box 4.2   Racism and textbooks

Proctor (cited in Birch, 1985) gives numerous examples to support the argument that many textbooks, particularly those concerned with history, are at least sometimes actively racist, both in intention and effect. Proctor gives as one example Manhattan Island being bought from the American Indians for only a few dollars. The current value of the island has been used as evidence of the 'stupidity' of the Indians. Yet as Proctor points out:

'To the Indians, the notion of a person *owning* land was ridiculous. The land cannot belong to one person, and why should one want to own it? The sale of Manhattan Island was a joke in Indian eyes. Somebody gave them four dollars to buy what cannot be possessed. It was like buying the sun to a European.'

More recently, Owusu-Bempah and Howitt (1994) have pointed out that in some leading *psychology* textbooks and elsewhere, black nations are still described in derogatory and deprecatory terms such as 'primitive', 'tribal', 'underdeveloped' and 'undeveloped'. In their view,

'Each and every psychologist needs to be able to question their "broadmindedness" ... There is little point in railing against the overt racists in psychology while at the same time ignoring matters closer to home'.

---

saw in Box 4.1, child-rearing practices can influence racial attitudes, with harsh, authoritarian discipline being linked to negative shifts in racial attitudes.

A number of researchers have looked at the extent to which directly experiencing prejudice and discrimination may help children to understand them and, as a result, reduce their occurrence. In one study, for example, McGuire (1969) showed that providing children with counter-arguments to attitudes and behaviours they might experience as adults lessens prejudice and discrimination. A well-documented example of this approach was taken by Jane Elliott, an American schoolteacher (Elliott, 1977).

As a way of helping her 9-year-old pupils understand the effects that prejudice and discrimination can have, she divided them into two groups on the basis of their eye colour. Elliott told the children that brown-eyed people are more intelligent and 'better' than those with blue eyes. Brown-eyed children, though in the minority, would therefore be the 'ruling class' over the inferior blue-eyed children and would be given extra privileges. The blue-eyed children were told that they would be 'kept in their place' by restrictions such as being last in line, seated at the back of the class, and being given less break time. They were also told that they would have to wear special collars as a sign of their low status.

Figure 4.1   Still from the film of Elliot's classroom experiment, in which wearing collars as an overt sign of low status was part of the discrimination sanctioned by the teacher

Within a short time, the blue-eyed children began to do more poorly in their schoolwork, became depressed and angry, and described themselves in negative ways. The brown-eyed group became mean, oppressed the others, and made derogatory statements about them. The next day, Elliott told the children that she had made a mistake and that it was really blue-eyed people who were superior. With the situation reversed, the pattern of prejudice and discrimination quickly switched from the blue-eyed children to the brown-eyed children as victims.

At the end of her demonstration, Elliott debriefed the children. She told them that its purpose was to provide them with an opportunity to experience the evils of prejudice and discrimination in a protected environment. Interestingly, the consequences of Elliott's demonstration were not short-lived. In a follow-up study of the children when they were 18, Elliott (1990) found that they reported themselves as being more tolerant of differences between groups and actively opposed to prejudice.

The implications of Elliott's informal demonstration were investigated by Weiner and Wright (1973). Their study is described in Box 4.3.

Box 4.3   Weiner and Wright's (1973) study

Weiner and Wright randomly assigned white 9-year-olds to either a 'green' or an 'orange' group, their group membership being indicated by an appropriately coloured armband. First, the 'green' pupils were labelled inferior and denied social privileges. After a few days, the labelling was reversed. Children in a second class were not treated in this way and served as a control group.

Once the children had experienced being in the 'green' and 'orange' conditions, they and the control group children were asked if they wanted to go on a picnic with black children from another school. Ninety-six per cent of children from the 'green–orange' group expressed a desire to go as compared with only 62 per cent of the control group children. It seems that the experience of prejudice and discrimination led the 'green–orange' children to think that discrimination on the basis of colour is wrong. This suggests that experience of being discriminated against can make children more aware of the sensitivities and feelings of members of outgroups.

The 'contact hypothesis'

People who are separated, segregated, and unaware of one another have no way of checking whether an interpretation of another group's behaviour is accurate. Because an interpretation of behaviour is likely to be consistent with a (negative) stereotype held about another group, the stereotype will be strengthened. Equally, if we do not know why members of a particular group behave the way they do, we are likely to see them as being more dissimilar from ourselves than is actually the case.

Related to this so-called *autistic hostility* is what Bronfenbrenner (1960) has called the *mirror-image phenomenon*. In this, enemies come to see themselves as being in the right (each has 'God on its side') and the other as being in the wrong. In the same way, each attributes to the other the same negative characteristics

Figure 4.2   The 'us' and 'them' mentality is a feature of the mirror-image phenomenon and autistic hostility

(the 'assumed dissimilarity of beliefs'). By enhancing or increasing contact between separated and segregated groups, prejudice and discrimination may be reduced for at least four reasons. These are described in Box 4.4.

Box 4.4   Some effects of enhanced contact between separated and segregated groups

One reason why increased contact might be effective is that it leads people to realise that their attitudes are actually more similar than they assumed. As discussed in Chapter 5, the recognition of similarity between people leads to increased liking and attraction. Another reason is that increased contact may have benefits through what Zajonc (1968) has called the *mere exposure effect* (according to which, the more we come into contact with certain stimuli, the more familiar and liked they become). Thirdly, favourable contact between two groups may lead to an opportunity to disconfirm the negative stereotypes held about them. Finally, increased contact may lead to a reduction in *outgroup homogeneity* (see page 28), because the outgroup members lose their strangeness and become more differentiated. As a result, they are seen as a collection of unique individuals rather than interchangeable 'units'.

It is generally agreed, however, that increased contact by itself is not sufficient to reduce prejudice, and may even have the effect of increasing prejudice. Despite evidence that we prefer people who are familiar, if this contact is between people who are consistently of the same *unequal* status, then 'familiarity may breed contempt'. As Aronson (1980) has noted, many whites in the United States have always had a great deal of contact with blacks, but with blacks in the role of dishwashers, toilet attendants, domestic servants, and so on. Contacts under these conditions may simply reinforce the stereotypes held by whites of blacks as being inferior.

Similarly, Amir (1994) has argued that the central issues to address are those concerning the important conditions under which increased intergroup contact has an effect, who is affected by it, and with respect to what particular outcomes. The first social psychologist to address at least some of these issues was Allport (1954). According to what has become known as the *contact hypothesis*:

'Prejudice (unless deeply rooted in the character structure of the individual) may be reduced by equal status contact between majority and minority groups in the pursuit of common goals. The effect is greatly enhanced if this contact is sanctioned by institutional supports (i.e. by law, custom or local atmosphere) and provided it is of a sort that leads to the perception of common interests and common humanity between members of the two groups.'

Most programmes aimed at promoting harmonious relations between groups that were previously in conflict have adopted Allport's view and stressed the importance of *equal status contact* and the *pursuit of common* (or *superordinate*) *goals*.

EQUAL STATUS CONTACT

One early study of equal status contact was conducted by Deutsch and Collins (1951). They compared two kinds of housing project, one of which was thoroughly integrated (blacks and whites were assigned houses regardless of their race) and the other segregated. Residents of both were intensively interviewed, and the researchers found that both casual and neighbourly contacts were greater in the integrated housing and that there was a corresponding decrease in prejudice among whites towards blacks. Other research (e.g. Wilner *et al.*, 1955) has shown that prejudice is particularly reduced in the case of next-door neighbours, an illustration of the effects of *proximity* (see Chapter 5, page 42).

Related to these studies are the findings reported by Minard (1952), Stouffer *et al.*, (1949) and Amir (1969). As mentioned in the previous chapter (see page 24), Minard studied white coalminers in the USA and found that whilst 80 per cent of his sample were friendly towards blacks *underground*, only 20 per cent were friendly *above ground*. This finding suggests that prejudice was reduced by the equal status contact between the two groups when they were working together, but that the *social norms* which operated above ground at that time did not permit equality of status. Likewise, Stouffer *et al.* (1949) and Amir (1969) found that inter-racial attitudes improved markedly when blacks and whites served together as soldiers in battle and on ships, but that their relationships were less good when they were at base camp.

Desegregation and equal educational opportunities

In the USA, much research has been conducted into the effects of desegregation in schools. The decision to desegregate schools was taken in 1954, at least partly as a result of research conducted by Clark and Clark (1947), which is described in Box 4.7 (see page 37). Whether integration is the best means for ensuring equal educational opportunities for children, and whether it actually reduces racial tension, have been hotly disputed. Box 4.5 considers some of the findings and issues.

Box 4.5   Desegregation in America's schools

According to some researchers, the continued academic underachievement of black students and inter-racial hostility between black and white students on many school campuses show that integration has failed to bring about equal educational opportunities and a lessening of racial tension. Supporters of integration, however, argue that this is because a reduction in racial tension and prejudice, and an improvement in black achievement, can occur *only* when school desegregation has been planned to promote equal status for majority and minority groups and has been implemented with the outspoken support of all authority figures involved. When these conditions are not met, as seems to be true in many cases, an increase in tension and prejudice should not be unexpected (Cook, 1984).

There is, however, evidence to suggest that desegregation may be working better than even contact hypothesis supporters believe. According to Braddock (1985), the literature on school desegregation suggests that the effects may actually be far-reaching and include lifelong social integration and occupational attainment for blacks (Crooks and Stein, 1991).

From the evidence considered, it would seem that if intergroup contact does reduce prejudice, then it is not because it encourages interpersonal friendship (as Deutsch and Collins would claim), but rather because of changes in the nature and structure of intergroup relationships. Brown and Turner (1981) and Hewstone and Brown (1986) argue that if the contact between individual groups is *interpersonal* (in that people are seen as individuals and group memberships are largely insignificant), any change of attitude may not generalise to other members of the respective group. So, and at the very least, people must be seen as typical members of their group if generalisation is to occur (Vivian *et al.*, 1994). The problem here is that if, in practice, 'typical' means 'stereotypical' and the stereotype is negative, reinforcement of the stereotype is likely to occur. Thus, any encounter with a 'typical' group member should be a pleasant experience (Wilder, 1984).

Pursuit of common goals

As was apparent in the previous chapter (see page 26), Sherif *et al.* (1961) were able to create conflict between two groups of children as a consequence of creating competition between them. The researchers initially attempted to resolve the conflict by having the children watch movies, attend a party, and eat meals together. However, this approach was unsuccessful and none of the situations, either individually or collectively, did anything to reduce the friction between the two groups. Indeed, the situations actually resulted in increased hostility between the groups.

However, another approach used by Sherif *et al.* to reduce the conflict between the two groups was more successful. This involved the creation of situations in which the problems that faced both groups could only be solved through *co-operation* between them (Deaux *et al.*, 1993). For example, the researchers arranged for the camp's drinking water supply to be cut off, with the only way of restoring it requiring both groups to work together. Similarly, on a trip to an overnight camp, one of the trucks carrying the boys got 'stuck', and the only way it could resume the journey was if all the boys pulled together on a large rope.

The researchers found that by creating these *super-ordinate goals* (goals that can only be achieved through co-operation), the group divisions gradually disappeared. Indeed, at the end of the experimental period, the boys actually suggested travelling home together on one bus. Sixty-five per cent of friendship choices were made from members of the *other* group, and the stereotypes that had been previously held changed to become much more favourable.

The findings reported by Sherif *et al.* have subsequently been replicated in a number of other similar studies (e.g. Clore *et al.*, 1978) in a variety of contexts (such as creating inter-racial sports teams: Slavin and Madden, 1979). However, the imposition of superordinate goals may not always be effective and may sometimes increase antagonism towards the outgroup if the co-operation fails to achieve its aims (Brown, 1996). It may also be important for groups engaged in co-operative ventures to have distinctive and complementary roles to play, so that each group's contributions are clearly defined. When this does not happen, liking for the other group may actually decrease, perhaps because group members are concerned with the integrity of the ingroup (Brown, 1996).

The pursuit of common goals has also been investigated in studies of co-operative learning in the classroom. One researcher who has been particularly involved with this approach is Aronson (e.g. 1992). Aronson was originally approached by the superintendent of schools in Austin, Texas, to give advice about how inter-racial prejudice could be reduced. Aronson *et al.* (1978) devised an approach to learning that involved mutual interdependence among the members of a class. This is described in Box 4.6.

Aronson originally studied white, black and hispanic students, who met for three days a week for a total of six weeks. At the end of this period, the students showed increased self-esteem, academic performance, liking for their classmates, and some inter-racial perceptions, compared with a control group given six

---

Box 4.6   The jigsaw classroom technique

In the *jigsaw classroom technique*, students (regardless of their race) are placed in a situation in which they are given material that represents one piece of a lesson to be learned. Each child must learn his or her part and then communicate it to the rest of the group. At the end of the lesson, all children are tested on the whole lesson and given an individual score. Thus, the children must learn the full lesson and there is complete *mutual interdependence* because each is dependent on the others for parts of the lesson that can only be learned from them.

---

weeks of traditional teaching. Aronson's method has been used in many classrooms with thousands of students, and the results are consistent in showing a reduction in prejudice (e.g. Slavin, 1985).

Figure 4.3   Pursuit of common goals: multi-racial children in harmony

Importantly, though, whilst the children who had actually worked together came to like each other better as individuals, this research has not been longitudinal and so the consequences of co-operative learning have only shown *short-term* benefits. Whether the changes last, and whether they *generalise* to other social situations is not clear. However, at least in the short term, the pursuit of common goals can be effective, especially with young children in whom prejudiced attitudes have not yet become deeply ingrained.

Racism and childhood identity

Earlier on in this chapter, socialisation and the reduction of prejudice were considered. According to Milner (1996, 1997), the development of children's racial attitudes has been seen as an essentially *passive* process in which parents and others provide behaviours which children then absorb and reproduce. Racial attitude development is seen as being the result of irresistible social and cultural factors which impinge on the child from a variety of sources, with the child's only active participation being an attempt to make 'cognitive sense' of the messages he or she receives.

Whilst Milner accepts that a variety of sources provide the *content* of children's racist attitudes, he argues that:

'there has been a tendency to make a rather facile equation between, on the one hand, children's racial attitudes, and culturally mediated racism on the other. It is as though we have said (a) "children have rather hostile racial attitudes", and (b) "our cultural products contain many instances of implicit or explicit racism", and therefore (a) must be caused by (b).'

Milner does not see sources such as children's books as containing enough 'raw material' in themselves to account for the development of their racial attitudes. In his view, children play an *active* role in the development of their racial awareness and rudimentary attitudes. Rather than solely absorbing the attitudes of adults in 'junior form', or seeking to construct a cognitively well-ordered world, they are motivated by *needs* to locate themselves and their groups within that social world 'in ways which establish and sustain positive self- and social-regard or identity'. This is consistent with social identity theory (see Chapter 3, page 28).

The principal need in a society with a competitive ethos (such as our own) is to understand the complexity of the social world and locate oneself at an acceptable station within it. Aligning oneself with a particular category might lead to social acceptance or to marginality or ostracism. Identification with a particular childhood category membership, then, has a positive aspect whose value is much sought after, and negative racial attitudes *may* fulfil this function for the majority-group child in a multiracial society. As Milner points out,

though, negative racial attitudes cannot (by definition) fulfil the same function for the minority group. This can be seen in the phenomenon of *misidentification*, which is described in Box 4.7.

Box 4.7   Misidentification

Clark and Clark (1947) asked black and white children aged between 3 and 7 years to choose a black or white doll to play with. Regardless of their own colour, the children consistently chose the white dolls, saying that they were prettier and nicer. These findings were replicated by other researchers, and it was also shown that the 'doll tests' are a valid measure of self-concept related to ethnic identification (Ward and Braun, 1972).

In other research, Morland (1970) found that when the level of actual discrimination increases, so self-contempt increases. Thus, more black children from Southern states in America chose a white child as a preferred playmate than was the case for black children from the Northern states. As Rowan (1978) has remarked:

'What this means is that when whites are taught to hate blacks, blacks themselves come to hate blacks – that is, themselves. When whites are taught that blacks are inferior, blacks come to see themselves as inferior. In order to cease to be inferior, they have (it sometimes seems to them) to cease to be black.'

The *self-denigration* by minority groups was addressed by civil rights and black politico-cultural movements that engendered a positive connotation about blackness with slogans like 'Black is Beautiful'. As a result of these movements, the misidentification phenomenon all but disappeared, even among young children who might not be expected to be attuned to the relevant cultural and political messages (Milner, 1997). But what about the majority group? As Milner notes:

'If it is true that majority-group children may actively seek, or be drawn to, a set of racial attitudes partly because the superior/inferior group relations they portray satisfies the developing need for a positive social identity, then this might seem to underscore both the inevitability and ineradicability of racism, among the majority group.'

However, Milner argues that many other things can serve the purpose of satisfying the need for a positive social identity (supporting a winning soccer team, for example), and so far from embedding racism deeper in the child's 'psychological economy', this notion actually undercuts the significance of childhood racism. For Milner, racist ideas may have more to do with the developing identity needs of children than with the objects of those attitudes, and may be rapidly superseded by other sources of status and self-esteem.

This would account for Pushkin and Veness's (1973) finding that racial attitudes peak in hostility around the age of six to seven and decline subsequently. Moreover, if racial attitudes were central in a child's identity, they would endure into adulthood, but (with a few exceptions) this does not seem to happen. That hostile racial attitudes may be transient phenomena

'would be encouraging for multiracial education and for the wider society' (Milner, 1997).

Conclusions

This chapter has examined a wide variety of approaches to the reduction of prejudice and discrimination. As was seen in the previous chapter, prejudice and discrimination cannot be explained in a simple and straightforward way. As a result, we should not be surprised to find, as we have, that the reduction of these phenomena is also not simple and straightforward.

SUMMARY

- Although there is evidence to suggest that the authoritarian personality is **self-perpetuating**, as in correlations between parents' and children's F scale scores, level of education is also correlated with authoritarianism. This implies that providing access to education would help to reduce prejudice.
- Changing child-rearing methods, by allowing children to express hostility, might also reduce prejudice by removing the need to displace it onto ethnic and other groups.
- According to the **frustration–aggression** and **relative deprivation theories**, prejudice and discrimination could be reduced by preventing frustration, lowering people's expectations, and providing less anti-social means of venting frustrations. However, the practical difficulties involved are immense.
- According to **conflict approaches**, replacing competition with **superordinate goals** will remove/prevent hostility, whilst **social categorisation** and **social identity approaches** imply that by making intergroup stereotypes more positive, and intergroup boundaries more flexible, group membership will become a less crucial part of the self-concept. In turn, positive evaluation of the ingroup would become less inevitable.
- According to **social learning theory**, children's negative attitudes towards various social groups are acquired from parents, teachers and peers who expose them to such attitudes and reward

them for expressing them. This can result in children's internalisation of their parents' prejudices.
- The mass media are another 'significant other' and if they portray particular groups in a demeaning way, it is hardly surprising that children come to see them as being inferior. History textbooks, for example, can be actively racist, and some psychology textbooks continue to describe black nations in derogatory ways.
- Discouraging parents from expressing prejudiced views and discriminatory behaviour should help to prevent these from developing. Parents could also encourage **self-examination** in their children, stressing the need to attribute behaviour to people as **individuals** rather than **group representatives**.
- Providing children with the opportunity to experience directly the evils of prejudice and discrimination in a protected environment may increase their understanding, as demonstrated by Elliot's 'blue eyes–brown eyes' experiment. The beneficial effects of that experience were evident nine years later.
- Weiner and Wright's more formal 'green–orange' experiment showed that the experience of being discriminated against can make children more aware of the sensitivities and feelings of outgroup members.
- When we are segregated and ignorant of other people, we rely on our (negative) stereotypes for interpreting another group's behaviour, and tend

to see them as being more dissimilar from ourselves than they really are (**autistic hostility**). Related to this is the **mirror-image phenomenon** and the 'assumed dissimilarity of beliefs'.

- Increasing contact between segregated groups can help people realise that their attitudes are actually more similar than they previously assumed, which can in turn increase attraction. This can also happen through the **mere exposure effect.**

- Favourable contact may also present opportunities for disconfirming negative stereotypes and a reduction in outgroup homogeneity, allowing outgroup members to be seen as unique individuals rather than interchangeable units.

- Increased contact by itself is not sufficient to reduce prejudice, and may even increase it. If the contact is between people who are consistently of the same **unequal status**, then stereotypes of the lower status group held by the higher status group may be reinforced.

- According to Allport's **contact hypothesis,** attempts to reduce conflict between groups must involve **equal status contact** and the **pursuit of common goals**.

- An early study by Deutsch and Collins of an integrated and a segregated housing project found that increased contact was associated with a corresponding decrease in anti-black prejudice. Other research has shown the effects of **proximity** on prejudice reduction.

- Minard's study of coalminers in the USA demonstrated the influence of **social norms** regarding the relative status of blacks and whites above and below ground. Similar findings were reported by Stouffer and Amir for the American armed forces.

- In the USA, there has been extensive research into the effects of **desegregation** in schools, and heated debate as to whether integration actually reduces racial tension and increases equal educational opportunities.

- According to supporters of integration, black students will continue to underachieve, and inter-racial hostility will continue to occur, unless desegregation has been planned to promote equal status for majority and minority groups and has the outspoken support of all the authority figures involved. Although these conditions are often not met, there is evidence that the positive effects of desegregation may be far reaching and long term.

- Intergroup contact reduces prejudice not through encouraging *interpersonal* friendship, but by changing the nature and structure of **intergroup relationships**. Where people are seen as individuals, and group memberships are largely insignificant, any change of attitude may not generalise to the group as a whole. Individuals must be seen as typical of their group, but this must not involve reinforcing negative group stereotypes.

- Sherif *et al.* initially tried, unsuccessfully, to reduce the conflict they created between two groups of children by getting them to do things together. They later succeeded, however, when they created **superordinate goals**, which can only be achieved through **co-operation**.

- These findings have been replicated many times in a variety of contexts. However, if co-operation fails to achieve its goals, antagonism towards the outgroup may increase, and it is important that each group's contributions are clearly defined.

- Aronson *et al.'s* approach to the study of co-operative learning in the classroom (the **jigsaw classroom technique**) involved **mutual interdependence** between students regardless of their race. Each child is tested on the whole lesson and is given an individual score, but each is dependent on the others for parts of the lesson that can only be learned from them.

- After white, black and hispanic students had met over a six-week period, they showed increased self-esteem, academic performance, liking for their classmates, and some inter-racial perceptions.

- Whilst these findings have been replicated with large numbers of students, they only tell us about the **short-term** benefits, and it is not clear whether they **generalise** to other social situations.

- According to Milner, children have been seen as **passively** absorbing and reproducing behaviours provided by parents and others. However, we cannot simply assume that children's hostile racial attitudes are caused by culturally mediated racism (implicit or explicit). Although the **content** of racial attitudes is provided by a variety of social/cultural sources, children play a much more **active** role in the development of their racial awareness and attitudes.

- Children are motivated by **needs** to locate themselves and their groups within their social world in ways that promote positive self- and social-identity. Adopting negative racial attitudes **may** help to achieve social acceptance for the majority-group child in a multiracial, competitive society.

- Negative racial attitudes cannot fulfil this function for minority-group children, as seen in **misidentification**. This was demonstrated in Clark and

Clark's study involving children's choice of a black or white doll, regarded as a valid measure of self-concept related to ethnic identification.

- Other research has shown that self-contempt among black children increases as the level of actual anti-black discrimination increases. According to Rowan, blacks come to hate themselves and see themselves as inferior. To cease being inferior, they think they have to stop being black, and this is reflected in doll choice and choice of playmates.
- This **self-denigration** by minority groups was addressed by civil rights and Black politico-cultural movements, leading to the near disappearance of misidentification, even among young children.
- Since racist attitudes are not the only means of achieving a positive social identity, racism among the majority group is neither inevitable nor ineradicable. Milner's belief that racist attitudes, have more to do with children's developing identity needs than with the objects of those attitudes, can account for the peaking of racial hostility at age 6–7. Generally, childhood racial attitudes do not endure into adulthood.

<h1 style="text-align:center">PART 2</h1>
<h2 style="text-align:center">Social relationships</h2>

THE FORMATION OF ADULT RELATIONSHIPS

Introduction and overview

According to Duck (1995), a leading researcher in the area, the study of interpersonal relationships is one of the most fertile and all-embracing aspects of social scientific research. This chapter, and the two that follow, aim to provide an introduction to the study of social relationships and examine how and why such relationships are formed, maintained and sometimes dissolved. Throughout these chapters, we will look at theories of adult interpersonal relationships, the components and effects of such relationships, and their individual, social and cultural variations.

This chapter is concerned with the formation of adult relationships, that is, how these relationships 'get started'. As we shall see, much of the data in this area comes from North American research, and both their quality and validity have been questioned. However, before we look at the research, and critiques of it, we will briefly consider affiliation, which can be seen as a precondition for relationship formation.

Affiliation

Affiliation is our basic need for the company of other people. According to Duck (1988), we are more affiliative and inclined to seek other people's company in some circumstances than others. These include moving to a new neighbourhood and the termination of a close relationship. One of the most powerful factors influencing affiliation is *anxiety*, as shown in Box 5.1.

Box 5.1 The effects of anxiety on affiliation

Schachter (1959) led female students to believe that they would be receiving electric shocks. Half were told that the shocks would be extremely painful (high anxiety condition) and half that they would not be at all painful (low anxiety condition). The students were then told that there would be a delay whilst the equipment was being set up, and that they could wait on their own or with another participant. Schachter found that two-thirds of those in the high anxiety condition chose to wait with another participant, whilst only one-third in the low anxiety condition chose this option.

In another experiment, Schachter told all the participants that the shocks would be extremely painful. This time, though, the members of one group were given the option of waiting alone or with another participant who would be receiving the shocks. Members of the second group were given the option of waiting alone or with a student who was waiting to see her teacher. Those in the first group preferred to sit with another participant, whilst those in the second group preferred to be alone. This suggests that if we have something to worry about, we prefer to be with others in the same situation.

The role of anxiety in affiliation has also been demonstrated in other studies. For example, Kulik and Mahler (1989) found that most patients awaiting coronary bypass surgery preferred to share a room with someone who had already undergone that operation, rather than with another patient who was waiting to undergo it. The main motive for this preference seemed to be the need for *information* in order to reduce the stress caused by the forthcoming operation (Buunk, 1996).

Forming relationships: interpersonal attraction

According to Clore and Byrne (1974), we are attracted to people whose presence is *rewarding* for us. These rewards may be direct (and provided by the other person) or indirect (the other person takes on the emotional tone of the surrounding situation). The more rewards someone provides for us, the more we should be attracted to them. Although rewards are not the same for everyone, a number of factors have been shown to be important in influencing the initial attraction between people through their reward value. These include proximity, exposure, familiarity, similarity, physical attractiveness, reciprocal liking, complementarity and competence.

PROXIMITY

Proximity means geographical closeness, and is a minimum requirement for attraction because the further apart two people live, the less likely it is that they will have the chance to meet, become friends or marry each other. In an early study on the effects of proximity, Festinger *et al.* (1950) found that students living in campus accommodation were most friendly with their next-door neighbours and least friendly with those at the end of the corridor. Students separated by four flats hardly ever became friends and, in two-storey flats, residents tended to interact mainly with people who lived on the same floor. On any one floor, people who lived near stairways had more friends than those living at the end of the corridor (see Figure 5.1).

Festinger *et al.'s* findings have been replicated in numerous studies. For example, home owners are more likely to become friendly with their next-door neighbours, especially when they share a drive (Whyte, 1956), and apartment dwellers tend to form relationships with those on the same floor (Nahemow and Lawton, 1975). At school, students are more likely to develop relationships with those they sit next to (Segal,

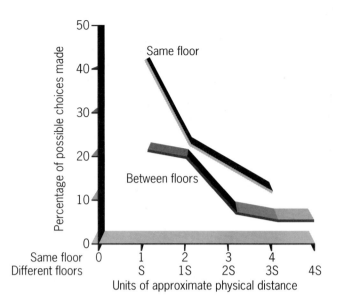

Figure 5.1   Data from Festinger *et al.'s* (1950) investigation. The 'units of approximate physical distance' refer to how many doors apart people lived. For example, 3S means three doors and a stairway apart (From Festinger *et al.*, 1950)

1974). We should, however, note that there are 'rules' governing physical proximity. Box 5.2 explores some of these.

Box 5.2   Physical proximity and personal space

In a number of studies, Sommer (1969) and his colleagues (e.g. Felipe and Sommer, 1966) showed that when a stranger sits next to or close to a person, that person experiences an unpleasant state of arousal. This is because his or her *personal space* – a term coined by Hall (1959) and conceptualised as a sort of 'invisible bubble' around a person in which it is unpleasant for others to be – has been invaded.

According to Hall we learn *proxemic rules*. These prescribe the physical distance that is appropriate between people in daily situations, and the kinds of situation in which closeness or distance is proper (see Figure 5.2). These rules are not the same in all cultures (Collett, 1993), and there are individual differences with regard to them, even within the same culture (violent criminals, for example, are more sensitive to physical closeness than non-violent criminals). Successful relationships may require an initial establishment of 'boundary understandings', that is, strangers must be invited into our personal space rather than 'invade' it.

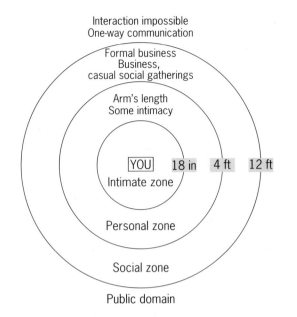

Figure 5.2   Hall's four zones of personal space (From Nicholson, 1977)

EXPOSURE AND FAMILIARITY

Proximity provides increased opportunity for interaction (*exposure*) which, in turn, increases how familiar others become to us (*familiarity*). Far from breeding *contempt*, the evidence suggests that familiarity breeds *contentment* unless we initially dislike something, in which case we tend to dislike it even more (Rubin, 1973; Grush, 1976). This is what Zajonc (1968) calls the *mere exposure effect*, and several studies have shown that there is a positive correlation between frequency of exposure to stimuli and liking for them (e.g. Moreland and Zajonc, 1982; Nuttin, 1987; Brooks and Watkins, 1989). Argyle (1983) has argued that increased exposure to, and familiarity with, others causes an increased polarisation of attitudes towards each other. Usually, this is in the direction of greater liking, but only if the interaction is as equals.

The impact of familiarity on attraction was demonstrated by Newcomb (1961). He found that whilst similarity of beliefs, attitudes and values (see below) was important in determining liking, the key factor was familiarity. So, even when students are paired according to the similarity or dissimilarity of their beliefs, attitudes and values, room-mates became friends far more often than would be expected on the basis of their characteristics.

Other research has shown that our preference for what is familiar even extends to our own facial appearance. For example, Mita *et al.*, (1977) showed people pictures of themselves as they appear to others and mirror-images (how we appear to ourselves when we look in a mirror). Most people preferred the latter – this is how we are used to seeing ourselves. However, their friends preferred the former – this is how others are used to seeing us. It seems, then, that in general we like what we know and what we are familiar with.

SIMILARITY

There is strong evidence to suggest that 'birds of a feather flock together', and research indicates that the critical similarities are those concerning *beliefs*, *attitudes*, and *values*. For example, Newcomb (1943) studied students at an American college which had a liberal tradition among teaching staff and senior students. Newcomb found that many students coming from conservative backgrounds adopted liberal attitudes in order to gain the liking and acceptance of their classmates. A selection of some of the research findings relating to similarity and attraction is described in Box 5.3.

> **Box 5.3   Some research findings relating to similarity and attraction**
>
> - We are more strongly attracted to people who share our attitudes. Moreover, the greater the proportion of shared attitudes, the greater the attraction.
> - The more dogmatic we are, the more likely we are to reject people who disagree with us.
> - When we believe that politicians share the same attitudes as us, we may fail to remember statements they made that *conflict* with our attitudes.
> - Some attitudinal factors are more important than others. One of the most important is religion.
>
> (Based on Byrne, 1971; Johnson and Judd, 1983; Howard *et al.*, 1987)

Rubin (1973) has identified several reasons for the importance of similarity. In his view, similarity is *rewarding* for at least five reasons. First, agreement may provide a basis for engaging in joint activities. Second, a person who agrees with us helps to increase our confidence in our own opinions and this enhances self-esteem. In Duck's (1992) view, the validation that friends give us is experienced as evidence of the accuracy of our personal construction of the world. Third, most of us are vain enough to believe that anyone who shares our views must be a sensitive and praiseworthy person. Fourth, people who agree about things that matter to them generally find it easier to communicate. Fifth, we may assume that people with similar attitudes to ourselves will like us, and so we like them in turn (a phenomenon called *reciprocal liking*: see page 46).

According to *balance theory* (Heider, 1946; Newcomb, 1953), people like to have a clear, ordered and consistent view of the world, so that all the parts 'fit together'. If we agree with our friends and disagree with our enemies, then we are in a state of balance (Jellison and Oliver, 1983). As Figure 5.3 shows, the theory predicts that two people (A and B) will like each other if their opinions about something (X) are the same. If A and B's evaluation of X is different, however, they will not like each other. This imbalance can be resolved either by A or B changing his or her opinion or by A and B disliking each other.

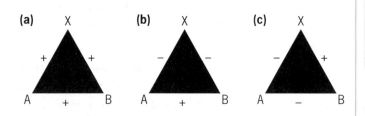

Figure 5.3   Balance theory predicts that two people, A and B, will like each other (+) if their opinions about something (X) are both favourable, as shown in (a), or unfavourable, as shown in (b). A and B will dislike each other if their opinions about X are different, as shown in (c) (After Heider, 1946; and Newcomb, 1953)

A slightly different approach to understanding the importance of similarity is provided by Rosenbaum (1986) in his *repulsion hypothesis*. Rosenbaum argues that whilst other people's agreement with our attitudes provides balance, this psychological state is not especially arousing. However, when people disagree with our attitudes, we experience arousal and discomfort as a result of the imbalance. In other words, disagreement has more effect than agreement (Crider *et al.*, 1989). So, whilst similarity is important, the role of dissimilarity in attraction should not be ignored.

PHYSICAL ATTRACTIVENESS

A large body of evidence supports the general view that physical attractiveness influences the impression we form of the people we meet. For example, research suggests that attractive-looking people are believed to have attractive personalities, such as being sexually warm and responsive, kind, strong, outgoing, nurturant, interesting, and so on (Dion *et al.*, 1972). Box 5.4 summarises the findings of some other research in this area.

> **Box 5.4   Some research findings relating to attractiveness**
>
> Compared with unattractive people, attractive people are:
>
> - more popular and sought after (Hatfield and Sprecher, 1986);
> - assumed to be higher in positive traits such as intelligence (Hatfield and Walster, 1985);
> - more likely to be employed even when their physical attractiveness is not a prerequisite for a job (Solomon, 1987);
> - perceived as happier, more sensitive, more successful, and more socially skilled (Hatfield and Sprecher, 1986).

Given the importance of *stereotypes* in influencing our first impressions of other people (see Chapter 2), it would seem that attractive people have a 'head start' in this early phase of relationship development (Solomon, 1987). However, it is not always in our best interests to be seen as highly attractive. For example, Dermer and Thiel (1975) found that female participants judged extremely attractive women to be egoistic, vain, materialistic, snobbish, and less likely to be successfully married.

Furthermore, although mock jury experiments and observational studies have shown that attractive people are more likely to be found innocent of crimes (Michelini and Snodgrass, 1980), there are exceptions to this. For example, if a woman is standing trial for fraud, accused of having charmed a man into giving her money for some non-existent cause, she is *more* likely to be found guilty if she is very attractive. In terms of attribution theory, her good looks may result in the jury being more likely to make a *correspondent inference* (see Chapter 1, page 2).

Albeit unconsciously, adults may treat children differently according to their physical appeal, and may expect good-looking children to be better behaved than less attractive ones (Stephan and Langlois, 1984). When the former do behave badly, their behaviour is more likely to be explained by adults in situational (it wasn't really their fault) rather than dispositional (something about them made them behave that way) terms (Dion, 1972). According to Dion and Dion (1995), stereotyping based on facial attractiveness appears at least as early as age six.

Interestingly, data exist suggesting that even infants as young as two months have a marked preference for attractive faces over unattractive ones. For example, Langlois *et al.* (1990) showed that when infants are presented with pairs of colour slides of adult faces rated by adults as being unattractive and attractive, they spend longer looking at the attractive face. According to Langlois *et al.* (1987), such a finding

> 'challenges the commonly held assumption that standards of attractiveness are learned through gradual exposure to the cultural standard of beauty and are merely "in the eye of the beholder"'.

Box 5.5 Who is attractive? The role of culture and gender

Different cultures have different criteria of what constitutes physical beauty. For example, chipped teeth, body scars, artificially elongated heads and bound feet have all been regarded as being attractive (Ford and Beach, 1951). In Western culture, definitions of beauty change over time, a particularly good instance of this being the 'ideal' figure for women. Traditionally, facial beauty has been generally regarded as more important in women than men. For men, stature (particularly height), a muscular body, and (at least at present) firm, rounded buttocks influence how attractive they are judged to be. (Jensen-Campbell *et al.*, 1995).

The above examples seem to show that it is impossible to define 'attractive' objectively. However, 'average', that is, not too big or too small, may be one way of moving away from a purely subjective definition. For example, Langlois and Roggman (1994) digitised the faces of a number of college students and used a computer to aver-

age them. Students judged the composite faces as more appealing than 96 per cent of the individual faces.

Brehm (1992) has argued that in the context of personal advertisements and commercial dating services, the primary 'resource' (or reward) offered by females seeking a male partner is still physical attractiveness, which matches what men actually seek from a female partner. However, Buss (1989) has argued that this is a universal phenomenon rather than one confined to Western culture. This issue is discussed further in Chapter 6 (see page 55).

What makes a pretty face?

In a study conducted by Bruce *et al.*, (1994), the relationship between facial distinctiveness and attractiveness was examined. The researchers found that the two variables were not correlated, and that 'distinctiveness' can be accounted for in terms of a physical deviation from the norm. Exactly what the 'norm' is was addressed by Perret *et al.* (1994). They asked white male and female undergraduates to rate each of 60 young adult white female faces for attractiveness.

After this, an 'average' composite was constructed from the photographs using the computer averaging method employed by Langlois and Roggman (see Box 5.5). An attractive composite was made from the 15 faces rated as being most attractive, and a highly attractive composite by exaggerating the shape of the attractive composite by 50 per cent. The composites were then rated by both female and male students. Both sexes preferred the attractive composite to the average one, and the highly attractive composite to the attractive one.

Figure 5.4   Computers can be used in a variety of ways to study facial attractiveness (From Perret *et al.*, 1994)

Perret *et al.* then attempted to replicate their findings cross-culturally. Young female Japanese adult faces were rated by Japanese and white raters, and the results did not differ from those found in the original study. The most attractive face generally had higher cheek bones, a thinner jaw, and larger eyes relative to the size of the face. There was also a shorter distance between the mouth and chin, and between the nose and mouth. These findings suggest that there is a systematic difference between an 'average' and an 'attractive' face, but casts doubt on the view that attractiveness is averageness.

There is emerging evidence to suggest that certain factors associated with physical attractiveness can cause psychological distress in those who do not possess them. An interesting example of this is described in Box 5.6.

Box 5.6   The psychological effects of hair loss

Research into impression formation indicates that bald and balding men are generally rated less favourably in terms of physical and social attractiveness, self-assertiveness, personal likeability and life success. Wells *et al.* (1995) wanted to know if men with hair loss suffer the kinds of psychological distress that might accompany such unfavourable impressions. The researchers studied 182 men of various ages and whose hair loss ranged from none to severe.

The participants were asked to complete a personality questionnaire which revealed that, irrespective of their age, the greater their hair loss, the more likely they were to report low self-esteem, feelings of depression and unattractiveness, and signs of neuroticism and psychoticism. These effects tended to be larger amongst the younger men.

The matching hypothesis

According to *social exchange theory* (Thibaut and Kelley, 1959; Blau, 1964; Homans, 1974; Berscheid and Walster, 1978), people are more likely to become romantically involved if they are fairly closely matched in their ability to reward one another. Ideally, we would all like to have the 'perfect partner' because, the theory says, we are all selfish. However, since this is impossible, we try to find a compromise solution. The best general bargain that can be struck is a *value-match*, that is, a subjective belief that our partner is the most rewarding we could realistically hope to find.

Several studies have attempted to test the matching hypothesis (Walster *et al.*, 1966; Dion and Berscheid, 1970; Berscheid *et al.*, 1971; Silverman, 1971; Murstein, 1972; Berscheid and Walster, 1974). What these studies show is that people rated as being of high, low or average attractiveness tend to choose partners of a corresponding level of attractiveness. Indeed, according to Price and Vandenberg (1979),

'the matching phenomenon (of physical attraction between marriage partners) is stable within and across generations'.

The findings from the various studies into the matching hypothesis imply that the kind of partner we would be satisfied with is one whom we feel will not reject us, rather than one whom we positively desire. Brown (1986), however, disagrees. In his view, the matching phenomenon results from a well-learned sense of what is 'fitting' rather than a fear of being rebuffed. For Brown, then, we learn to adjust our expectations of rewards in line with what we believe we have to offer others. A novel approach to the matching hypothesis is described in Box 5.7 (see opposite).

RECIPROCAL LIKING

In *How to Win Friends and Influence People*, Carnegie (1937) advised people to greet others with enthusiasm and 'praise' if we wanted them to like us. It is certainly a pleasant experience when someone pays us compliments and generally seems to like us. Indeed, we often respond by saying 'flattery will get you everywhere'. Research suggests that we tend to respond in kind, or *reciprocate*, when we are the recipients of compliments and liking (Byrne and Murnen, 1988), and that this often influences those to whom we respond to like us even more (Curtis and Miller, 1988).

According to Aronson's (1980) *reward–cost principle*, we are most attracted to a person who makes entirely positive comments about us on several occasions, and least attracted to one who makes entirely negative comments. This, however, is not particularly surprising or interesting. More interesting is Aronson and Linder's (1965) *gain–loss theory*. According to this, someone who starts off by disliking us, and then comes to like us, will be more liked than someone who likes us from the start. Equally, someone who begins by liking us and then adopts a negative attitude towards us will be disliked more than someone who dislikes us from the start.

Box 5.7 'Mate selection' in twins

The term 'mate selection' refers to choosing someone we hope will be our lifetime partner. Because identical twins share the same genes and, typically, the same environment, their choice of a mate might be expected to be similar. However, using 738 sets of identical twins, Lykken and Tellegren (1993) found that this was not the case, and the spouses of an identical twin-pair were hardly more likely to be similar than were spouses of random pairs of same-sex adults. When the researchers asked the twins how they felt about their co-twin's choice of mate, less than half the twins (of both sexes) reported that they were attracted to their co-twin's choice. Indeed, just as many reported negative attitudes.

Lykken and Tellegren argue that if people adopt reasonably discriminating criteria to guide mate selection, then those of identical co-twins should be more similar (even though these criteria will differ from person to person). The evidence, though, suggests that whilst we do tend to choose from among people like ourselves, identical twins are not likely to be drawn to the same choice. According to Lowe (1994), this suggests that

'although most human choice behaviour is fairly rational, the most important choice of all – that of a mate – seems to be an exception'.

COMPLEMENTARITY

As was seen in the section on similarity, 'birds of a feather flock together'. But do 'opposites attract'? There is a little evidence to support the view that some relationships are based on *complementarity* rather than similarity. For example, Winch (1958) found a tendency for each partner in a marriage to possess needs or traits that the other lacked (and he termed this *complementarity of needs*: see Chapter 6, page 55). In Winch's study, women who displayed a need to be nurturant were often married to men who needed to be nurtured.

If complementarity does occur in relationship formation, it is likely that this is because opposing traits reinforce each other and benefit both individuals. However, apart from Winch's research, the evidence for complementarity is weak (Nias, 1979), and it is more likely that complementarity develops during a relationship (Rubin, 1973). However, there is stronger evidence for complementarity of *resources* (see Chapter 6, page 55).

COMPETENCE

Whilst it is generally the case that we are more attracted to competent than incompetent people, there are exceptions to this. For example, when a highly talented male makes an embarrassing error, we come to like him more (Aronson *et al.*, 1966). Presumably, this is because the error indicates that, like the rest of us, he is 'only human'. Additionally, Aronson *et al.* found that when a person of average ability makes an error, he is liked less, and his error is seen as being just another example of his incompetence. These findings seem to be confined to men (Deaux, 1972), possibly because men are more competitive and like other competent people better when they show a weakness.

Duck's critique of the research

As noted in the introduction to this chapter, the quality and validity of the data of research into relationship formation have been questioned. One of the major critics has been Duck (1995), who argues that much of the research is

'typically based on scrutiny of the point of interaction at which the partners were, at best, strangers to each other. The studies [use] college students, for the most part, and [focus] only on immediate judgements of attractiveness or expressions of desire to see the other person again – [and are] rarely followed up or checked for correspondence to later realities of actual interaction or second meetings'.

Duck has called for appropriate caution to be taken about such data, and for the scope of research to be broadened beyond studies of 'initial attraction'. He cites areas such as commuter marriages (Rohlfing, 1995), relationships conducted across electronic mail (Lea and Spears, 1995), and relationships among the elderly (Blieszner and Adams, 1992) as areas attracting recent interest. For Duck,

'those who became irritated by the early work, and hence convinced that the topic had no insights to offer our deeper understanding of the human condition, were perhaps as right to be indignant as were those of us who thought it could be done better at the time and hoped to change things'.

Duck's review of the ever-growing literature in this area indicates that the study of social relationships has recovered from what he describes as 'the [biased] discussions … that used to make up the bulk of … our social psychology textbooks'. Whilst a general text such as this cannot even briefly review *all* of the areas currently under investigation, the following two chapters

at least begin to look at the wider concerns of social relationships research.

Conclusions

This chapter has looked at social psychological research into the formation of adult relationships. Many factors have been shown to influence the initial attraction between people, although the research conducted in this area has been subjected to criticism.

SUMMARY

- **Affiliation** represents a precondition for relationship formation, and is our basic need for other people's company. This need is more apparent in some circumstances than others.
- The role of **anxiety** in affiliation was demonstrated by Schachter's experiments involving female students who believed they were going to receive electric shocks. The results suggest that, when anxious, we prefer the company of others in the same situation. The main motive for this preference may sometimes be the need for stress-reducing **information.**
- According to Clore and Byrne, we are attracted to people who **reward** us, either directly or indirectly, and the greater the rewards, the greater the attraction. Whilst rewards are not the same for everyone, several factors have been shown to influence initial attraction through their reward value.
- **Proximity** is a minimum requirement for attraction, since people must meet if they are to become friends or marry. Festinger *et al.*'s study of friendship patterns amongst students living in campus accommodation showed the importance of proximity. These results have been replicated many times, with neighbours, apartment dwellers and school students.
- Sommer's research demonstrated the unpleasant state of arousal caused by a stranger's invasion of our **personal space.** According to Hall, we learn **proxemic rules**, which prescribe appropriate distances between people in daily situations. These rules differ both between cultures and between individuals within the same culture. Successful

relationships may require initial 'boundary understandings'.
- Proximity provides increased opportunity for **exposure** to others, thus increasing **familiarity**. In turn, familiarity appears to breed **contentment.** There is considerable support for Zajonc's **mere exposure effect** and, according to Argyle, increased exposure to, and familiarity with, others produces increased liking, as long as the interaction is as equals.
- Newcomb found that when students are paired according to the similarity/dissimilarity of their beliefs, attitudes and values, room-mates become friends far more often than their characteristics would lead us to expect. This demonstrates the impact of familiarity. This preference for what is familiar extends to our own facial appearance.
- Several studies, have shown the importance of **similarity**, particularly of **beliefs, attitudes** and **values.** Similarity of religion seems to be especially important.
- According to Rubin, similarity is **rewarding** because agreement may provide a basis for joint activities. Also, someone agreeing with us helps to increase our confidence in our opinions which enhances self-esteem.
- We are also likely to see people who agree with us as sensitive and praiseworthy, as well as easier to communicate with. Through **reciprocal liking,** we like people who share our attitudes based on the assumption that they will like us.
- According to **balance theory**, we like to have an ordered and consistent view of the world. Two people, A and B, will like each other if both their

opinions about something are favourable or un-favourable, but they will dislike each other if their opinions differ.

- According to Rosenbaum's **repulsion hypothesis**, whilst others' agreement with our attitudes provides balance, the imbalance produced by their disagreement is more psychologically arousing. So, as important as similarity is, dissimilarity is also important.

- There is considerable evidence that **physical attractiveness** influences the impressions we form of others. Compared with unattractive people, attractive-looking people are seen as having attractive personalities, being more intelligent, happier, sensitive, successful and socially skilled, and are more popular and sought after.

- Given the importance of **stereotypes** in impression formation, attractive people seem to have an advantage in the initial stages of relationship development. However, in mock jury experiments, a very attractive woman accused of fraudulently charming a man into giving her money is **more** likely to be found guilty (the jury is more likely to make a **correspondent inference**).

- Adults may unconsciously expect good-looking children to be better behaved than less attractive ones. When the former do behave badly, adults are more likely to make situational than dispositional attributions.

- Different cultures clearly have different criteria of what constitutes physical beauty, and these change over time in Western culture, as in definitions of the 'ideal' figure for women.

- According to Buss, men universally seek physical attractiveness in women, and this is not confined to Western culture, as demonstrated in personal advertisements and commercial dating services.

- Whilst it is impossible to define 'attractive' objectively, Langlois and Roggman's use of digitised 'average' faces is one alternative to a purely subjective definition.

- Bruce *et al.* found that attractiveness is not correlated with facial distinctiveness, which can be explained in terms of a physical deviation from the norm. Perret *et al.*'s findings with both American and Japanese participants suggest that this norm is best defined in terms of an exaggeration of averageness. There also seems to be a systematic difference between an average and an attractive face.

- Lacking certain factors associated with physical attractiveness (such as having a full head of hair),

and hence being perceived less favourably by others, can cause psychological distress.

- According to **social exchange theory**, people are more likely to become romantically involved the more closely matched they are in their ability to reward each other. Since it is impossible to find the perfect partner, we settle for a **value-match** (the **matching hypothesis**).

- Several studies have found that people rated as being of high, low or average attractiveness tend to choose partners of a corresponding level of attractiveness. In married couples, the matching phenomenon appears to be stable within and across generations.

- Instead of the matching phenomenon reflecting a fear of rejection, Brown believes that we learn to adjust our expectations of reward in line with what we believe we have to offer others.

- Research suggests that we tend to **reciprocate** when others pay us compliments and show they like us (**reciprocal liking**). According to Aronson's **reward–cost principle**, we are most attracted to people who make entirely positive comments about us, and least attracted to those who make entirely negative comments.

- More interestingly, Aronson and Linder's **gain–loss theory** claims that someone who starts off by disliking us and then comes to like us will be liked more than someone who likes us from the start. The reverse is true for someone who likes us initially, then comes to dislike us.

- There is some evidence that relationships can be built on **complementarity of needs** rather than similarity. However, the little evidence that exists suggests that complementarity develops during a relationship and, rather than personality traits, it involves resources such as physical beauty and money.

- Whilst we generally prefer competent to incompetent people, a highly competent person who makes an embarrassing mistake may be liked most of all, and an incompetent person who makes the same mistake may be the least liked. These findings seem to be confined to men, who are more competitive than women.

- According to Duck, most studies involve college students, focusing on first meetings and judgements of initial attraction, with little follow-up of how the relationship subsequently progresses.

- Areas currently being investigated include commuter marriages, relationships conducted across electronic mail, and relationships among the elderly.

THE MAINTENANCE OF ADULT RELATIONSHIPS

Introduction and overview

The previous chapter looked at some of the factors that influence the extent to which we are attracted to others and hence make it likely that we will try to form relationships with them. Our aim in this chapter is to look at how relationships are maintained. Some of the factors discussed in the previous chapter apply here as well. For example, Byrne (1971) found that the greater the similarity between a couple, the more likely it was that a relationship endured. This was shown to be the case for a variety of groups including school children and adult alcoholics! Before we look at theory and research into the maintenance of relationships, however, we will briefly consider the distinction between liking and loving, and cross-cultural conceptions of love.

Liking and loving

According to Rubin (1973), liking and loving are not the same. For Rubin, liking is the positive evaluation of another and consists of respect and affection. Rubin sees loving as being more than an intense liking. In his view, loving is qualitatively different and is composed of *attachment, caring,* and *intimacy.* Attachment is the need for the physical presence and support of the loved one. Caring is a feeling of concern and responsibility for the loved one. Intimacy is the desire for close and confidential contact, and wanting to share certain thoughts and feelings with the loved one more fully than with anyone else. Rubin's idea of caring corresponds to Fromm's (1962) definition of love as 'the active concern for the life and growth of that which we love'.

Much of the support for Rubin's distinction between liking and loving comes from people's responses on scales he devised to measure them. Some sample items

from the scales are shown in Table 6.1. Rubin's research has revealed a number of interesting findings. For example, lovers tend to give similar but not identical positive responses to items on both scales. So, we tend to like the people we love, but the relationship is not perfect. Also, people who score high on the love scale are more likely to say that they expect to marry their partners. This means that love is correlated with an anticipated permanent relationship.

Table 6.1   Some items from Rubin's (1973) Liking scale and Love scale

Respondents are asked to indicate if a particular statement reflects accurately their perception about another person.

Liking scale
1. I think that ____ is unusually well adjusted.
2. I have great confidence in ____'s good judgement.
3. ____ is the sort of person whom I myself would like to be.

Love scale
1. If ____ were feeling bad, my first duty would be to cheer him/her up.
2. I feel that I can confide in ____ about virtually everything.
3. If I could never be with ____ I would feel miserable.

The Love scale can also be applied to same-sex friends. Here, Rubin found that females reported loving their friends more than men did. Other research has shown that women's friendships tend to be more intimate than men's, and that women engage in more spontaneous joint activities and more exchange of confidences. According to Rubin and McNeil (1983), loving for men may be channelled into single, sexual relationships, whilst women may be better able to experience attachment, caring and intimacy in a wider range and variety of relationships.

It has been argued that a concept like love cannot be measured at all, let alone by using pencil-and-paper devices. Rubin, though, has shown that partners who are high on the Love scale engage in more eye contact than dating couples who are lower on it. For Rubin (1973), this is good evidence that the Love scale has at least some validity.

TYPES OF LOVE

For some researchers, love is a label that we learn to attach to our own state of physiological arousal. However, for most of the time love does not involve intense physical 'symptoms', and it is perhaps better to view it as a sort of attitude that one person has towards another (Rubin and McNeil, 1983). It seems likely that the sort of love a couple married for 50 years experience is different from that of a couple at school who are 'going steady'. So how many types of love are there?

Berscheid and Walster (1978) have made a distinction between *romantic love* and *companionate love*. Romantic love (which has also been called *passionate* love) is characterised by intense feelings of tenderness, elation, anxiety, and sexual desire. It is also associated with increased activity in the sympathetic branch of the autonomic nervous system. According to Hatfield and Rapson (1987):

'passionate love is like any other form of excitement. By its very nature, excitement involves a continuous interplay between elation and despair, thrills and terror ... Sometimes men and women become entangled in love affairs where the delight is brief, and pain, uncertainty, jealousy, misery, anxiety, and despair are abundant. Often, passionate love seems to be fuelled by a sprinkling of hope and a large dollop of loneliness, mourning, jealousy, and terror'.

Romantic love usually occurs early in a relationship but does not last very long. Companionate love (which is sometimes called *true love* or *conjugal love*) is the affection that remains after the passion of romantic love has subsided, and is essential if a relationship is to be maintained. Companionate love is less intense than romantic love and involves thoughtful appreciation of one's partner. It is also characterised by a tolerance for weaknesses and a desire to solve conflicts and difficulties in a relationship (Rubenstein, 1983).

According to Sternberg (1986, 1988), love has three basic components, these being *intimacy, passion* and *decision/commitment*. The presence or absence of these three components produces the different types of love shown in Box 6.1 (Table 6.2).

Box 6.1   Sternberg's triangular theory of love.

Intimacy is the emotionally based part of love, that is, the feelings of closeness, connectedness and bondedness in loving relationships.

Passion is the motivational component of love, the drives that lead to romance, physical attraction and sexual consummation.

Decision/commitment is the cognitive 'controller' in a loving relationship. The short-term decision involves acceptance of such a relationship. The long-term aspect involves the commitment to maintain the relationship.

Table 6.2

Kind of love	Component		
	Intimacy	Passion	Decision/ commitment
Non-love	Absent	Absent	Absent
Liking	Present	Absent	Absent
Infatuated love	Absent	Present	Absent
Empty love	Absent	Absent	Present
Romantic love	Present	Present	Absent
Companionate love	Present	Absent	Present
Fatuous love	Absent	Present	Present
Consummate love	Present	Present	Present

Consider, for example, *infatuated love*. This includes those relationships which we describe as being 'love at first sight'. The love is aroused by passion, but there is no intimacy or decision/commitment. Such relationships can rise almost instantaneously and end just as quickly.

Sternberg's theory helps us to understand the various relationships we have by looking at the three dimensions. We should, however, note that most loving relationships will fit between the categories because the various components of love are expressed along continua, not discretely (Houston *et al.*, 1991). We should also note that alternatives to Sternberg's theory exist, most notably the six basic love styles identified by Hendrick *et al.* (1988), which recognise that 'love' means different things to different people, even to the partners themselves (Bellur, 1995).

LOVE ACROSS CULTURES

According to Moghaddam *et al.* (1993), much of the theory and research relating to social relationships is a reflection of the dominant values of North America, from where a large number of theories and an even larger number of studies originate.

Box 6.2   The importance of cross-cultural analyses

Goodwin (1995) has argued that cross-cultural analyses of relationships are important for at least three reasons. First, they allow competing theories to be compared and assessed according to whether they are universal or the products of particular cultural or historical conditions. Second, contact between people from different cultural backgrounds is increasing in both frequency and intensity. As people acculturate to a new society, their relationships with those around them are important in determining their psychological well-being. Third, increasing business and leisure contacts raise important issues about cross-cultural communications, and understanding the rules of commerce in different cultures is an important part of a business person's armoury.

One of the main dimensions on which cultures differ is *individualism–collectivism*. Individualism places greatest emphasis on personal achievement and self-reliance. Collectivism, by contrast, places priority on the welfare and unity of the group (Bellur, 1995). Although Goodwin (1995) has argued that this division is a somewhat simplified one (because some cultures seem to be highly individualist in some settings and more collectivist in others), he believes that it can be useful in helping to summarise some of the cross-cultural variations in personal relationships.

Goodwin argues that love, 'at least in its passionate stomach churning Hollywood manifestation', is largely a Western and individualistic phenomenon and that in Western cultures, marriage is seen as the culmination of a 'loving' relationship. In those cultures where 'arranged marriages' occur, the relationship between love and marriage is the other way around, and marriage is seen as the basis on which to explore a loving relationship (Bellur, 1995). As Bellur notes, the cultural background in which people have learned about love is important in shaping their concept of love.

The fact that love is seen as something that will develop in the arranged marriage does not necessarily mean that such a marriage will be unhappy. Indeed, evidence suggests that such marriages may produce more happiness than 'love' marriages. For example, Gupta and Singh (1992) found that couples in India who married out of love reported diminished feelings of love if they had been married for more than five years. By contrast, those who had undertaken arranged marriages reported more love if they were not newly weds.

As Bellur (1995) observes, these findings reveal that 'passionate love cools over time' and that 'there is scope for love to flourish within an arranged marriage'. In the case of those cultures in which arranged marriages occur, then, courtship is accepted to a certain degree, but love is left to be defined and discovered after marriage.

Stage theories of relationships

As we all know and expect, relationships develop and change over time. Indeed, relationships which stagnate, especially if sexual/romantic in nature, may well be doomed to failure (Duck, 1988: see Chapter 7). A number of theories that chart the course of relationships have been proposed. These typically cover both sexual and non-sexual relationships, although they sometimes make specific mention of marriage/marriage partners.

KERCKHOFF AND DAVIS'S 'FILTER' THEORY

According to Kerckhoff and Davis (1962), relationships pass through a series of 'filters'. They base this claim on a comparison between 'short-term couples' (less than 18 months) and 'long-term couples' (more than 18 months). Similarity of *sociological* (or *demographic*) variables (such as ethnic, racial, religious, and social class groups) determines the likelihood of people meeting in the first place. To some extent, our choice of friends and partners is made for us because, to use Kerckhoff's (1974) term, 'the field of availables' (the range of people who are realistically, as opposed to theoretically, available for us to meet) is reduced by social circumstances.

The next 'filter' involves people's *psychological* characteristics and, specifically, agreement on basic values.

Kerckhoff and Davis found this to be the best predictor of a relationship becoming more stable and permanent. Thus, those who had been together for less than 18 months tended to have a stronger relationship when the partners' values coincided. With couples of longer standing, though, similarity was not the most important factor. In fact, *complementarity of emotional needs* was the best predictor of a longer term commitment, and this constitutes the third 'filter'.

MURSTEIN'S STIMULUS–VALUE–ROLE (SVR) THEORY

Murstein (1976, 1987) sees intimate relationships proceeding from a *stimulus* stage, in which attraction is based on external attributes (such as physical appearance), to a *value* stage, in which similarity of values and beliefs becomes much more important. Then, relationships proceed to a *role* stage, which involves a commitment based on successful performance of relationship roles, such as husband and wife. Although all of these factors have some influence throughout a relationship, each one assumes its greatest significance during one particular stage, as shown in Figure 6.1.

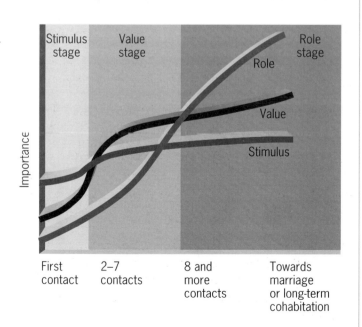

Figure 6.1   States of courtship in Murstein's SVR theory (From Gross, 1996)

LEVINGER'S THEORY

For Levinger (1980), relationships pass through five stages rather than the three proposed by Murstein. These are acquaintance or initial attraction, building up the relationship, consolidation or continuation, deterioration and decline, and ending. At each stage there are positive factors that promote the development of the relationship, and corresponding negative factors that prevent its development or cause it to fail.

For example, and as seen in the previous chapter, repeated interaction with someone makes initial attraction more likely, whilst infrequent contact makes it much less likely. Similarity of attitudes and other characteristics helps a relationship to build, whilst dissimilarity makes building difficult (Levinger's second stage), and so on. The major limitation of Levinger's theory and, indeed, other stage theories, is that there is only weak evidence for a fixed sequence of stages in interpersonal relationships (Brehm, 1992). As a result, Brehm suggests that it is better to talk about 'phases' that take place at different times for different couples.

What keeps people together?

If we consider what all our important relationships have in common, we would find that all are rewarding for us and yet all can at times be complex, demanding, and even painful. If all relationships involve both positive and negative aspects, then what determines our continued involvement in them?

SOCIAL EXCHANGE THEORY

Social exchange theory was mentioned briefly in the previous chapter (see page 46). It provides a general framework for analysing all kinds of relationship, both intimate and non-intimate, and is really an extension of reward theory (also discussed briefly in the previous chapter, see page 46).

According to Homans (1974), we view our feelings for others in terms of profits, that is, the amount of reward obtained from a relationship minus the cost. The greater the reward and lower the cost, the greater the profits and hence the attraction. Blau (1964) argues that interactions are 'expensive', in the sense that they take time, energy and commitment, and may involve unpleasant emotions and experiences. Because of this, what we get out of a relationship must be more than what we put into it.

Figure 6.2   According to social exchange theory, we stay in relationships which are 'profitable' for us. Different individuals will define the costs and rewards involved in different ways

In the same way, Berscheid and Walster (1978) have argued that in any social interaction there is an exchange of rewards (such as affection, information and status), and that the degree of attraction or liking will reflect how people evaluate the rewards they have received relative to those they have given. However, whether or not it is appropriate to think of relationships in this economic, and even capitalistic, way has been hotly debated, as shown in Box 6.3.

Box 6.3   Are relationships really seen in economic terms?

Social exchange theory sees people as being fundamentally selfish, and views human relationships as being based primarily on self-interest. Like many theories in psychology, social exchange theory offers us a *metaphor* for human relationships and should not be taken too literally. However, although we like to believe that the joy of giving is as important as the desire to receive, it is true that our attitudes towards other people are

determined to a large extent by our assessments of the rewards they hold for us (Rubin, 1973).

Equally, though, Rubin does not believe that social exchange theory provides a complete, or even adequate, account of human relationships. In his view:

'Human beings are sometimes altruistic in the fullest sense of the word. They make sacrifices for the sake of others without any consideration of the rewards they will obtain from them in return'.

Altruism is most often and most clearly seen in close interpersonal relationships (and is discussed further in Chapter 12).

Consistent with Rubin's view, some researchers (e.g. Brown, 1986) distinguish between 'true' love and friendship (which are altruistic), and less admirable forms which are based on considerations of exchange. For example, Fromm (1962) defines true love as giving, as opposed to the false love of the 'marketing character', which depends upon expecting to have favours returned. Support for this distinction comes from Mills and Clark (1980), who identify two kinds of intimate relationship. In the *communal couple*, each partner gives out of concern for the other. In the *exchange couple*, each keeps mental records of who is 'ahead' in the relationship and who is 'behind'.

EQUITY THEORY

Social exchange theory is really a special case of a more general account of human relationships known as equity theory. The extra component in equity theory that is added to reward, cost and profit is *investment*. For Brown (1986),

'a person's investments are not just financial; they are anything at all that is believed to entitle him [or her] to his [or her] rewards, costs, and profits. An investment is any factor to be weighed in determining fair profits or losses'.

Equity means a constant ratio of rewards to costs or profit to investment. In other words, it is concerned with *fairness* rather than equality. Equity theory does not see the initial ratio as being important. Rather, it is the changes in the ratio of what is put into a relationship and what is got out that cause changes in the way we feel about it. For example, we might feel that it is fair and just that we should give more than we get, but if we start giving very much more than we did and receiving very much less, we are likely to become dissatisfied with the relationship.

Some versions of social exchange theory do actually take account of factors other than the simple and crude profit motives of social interactors. One of these is described in Box 6.4.

Box 6.4   The concepts of comparison level and comparison level for alternatives

The concepts of comparison level (CL) and comparison level for alternatives (CL alt.) were introduced by Thibaut and Kelley (1959). CL is essentially the average level of rewards and costs that a person is used to in relationships, and is the basic level that is expected to be obtained in any future relationship. So, if a person's reward:cost ratio falls below his or her CL, the relationship will be dissatisfying. If it is above the CL, the relationship will be satisfying.

CL alt. is essentially a person's expectation about the reward:cost ratio which could be obtained in other relationships. If the ratio in a relationship exceeds the CL alt., then a person is doing better in it than he or she could do elsewhere. As a result, the relationship should be satisfying and likely to continue. If CL alt. exceeds the reward:cost ratio, then a person is doing worse than he or she could do elsewhere. As a result, the relationship should be dissatisfying and unlikely to continue.

The concept of CL alt. implies that the endurance of a relationship (as far as one partner is concerned) could be due to the qualities of the other partner and the relationship, *or* to the negative and unattractive features of the perceived alternatives, *or* to the perceived costs of leaving. This, however, still portrays people as being fundamentally selfish, and many social psychologists (e.g. Duck, 1988) prefer to see relationships as being maintained by an equitable distribution of rewards and costs for both partners. In this approach, people are seen as being concerned with the equity of outcomes both for themselves and their partners.

Murstein *et al.* (1977) have argued that concern with either exchange or equity is negatively correlated with marital adjustment. According to Argyle (1988), people in close relationships do not think in terms of rewards and costs at all, until they start to feel dissatisfied.

Murstein and MacDonald (1983) have argued that the principles of exchange and equity play a significant role in intimate relationships. However, they believe that a conscious concern with 'getting a fair deal', especially in the short term, makes compatibility (see page 56) very hard to achieve, and that this is true for friendship and, especially, marriage (see Box 6.3 and Mills and Clark's *exchange couple*).

THE ROLE OF COMPLEMENTARITY

As mentioned in the previous chapter, complementarity refers to the reinforcement of opposing traits to the mutual benefit of both individuals in a relationship. According to Winch (1958), happy marriages are often based on each partner's ability to fulfil the needs of the other (*complementarity of emotional needs)* and, as noted in the previous chapter, Winch obtained some empirical support for this.

Whilst evidence for complementarity of needs is weak, it is stronger for *complementarity in resources* (Brehm, 1992). As has been seen elsewhere, men seem to give a universally higher priority to 'good looks' in their female partners than do women in their male partners. In the case of being a 'good financial prospect' and having a 'good earning capacity', however, the situation is reversed.

Sociobiological theory

According to Buss (1988, 1989), these differences between the sexes 'appear to be deeply rooted in the evolutionary history of our species'. Buss bases this claim on a study of 37 cultures involving over 10 000 people. In his view, the chances of reproductive success should be increased for men who mate with younger, 'healthy' adult females as opposed to older, 'unhealthy' ones. Fertility is a function of a female's age and health, which affects pregnancy and her ability to care for her child.

Since reproductive success is crucial to the survival of a species, natural selection should favour those mating patterns that promote the survival of the offspring. Men often have to rely on a woman's physical appearance in order to estimate her age and health, with younger, healthier women being perceived as more attractive. For women, mate selection depends on their need for a provider to take care of them during pregnancy and nursing. Men who are seen as powerful and controlling resources that contribute to the mother and child's welfare will be seen as especially attractive.

Figure 6.3   Sociobiologists argue that men's desire for attractive female partners, and women's desire for good providers, represents a universal sex difference rooted in human evolutionary history

power' by both men *and* women. Finally, Buss's argument fails to account for homosexual relationships (see, for example, Kitzinger and Coyle, 1995). Such relationships clearly do not contribute to the survival of the species, despite being subject to many of the same sociopsychological influences involved in heterosexual relationships (Brehm, 1992).

THE ROLE OF COMPATIBILITY IN MAINTAINING RELATIONSHIPS

As far as it exists, complementarity can be seen as a component of *compatibility*. However, and as was seen in the previous chapter, evidence for the importance of similarity in the formation of relationships is much greater. The evidence also suggests that similarity plays a much greater role in *maintaining* relationships.

> **Box 6.5   The role of similarity in relationship maintenance**
>
> Hill *et al.* (1976) studied 231 steadily dating couples over a two-year period. At the end of this period, 103 (or 45 per cent) had broken up and when interviewed often mentioned differences in interests, background, sexual attitudes, and ideas about marriage as being responsible. By contrast, those who were still together tended to be more alike in terms of age, intelligence, educational and career plans, as well as physical attractiveness.
>
> Hill *et al.* found that the maintenance or dissolution of the relationship in the couples they studied could be predicted from initial questionnaire data collected about them. For example, about 80 per cent of those who stayed together described themselves as being 'in love', compared with 56 per cent of those who did not stay together.
>
> Of couples in which both members initially reported being equally involved in the relationship, only 23 per cent broke up. However, where one member was much more involved than the other, 54 per cent broke up. The latter type of couple is a highly unstable one in which the person who is more involved (putting more in but getting less out) may feel dependent and exploited. The one who is less involved (putting less in but getting more in return) may feel restless and guilty (which implies some sense of fairness).

There are, however, a number of drawbacks to sociobiological theory in this regard. For example, it seems to take male–female relationships out of any cultural or historical context (captured by the use of the term 'mate selection'). According to Sigall and Landy (1973), it is equally plausible to argue that women have been forced to obtain desirable resources through men because they have been denied direct access to political and economic power. Sigall and Landy argue that, traditionally, a woman has been regarded as the property of a man, wherein her beauty increases his status and respect in the eyes of others.

Importantly, Buss ignores the fact that in his cross-cultural study, 'kind' and 'intelligent' were universally ranked above 'physically attractive' and 'good earning

Other research has confirmed the general rule that the more two people in a relationship see themselves as being like one another, the more likely it is that the relationship will be maintained. Thus, individuals who have similar needs (Meyer and Pepper, 1977), similar attitudes, likes and dislikes (Newcomb, 1978), and are similar in attractiveness (White, 1980), are more likely to maintain a relationship than dissimilar individuals.

Another way of looking at compatibility is *marital satisfaction*. In a review of several studies that have looked at marital satisfaction and communication, Duck (1992) found that happy couples give more positive and consistent non-verbal cues than unhappy couples, express more agreement and approval for the other's ideas and suggestions, talk more about their relationship, and are more willing to compromise on difficult decisions.

The importance of positive interactions was shown by Spanier and Lewis (1980). They propose that there are three main components in relationships that are maintained. These are 'rewards from spousal interaction', satisfaction with lifestyle, and sufficient social and personal resources. The rewards identified by Spanier and Lewis include regard for one's partner and emotional gratification. When these elements are positive, spouses or partners are more likely to report that they are satisfied with their relationship, and the relationship is more likely to endure (Houston *et al.*, 1991).

Conclusions

Our continued involvement in relationships has been addressed by a number of researchers, and several theories of relationship maintenance have been advanced. Complementarity and compatibility also play an important role in maintaining relationships.

SUMMARY

- Some of the factors relevant to understanding the formation of relationships also apply to understanding their maintenance. A couple's similarity is related to how likely they are to remain together.
- According to Rubin, liking and loving are qualitatively different. Loving involves **attachment, caring** and **intimacy.**
- Much of the support for Rubin's distinction between liking and loving comes from people's responses to his Liking and Love scales. Lovers tend to give similar, but not identical, positive responses to items on both scales, and there is a correlation between love and an anticipated permanent relationship.
- Rubin also found that females reported loving their same-sex friends more than men did. This is consistent with other research showing that women's friendships tend to be more intimate and more varied than men's, for whom loving may be channelled into single, sexual relationships.
- Partners who score high on the Love scale engage in more eye contact than those who score low. For Rubin, this represents some evidence for the Love scale's validity.

- Most of the time, love does not involve intense physiological arousal, and a number of different types of love have been identified, including **romantic (passionate) love** and **companionate (true/conjugal) love**.
- Romantic love involves intense feelings of tenderness, elation, anxiety and sexual desire, and is associated with increased activity in the sympathetic branch of the autonomic nervous system. It usually occurs early in a relationship and is short-lived. Companionate love is the affection that remains after the passion of romantic love has passed, and is essential for the maintenance of a relationship.
- According to Sternberg, the basic components of love are **intimacy** (the emotionally based part), **passion** (the motivational component) and **decision/commitment** (the cognitive 'controller'). The presence or absence of these components produces several different types of love, including **infatuated, romantic, companionate, fatuous** and **consummate**.
- Our understanding of social relationships is a reflection of the dominant values of North America, from where most of the theories and studies originate. Cross-cultural studies allow

competing theories to be assessed in terms of whether they are universal, or the products of particular cultural or historical conditions.

- A major dimension on which cultures differ is **individualism–collectivism.** The former stresses personal achievement and self-reliance, whilst the latter stresses the welfare and unity of the group. Although particular cultures often display characteristics of both, passionate love is largely a Western and individualistic phenomenon, with marriage being seen as the culmination of a loving relationship. The reverse is true of cultures that favour arranged marriages, with marriage being seen as the basis on which love can develop.

- Arranged marriages may produce more happiness than 'love' marriages. Courtship is accepted in cultures such as India to a certain degree, but love is left to be defined and discovered after marriage.

- Relationships are expected to change and develop over time, and their stagnation may be a major cause of their failure, especially romantic relationships. Several theories try to account for relationship development, both sexual and non-sexual.

- Kerckhoff and Davis's **filter theory** was based on comparison between short-term and long-term couples. Similarity of **sociological/demographic** variables determines how likely people are to meet in the first place. The 'field of availables' is reduced by social circumstances and constitutes the first filter.

- The second filter involves people's **psychological** characteristics, specifically, agreement about basic values. Short-term couples tended to have a stronger relationship when their values coincided. Finally, the best predictor of a longer term commitment among the long-term couples was **complementarity of emotional needs**.

- According to Murstein's **stimulus–value–role (SVR) theory**, intimate relationships pass from a **stimulus** stage (external attributes, such as physical appearance, are most important) to a **value** stage (similarity of values and beliefs assumes greater importance) to a **role** stage (a commitment based on successful performance of relationship roles, such as husband and wife). Each factor becomes most significant at one particular stage.

- For Levinger, acquaintance/initial attraction is followed by build-up of the relationship, after which consolidation/continuation takes place, followed by deterioration/decline and ending. At each stage, there are both positive and negative factors, either promoting or preventing the relationship's development.

- All stage theories suffer from the same limitation, namely the weak evidence for a fixed sequence of stages. Brehm prefers to talk about phases that occur at different times for different couples.

- **Social exchange theory** provides a general framework for analysing all kinds of relationship, and is really an extension of reward theory. According to Homans, we view our feelings for others in terms of profits, and the greater the profits, the greater the attraction. For Blau, interactions are expensive, so that what we get from a relationship must exceed what we put into it.

- According to Berscheid and Walster, all social interactions involve an exchange of rewards. The degree of liking or attraction will reflect how we evaluate the rewards we have received relative to those we have given.

- All versions of social exchange theory see people as fundamentally selfish. Whilst social exchange theory offers a **metaphor** for human relationships, it is probably true that our attitudes towards others are largely determined by how we assess the rewards they can offer us. However, we are capable of genuine altruism, and this is most clearly seen in close interpersonal relationships.

- Some researchers distinguish between true love and friendship (which are altruistic) and those forms based on considerations of exchange. In support of this distinction, Mills and Clark found evidence for **communal** and **exchange couples**.

- Social exchange theory is really a special case of a more general account of human relationships called **equity theory**, which adds the concept of **investment** to those of reward, cost and profit. The central idea is **fairness** in relation to the reward–cost/profit–investment ratio, rather than equality. It is changes in this ratio that determine how we feel about a relationship, not the initial ratio.

- Thibaut and Kelley's version of social exchange theory takes into account factors other than the crude profit motive, in particular the concepts of comparison level (CL) and comparison level for alternatives (CL alt.). The latter implies that the endurance of a relationship (for one of the partners) could be due to the qualities of the other partner and the relationship, **or** to the negative features of the perceived alternatives, **or** to the perceived cost of leaving.

- Murstein *et al.* see concern with either exchange or equity as negatively correlated with marital adjustment, and Argyle claims that concern with rewards and costs is a sign of dissatisfaction with the relationship. Similarly, Murstein and MacDonald believe that a conscious concern with getting a fair deal makes compatibility very hard to achieve, especially in marriages.

- Whilst evidence for **complementarity of needs** is weak, it is stronger for **complementarity in resources**. Based on his study of 37 cultures, Buss claims that the universal preference of men for physical beauty in their female partners, and women's preference for their male partners to be a good financial prospect, are deeply rooted in the evolutionary history of the human species.

- According to **sociobiological theory**, the chances of reproductive success should be increased for men who mate with younger, healthy, adult females. A woman's physical appearance is often the only indication of her fertility, hence younger, healthier women are seen as more attractive. For women, mate selection depends on their need for a provider to protect them during pregnancy and nursing, hence powerful men who control relevant resources will be seen as attractive.

- This account takes male–female relationships out of any cultural or historical context. According to Sigall and Landy, women may be trying to gain access to political and economic power indirectly through men, since they are denied more direct access and have traditionally been regarded as men's property. Buss's argument also fails to account for homosexual relationships.

- Similarity plays a much greater role than complementarity in **compatibility** and the maintenance of relationships. As far as **marital satisfaction** is concerned, Duck's review found that compared with unhappy couples, happy couples give more positive and consistent non-verbal cues, express more agreement with the other's ideas, talk more about their relationship, and are more willing to compromise on difficult decisions.

THE DISSOLUTION OF ADULT RELATIONSHIPS

Introduction and overview

Having considered the formation and maintenance of adult relationships in the previous two chapters, we conclude this section by looking at the dissolution of such relationships. As we shall see, there are many positive effects associated with being in a relationship and many negative effects follow its dissolution (break-up). This chapter looks at what social psychological research has discovered about the effects of relationship dissolution and why some relationships are dissolved.

Some positive effects of relationships

As long ago as 1885, William Farr, then Superintendent of the Statistical Department of the Registrar General's Office for England, advanced the view that mortality is affected by mental status (Cramer, 1995). Having studied mortality rates for single, married and widowed women, Farr concluded that marriage

'is a healthy state. The single individual is more likely to be wrecked on his voyage than the lives joined together in matrimony' (cited in Humphreys, 1975).

Farr also found that the difference between the single and the married state was more striking for men than for women, and contemporary research has generally confirmed his conclusions about marriage. For example, Hu and Goldman (1990) showed that married people tend to live longer than unmarried people, whilst Cramer (1994) found that married people are happier, healthier and have lower rates of various mental disorders than the single, widowed or divorced (see pages 63–64).

We should also note Cochrane's (1996) finding that the data for England show that age for age, a person is 22 per cent more likely to die in a given year if he or she is single rather than married and 30 per cent more likely if divorced. A number of explanations for these data have been advanced and three of these are summarised in Box 7.1.

Box 7.1 Explaining the beneficial effects of marriage

Kessler and Essex (1982) found that married people in their sample rated significantly higher in terms of their self-esteem, and it could be that marriage provides people with some sort of 'protection' from mental ill-health in the same way that a healthy diet protects against physical illness (Cochrane, 1996). Such protection may come from the intimacy and security provided by a relationship, home-building, sexual satisfaction, and so on. Marriage may also contribute to psychological well-being and the *prevention* of stress, rather than its cause, by, for example, the provision of social support.

As Cochrane has noted, these two explanations assume that marital status causes variations in mental health status. An alternative approach, called the *selection for marriage hypothesis*, suggests that mental health status causes marital status. According to this hypothesis, a predisposition to illness reduces the likelihood of a person marrying, either because an unwell person is not motivated to marry and/or because he or she is an unattractive proposition to potential spouses.

Whichever of the explanations we accept, on the basis of the findings relating to marriage and physical and mental health, we might expect people to continue in a relationship for as long as possible! So how and why do relationships go wrong?

Marital unhappiness and divorce

Duck (1988, 1992) has identified several factors which make it more likely that a marriage will end in either unhappiness or divorce. These are shown in Box 7.2.

Box 7.2   Factors contributing to marital unhappiness and divorce

- Marriages in which the partners are younger than average tend to be more unstable. This can be related to Erikson's (1963) concept of intimacy, whereby teenage marriages, for example, involve individuals who have not yet fully established their sense of identity and so are not ready for a commitment to one particular person. Additionally, there seems to be a relationship between the rising divorce rate and early parenthood, which gives young couples little time to adjust to their new relationship and the responsibilities of marriage. The arrival of a baby brings added financial and housing problems (Pringle, 1986).
- Marriages between couples from lower socioeconomic groups and lower educational levels tend to be more unstable. These are also the couples who tend to have children very early on in their marriage.
- Marriages between partners from different demographic backgrounds (race, religion, and so on) also tend to be more unstable. This finding can be related to Kerckhoff and Davis's 'filter' theory, considered in Chapter 6 (see page 52).
- Marriages also tend to be more unstable between people who have experienced parental divorce as children or who have had a greater number of sexual partners than average before marriage.

Relationships are, of course, highly complex, and it is important to remember that the factors identified in Box 7.2 cannot on their own completely explain why marriage break-ups occur (Duck, 1995). For example, only a proportion of marriages involving the young, those from lower socioeconomic groups, or different demographic backgrounds, actually end in divorce. Equally, many divorces occur between couples who do not fit the descriptions given in Box 7.2. There is a link between *communication strategies* employed early on in married life and subsequent marital unhappiness, with manipulative and coercive styles being a good predictor of the dissatisfaction experienced by wives but *not* by husbands (McGhee, 1996).

Brehm (1992) identifies two broad types of cause of marital unhappiness and divorce, these being *structural* (which includes gender, the duration of the relationship, the presence of children, and the role strain created by competing demands of work and family) and *conflict resolution*.

GENDER DIFFERENCES

Men and women appear to differ in their perceptions of a relationship's problems. In general, women report more problems, and there is evidence to suggest that the degree of female dissatisfaction is a better predictor than male unhappiness of whether the relationship will end. This could mean that women are more sensitive to relationship problems than men. Alternatively, it could be that men and women enter into relationships with different expectations and hopes, and that those of men are generally fulfilled to a greater extent than those of women.

Consistent with this possibility is evidence of gender differences in the specific types of relationship problems reported. For example, whilst men and women who are divorcing are equally likely to cite communication problems as a cause for the dissolution of their relationship, women stress basic unhappiness and incompatibility more than men do. Again, men seem to be particularly upset if there is 'sexual withholding' by a female partner, whilst women are distressed by a male partner's aggression.

DURATION OF RELATIONSHIPS AND THE PASSAGE OF TIME

The longer partners have known each other before they marry, the more likely they are to be satisfied in their marriage and the less likely they are to divorce. However, couples who have cohabited before marriage report fewer barriers to ending the marriage, and the longer a relationship lasts, the more likely it is that people will blame their partners for negative events.

Two major views of changes in marital satisfaction are provided by Pineo's (1961) *linear model* and Burr's

(1970) *curvilinear model*. According to the linear model, there is an inevitable fading of the romantic 'high' of courtship before marriage. The model also proposes that people marry because they have achieved a 'good fit' with their partner, and that any changes occurring in either partner will reduce their compatibility. For example, if one partner becomes more self-confident (which, ironically, may occur through the support gained from the relationship), there may be increased conflict between two equals who now compete for 'superiority' in the relationship. The linear model of marital satisfaction, which is supported by at least some evidence (Blood and Wolfe, 1969), is shown in Figure 7.1.

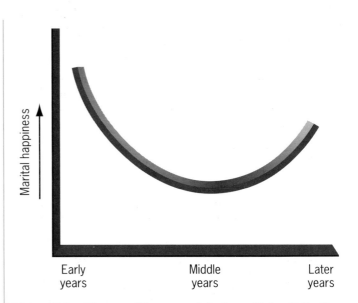

Figure 7.2   The curvilinear model of marital satisfaction (From Gross, 1996, and based on Brehm, 1992)

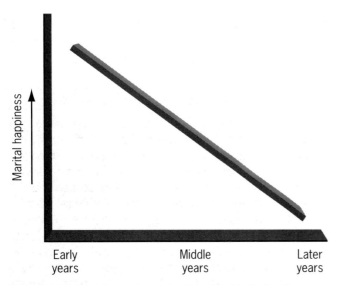

Figure 7.1   The linear model of marital satisfaction (From Gross, 1996, and based on Brehm, 1992)

The curvilinear model of martial satisfaction, shown in Figure 7.2, proposes that marital happiness is greatest in the earliest years of marriage, reaches a low in the middle years, and then begins to rise again in the later years. The middle years of marriage are often associated with the arrival and departure of children. The model proposes that marital happiness declines when children are born and during their growing up, but increases as they mature and leave home. However, whilst it is generally agreed that a decline in marital happiness begins in the early years, whether happiness increases or merely 'levels off' is a matter of debate.

Gilford and Bengston (1979) argue that it is an over-

simplification to talk about marital 'satisfaction' or 'happiness'. In their view, it is much more productive to look at the *pattern of positive rewards* and the *pattern of negative costs* that occur in a marriage. The early years of marriage are associated with very high rewards and very high costs. In the middle years, there is a decline in both, whilst in the later years there is a continuing decline in costs and an increase in rewards.

CONFLICT RESOLUTION

According to Duck (1988), some kind and degree of conflict is probably inevitable in all kinds of relationship. However, the process of resolving conflicts can often be a positive one that promotes the growth of the relationship (Wood and Duck, 1995). The important question is not whether there is conflict, but *how* this conflict can best be dealt with. Unfortunately, the recurrence of conflicts, indicating a lack of agreement and an inability to resolve the conflict's underlying source, may lead the partners to doubt each other as 'reasonable persons'. This might lead to a 'digging in of the heels', a disaffection with each other, and, ultimately, a 'strong falling out'.

Bradbury and Fincham (1990) have argued that happy and unhappy couples resolve their conflicts in typically different ways, and that these can be understood as different *attributional patterns* (see Chapter 1). Happy couples use what Bradbury and Fincham call a *relationship-enhancing* attributional pattern in which a partner's negative behaviour is explained in terms of situational and other variable causes. By contrast, unhappy couples use a *distress-maintaining* attributional pattern in which a partner's negative behaviour is explained in terms of underlying and unchanging personality dispositions, as shown in Figure 7.3.

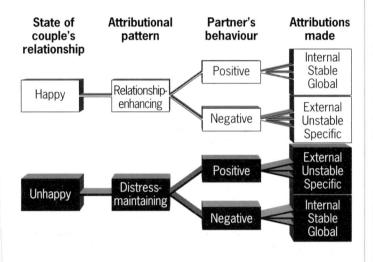

Figure 7.3   Attributions made by happy and unhappy couples according to Bradbury and Fincham (1990) (From Gross, 1996, and based on Brehm, 1992)

RULE-BREAKING AND DECEPTION

Argyle and Henderson (1984) have conducted many studies looking at the *rules* used by people in different types of relationship. By rules, they mean shared opinions or beliefs about what should and should not be done. According to Argyle and Henderson, the two major functions of rules are to regulate behaviour in order to minimise potential sources of conflict, and to check on the exchange of rewards which motivate people to stay in a relationship. Their research has uncovered a number of rules which are thought to apply to all or most types of relationship, such as 'respecting other people's privacy', 'not discussing what has been said in confidence' and 'being emotionally supportive'.

Additional rules apply in particular types of relationship. Argyle's research suggests that relationships fall into clusters, with similar rules applying within a particular cluster. One such cluster includes spouse, sibling and close friends, whilst another includes doctor, teacher and boss. *Deception* is probably the most

important rule that should not be broken, However, what counts as deception will depend on the nature of the relationship: if we cannot trust a friend or a partner, then the relationship is almost certainly doomed.

Some effects of relationship dissolution

In a review of the research, Duck (1992) found that people in disrupted relationships are more susceptible than others of the same sex and age group to coronary heart disease, alcoholism, drug dependence, and sleep disturbances. The relationship between marital status and vulnerability to mental disorders has been extensively investigated by Cochrane (1983, 1996), who found that marital status is one of the strongest correlates of risk of mental health hospital admissions.

Box 7.3   Marital status and mental health

Allowing for age differences, Cochrane suggests that the divorced are five-and-a-half times more likely than the married to be admitted to a mental hospital in any one year. Stress could account for this, as the relationship between stress and illness is strongly supported by evidence. Additionally, a loss of the 'protective' factors mentioned on page 60 could also be important. Even the 'selection for marriage' hypothesis might have something to contribute given that, with about 40 per cent of British marriages ending in divorce, divorce is becoming 'normal'.

However, there may be an important gender difference regarding the effects of divorce, depending on the point of the dissolution process being considered. Whilst much has been made of the detrimental effects of divorce on men, as opposed to women, these usually occur *after* the relationship has ended. Men discover that they miss the emotional support that marriage can provide and that on their own they have very little opportunity to express feelings to friends around them.

In the case of women, it is the stage *before* divorce, during marital stress, when they are far more likely to become depressed than men. That is the point when marriage is probably worse for female mental stability than divorce itself.

A survey carried out by Fincham (1997), involving over a 100 couples, compared levels of marital discord and depression symptoms in men and women. According to Fincham (cited in Cook, 1997),

> 'Our result suggests something pretty clear and robust and raises all sorts of interesting questions. It is widely believed that marriage protects men from mental health problems but if you look at women you find the opposite'.

The situation for men (depression predicted marital stress) represents the mirror-image of what happens for women, for whom marital stress predicted depressive symptoms. Women seem to value relationships more than men, and when the martial relationship is not working, this can cause depression.

According to Fincham, women may feel greater responsibility for making the relationship work, so that when it does not, they blame themselves and this makes them more susceptible to depression (see Chapter 1, page 9).

As McGhee (1996) has observed, however, there is much evidence to suggest that the social support given to people following the dissolution of a relationship can *reduce* the probability of psychological distress and ill-health. For example, Buehler and Legge (1993) found that companionship and other reassurance to self-esteem improved the level of psychological well-being in a sample of 144 women with children. If women are better at confiding in others (especially other women: see Chapter 6), they are more likely to receive social and emotional support following divorce, whereas men are more likely to be socially and emotionally isolated.

The process of relationship dissolution

As noted elsewhere, relationships are highly complex, and this is as true of relationship dissolution as it is of the formation and maintenance of relationships. The complexity of relationship dissolution is evident not just in the case of marriage, but in all sorts of relationships, such as friendships and sexual relationships. The complexity is even greater if the relationship is a long-term one that has embraced many parts of a person's emotional, communicative, leisure and everyday life (Duck, 1988).

One useful way of looking at the break-up of a relationship is to regard it as a *process*, rather than an event, which takes place over a period of time. For Duck (1988),

> 'breaking up is not only hard to do, but also involves a lot of separate elements that make up the whole rotten process'.

Several models of the stages through which relationships pass as they dissolve have been proposed. As McGhee (1996) has noted, if there are aspects that characterise many, if not all, dissolving relationships, it might be possible to identify the kinds of counselling or other 'repair work' that might work best for dissatisfied couples who want to avoid dissolving the relationship. Such models are, therefore, of more than theoretical importance.

LEE'S MODEL

Lee (1984) has proposed that there are five stages in pre-marital romantic break-ups. First of all, *dissatisfaction* (D) is discovered. This dissatisfaction is then *exposed* (E). Some sort of *negotiation* (N) about the dissatisfaction occurs, and attempts are made to *resolve* (R) the problem. Finally, the relationship is *terminated* (T). Lea surveyed 112 premarital break-ups and found that (E) and (N) tended to be experienced as the most intense, dramatic, exhausting and negative aspects of the whole experience.

Those who skipped these stages, by just walking out of the relationship, reported feeling less intimate with their ex-partner, even when the relationship had been progressing smoothly. Lee also found that in those cases where the passage from (D) to (T) was particularly prolonged, people reported feeling more attracted to their ex-partner and experienced the greatest loneliness and fear during the break-up.

DUCK'S MODEL

Duck (1982, 1988) has proposed a model of relationship dissolution that consists of a number of phases, each of which is initiated when a threshold is broken. The model is summarised in Table 7.1. The first, *intrapsychic phase*, begins when one of the partners sees him or herself as being unable to stand the relationship any more. This initiates a focus on the other partner's behaviour, and an assessment of the adequacy of the partner's role performance. Also, the individual begins to assess the negative aspects of being in the relationship, considers the costs of withdrawal, and assesses the positive aspects of being in an alternative relationship. Duck uses the term 'intrapsychic' because the processes are occurring only in the individual's head and have not shown themselves in actual behaviour.

The next threshold is when the individual considers him or herself as being justified in withdrawing from the relationship. This leads to the *dyadic phase*, and involves the other partner. Here, the dissatisfied individual must decide whether to confront or avoid his or her partner. When a decision has been made to confront the partner, negotiations occur about, for example, whether the relationship can be repaired and the joint costs of withdrawal or reduced intimacy.

If the negotiations in the dyadic phase are unsuccessful, the next threshold is when the dissatisfied partner determines that he or she means the relationship to end. This leads to the *social phase*, so-called because it involves consideration of the social implications of the relationship's dissolution. This state of the relationship is made public, at least within the individual's own social network, and publicly negotiable face-saving/blame-placing stories and accounts of the relationship's breakdown may be given. 'Intervention teams', such as family or very close friends, may be called in to try to bring about a reconciliation.

Unless the 'intervention teams' are successful, the next threshold is when the dissolution of the relationship becomes inevitable. This leads to the final *grave-dressing phase*. In this, the partners attempt to 'get over' the relationship's dissolution and engage in their own 'post-mortem' about why the relationship dissolved, a version of events which is then given to friends and family. Each partner needs to emerge from the relationship with an intact reputation for relationship reliability.

'Dressing the grave' involves 'erecting a tablet' which provides a credible and socially acceptable account of the life and death of the relationship. Whilst helping to save face, it also serves to keep alive some memories and to 'justify' the original commitment to the ex-partner. In Duck's (1988) words:

'Such stories are an integral and important part of the psychology of ending relationships ... By helping the person get over the break-up, they are immensely significant in preparing the person for future relationships as well as helping them out of old ones'.

Table 7.1 A summary of the phases involved in Duck's (1982, 1988) model of relationship disolution

Breakdown–dissatisfaction with relationship

Threshold: '*I can't stand this any more*'

INTRAPSYCHIC PHASE
Personal focus on partner's behaviour
Assess adequecy of partner's role performance
Depict and evaluate negative aspects of being in the relationship
Consider costs of withdrawal
Assess positive aspects of alternative relationships
Face 'express/repress dilemma'

Threshold: '*I'd be justified in withdrawing*'

DYADIC PHASE
Face 'confrontation'
Confront partner
Negotiate in 'our relationship talks'
Attempt repair and reconciliation?
Assess joint costs of withdrawal or reduced intimacy

Threshold: '*I mean it*'

SOCIAL PHASE
Negotiate-dissolution state with partner
Initiate gossip/discussion in social network
Create publicly negotiable face-saving/blame-placing stories and accounts
Consider and face up to implied social network effect, if any
Call in intervention team

Threshold: '*It's now inevitable*'

GRAVE-DRESSING PHASE
'Getting over' activity
Retrospective; reformative post-mortem attribution
Public distribution of own version of break-up

(From Gross, 1996)

As well as the models proposed by Lee and Duck, several others have been advanced to explain the process of relationship dissolution. Rusbult's (1987) *exit–voice–loyalty–neglect model* is described in Box 7.4 (see page 66).

More recently, Felmlee (1995) has proposed what she calls the *fatal attraction model of relationship breakdown*. Felmlee argues that the perceived characteristics in a person that initially attract someone to him or her are the very characteristics that lead to the breakdown of a relationship. So, a characteristic that initially makes a person appear 'exciting', say, to another, later on makes that person 'unpredictable', and the relationship breaks down because of this perceived unpredictability.

Box 7.4   Rusbult's exit–voice–loyalty–neglect model

According to Rusbult, there are four basic responses to relationship dissatisfaction. These are:

- *exit* (leaving the relationship)
- *neglect* (ignoring the relationship)
- *voice* (articulating concerns)
- *loyalty* (staying in the relationship and accepting the situation and the other's behaviour).

The two active strategies in the face of dissatisfaction are exit and voice, whilst the two 'passive' strategies are neglect and loyalty. Exit and neglect are 'destructive', whilst voice and loyalty are 'constructive'. The characteristics of these strategies are shown below.

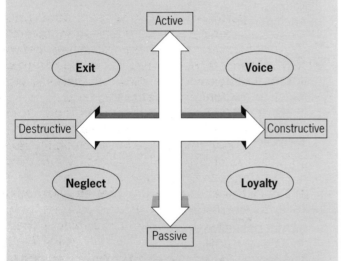

Figure 7.4   Rusbult's exit-voice-loyalty-neglect model

According to McGhee (1996), the usefulness of this model and the accuracy of its predictions about which type of couple will engage in which type of strategy have been supported by studies conducted in both Britain (Goodwin, 1991) and America (Rusbult, 1987).

(From McGhee, 1996.)

Marital reconciliation

We have looked in detail at the process of relationship breakdown. Other research has examined the factors that are involved in marital reconciliation and which might predict successful reconciliation. One study that has explored the issue of marital reconciliation is described in Box 7.5.

Box 7.5   Wineberg's (1994) study of marital reconciliation

Wineberg studied 506 white women who had attempted a reconciliation in their first marriage. Women who had made a 'successful' reconciliation, and were still married a year after their reconciliation, were compared with those who had made an 'unsuccessful' reconciliation and were separated/divorced within a year of the attempted reconciliation. Wineberg found that, overall, 30 per cent of reconciliations were successful, and that important factors linked with the reconciliation included:

- both partners being of the same religion (especially if one partner had changed religion in connection with the marriage);
- cohabitation with a partner before marriage;
- marriage with a partner of the same age.

Different factors were associated with marital dissolution, including age at separation, duration of marriage, and education. Wineberg argues that whilst these factors may be reflected in the decision to separate, other factors may have a bearing on whether an attempted reconciliation is successful. Amongst these are social and religious ties, advice from family and friends, and life after separation.

Conclusions

Whilst various studies, and models that have been derived from them, have made a significant contribution to our understanding of the breakdown and dissolution of relationships, much remains to be investigated. For example, this chapter has concentrated on the breakdown of heterosexual relationships. Whether homosexual relationship dissolution involves the same processes remains to be discovered. As McGhee (1996) has noted:

'We know much, much more now about how relationships become unsatisfactory and break down than we did even 10 years ago, and yet like so many areas in social psychology, what we do know now is but an infinitesimal fraction of what remains to be known'.

SUMMARY

- As long ago as 1885, the study of mortality rates showed that married people were less likely to die than the single or widowed, and this difference was more striking for men than for women. These conclusions have been confirmed by contemporary research. Not only do married people live longer, but they are happier, healthier and have lower rates of various mental disorders than the single, widowed or divorced.

- The finding that married people show significantly higher self-esteem suggests that marriage may protect people from mental ill-health. This may derive from the intimacy and security of the marital relationship. Marriage may also help to **prevent** stress through providing social support.

- Whilst these explanations assume that marital status causes variations in mental health status, the **selection for marriage hypothesis** turns this around, so that a predisposition to illness reduces the likelihood that someone will marry.

- Duck has identified several factors which make it more likely that a marriage will end in either unhappiness or divorce. Marriages will be more unstable if the partners are younger than average, perhaps because the individuals have not yet achieved a sense of identity (and so are not ready for intimacy), and also because of the often early arrival of a baby.

- Marriages between couples from lower socioeconomic groups and lower educational levels, and between partners from different demographic backgrounds, also tend to be more unstable. This is true also for those who have had many pre-marital sexual partners and whose parents divorced.

- These factors cannot on their own completely explain marriage break-ups. Only a proportion of marriages involving couples who fit these descriptions actually break up, and, conversely, divorces occur between couples who do not fit them.

- According to Noller *et al.*, there is a link between **communicative strategies** used early in married life and subsequent unhappiness. Manipulative and coercive styles predict wives' dissatisfaction but not husbands'.

- Brehm identifies two broad types of cause for marital unhappiness and divorce: **structural** (including gender, the duration of the relationship, presence of children, and role strain) and **conflict resolution**.

- There appear to be **gender differences** in perceptions of relationship problems, with women reporting more problems overall. The degree of female dissatisfaction seems to be a better predictor of whether the relationship will end, which could reflect the different hopes and expectations that men and women bring with them into their marriage.

- Consistent with the possibility that men's expectations are generally fulfilled more than women's is evidence of gender differences in the specific types of problems reported. For example, women stress basic unhappiness and incompatibility more than men do.

- The longer partners have known each other prior to marriage, the less likely they are to divorce. However, partners who have cohabited before marrying report fewer barriers to getting divorced. Blaming one's partner for negative events is also more likely the longer a relationship lasts.

- According to Pineo's **linear model**, there is an inevitable decline in the romantic love of courtship and there may be a decrease in compatibility during the course of the marriage due to a reduction in the 'fit' between the partners.

- Burr's **curvilinear model** provides an alternative view, whereby marital happiness is greatest in the earliest years, reaches a low in the middle years, then begins to rise again in the later years. These ups and downs are associated with the arrival, growing up, and leaving home of children.

- Gilford and Bengston argue that rather than talking about marital satisfaction or happiness, we should look at the **pattern of positive rewards** and **negative costs** that occurs at different points in marriage

- According to Duck, whilst conflict is inevitable in all kinds of relationship, **conflict resolution** can often be a positive process which promotes the growth of the relationship. However, recurring conflicts suggest failure to resolve the underlying cause and may lead the partners to doubt each other as reasonable persons.

- According to Bradbury and Fincham, happy and unhappy couples display very different **attributional patterns** when resolving their conflicts. This is **relationship-enhancing** in the case of happy couples and **distress-maintaining** in the case of unhappy couples.

- Argyle and Henderson have identified a number

of relationship **rules**, whose main functions are to regulate behaviour so as to minimise conflict and to check on the exchange of rewards. Whilst many rules apply to all or most types of relationship, additional rules apply in particular types or clusters of relationship. **Deception** is probably the most important rule, although how this is defined will depend on the nature of the relationship.

- According to Duck, people in disrupted relationships are more likely to suffer coronary heart disease, alcoholism, drug dependence, and sleep disturbances than others of the same age and sex. Cochrane reports that marital status is one of the strongest correlates of risk of mental health hospital admissions.

- Stress, loss of the protective nature of marriage, as well as the selection for marriage hypothesis, could all help to explain why the divorced are much more likely than the married to be admitted to a mental hospital in any one year.

- However, whilst most of the harmful effects suffered by men occur **after** the relationship has ended, women are far more likely to become depressed **before** divorce, during marital stress. This could be explained in terms of the greater responsibility women feel for making the relationship work, and their tendency to blame themselves if it fails.

- Whilst men are more likely to be socially and emotionally isolated following divorce, women are better at confiding in others and so are more likely to receive social and emotional support, which can **reduce** the probability of psychological ill-health.

- Relationship dissolution is complex, especially if the relationship has been long-term and has embraced many parts of a person's emotional, communicative, leisure and everyday life.

- Dissolution is best thought of as a **process**, rather than an event. Models that try to identify the stages which all relationships pass through as they break up can have practical implications, such as the kind of counselling that might be most useful.

- Lee proposes five stages in premarital romantic break-ups: **dissatisfaction** (D) is discovered then **exposed** (E), followed by some sort of **negotia-**tion (N) about the dissatisfaction and attempts to **resolve** (R) the problem, with the relationship finally being **terminated** (T).

- Whilst (E) and (N) were generally the most unpleasant stages, those who skipped them reported feeling less intimate with their partner, even at the height of the relationship. Where the passage from (D) to (T) was particularly prolonged, people reported greater attraction to their ex-partner and experienced the greatest loneliness and fear during the break-up.

- Duck's model comprises several phases, each of which is initiated when a threshold is broken. The **intrapsychic phase** begins when one of the partners cannot stand the relationship any more. When the individual comes to feel justified in withdrawing, the **dyadic phase** is reached. Unsuccessful negotiations during this phase lead to the next threshold ('I mean it'), which leads in turn to the **social phase**.

- Unless the 'intervention teams' of family and close friends are successful, the 'It's now inevitable' threshold is reached, leading to the final **grave-dressing phase**. This involves providing a credible account of why the relationship died, which helps to save face and justify the relationship. Crucially, these accounts help prepare the person for future relationships.

- Rusbult's **exit–voice–loyalty–neglect model** identifies four basic responses to relationship dissatisfaction, which can be placed on an active– passive and a destructive–constructive dimension. It has received support from both American and British research.

- Felmlee's **fatal attraction model of relationship breakdown** claims that the perceived characteristics that initially attract us to someone are also those that lead to the breakdown of the relationship.

- Wineberg's study of marital **reconciliation** found that relevant factors included both partners being of the same religion and age, and cohabitation with the partner before marriage. Different factors were associated with marital dissolution, such as age at separation, duration of marriage, and education.

PART 3
Social influence

CONFORMITY

Introduction and overview

In his *Letter to Lucalius*, a philosophical tract written in AD 63–65 about providence and fate, Seneca observed that 'it is too easy to go over to the majority'. Psychologists have defined *conformity* in a number of ways. For Crutchfield (1955), it is 'yielding to group pressure', whilst Mann (1969) argues that whereas this is its essence, 'it may take different forms and be based on motives other than group pressure'. Zimbardo and Leippe (1991) see conformity as

'a change in belief or behaviour in response to real or imagined group pressure when there is no direct request to comply with the group nor any reason to justify the behaviour change'.

What the definitions above have in common is that they all make reference to *group pressure*, although none of them specifies particular groups with particular beliefs or practices. Rather, it is the pressure exerted by *any* group which is important to a person at any given time that is seen as being influential. The groups may be composed of 'significant others', such as family or peers (so-called *membership groups*), or may be groups whose values a person admires or aspires to, but is not actually a member of (so-called *reference groups*). Conformity, then, does not imply adhering to any particular set of attitudes or values (such as traditional middle class or bourgeois). Instead, it involves yielding to the real or imagined pressures of *any* group regardless of its majority or minority status (van Avermaet, 1996).

Experimental research into conformity began in the early 1930s, and the phenomenon continues to attract research interest today. Our aim in this chapter is to review what is known about conformity to the real or imagined pressures from others.

Figure 8.1

Experimental studies of conformity

In an experiment conducted in 1935, Sherif had participants make estimates of the amount by which a spot of light in an otherwise darkened room appeared to move (a phenomenon known as the *autokinetic effect*, which occurs because of the absence of a reference point). In one experiment, participants first made their estimates privately and then as members of a group. Sherif found that individual estimates converged, and became more alike. Thus, a *group norm* developed, which represented the average of the individual estimates, as shown in Figure 8.2 (see over).

Whilst Sherif believed that his study demonstrated conformity, Asch (1951) disagreed. According to Asch, the

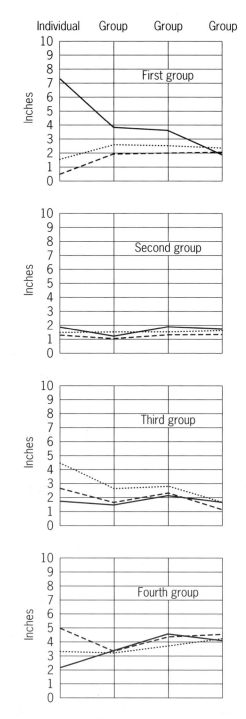

Figure 8.2 **Median judgements of the apparent movement of a stationary point of light given by participants in Sherif's (1935) experiment. In the data shown, participants first made their estimates alone ('individual') and then in groups of three on three occasions ('group'). The figure shows the estimates given by four groups. Sherif also found that when the procedure was reversed, that is, participants made three estimates in groups followed by an estimate alone, the 'individual' estimates did not deviate from one another (From Sherif, 1936)**

fact that Sherif's task was ambiguous, in that there was no right or wrong answer, made it difficult to draw conclusions about conformity in group situations. In Asch's view, the best way to measure conformity was in terms of a person's tendency to agree with other people who unanimously give the *wrong answer* on a task which has an obvious and unambiguous solution. Asch devised a simple perceptual task that involved participants deciding which of three comparison lines of varying length matched a standard line. An example is shown in Figure 8.3.

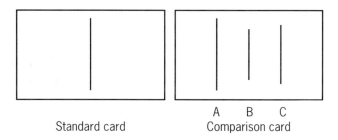

Figure 8.3 **An example of the task devised by Asch**

In a pilot study, Asch tested 36 participants on an individual basis using 20 slightly different versions of the task shown in Figure 8.3. Since the participants made a total of only three mistakes in the 720 trials (an error rate of 0.42 per cent), Asch concluded that the tasks were simple and the answers to them obvious and unambiguous. Asch's procedure for studying conformity was ingenious and, because the basic set-up can be adapted to investigate the effects that different variables have on conformity, it is known as the *Asch paradigm*.

Box 8.1   The Asch paradigm

Some of the participants who had taken part in Asch's pilot study (see text), were requested to act as 'stooges' (or confederates). The stooges were told that they would be doing the tasks again, but this time in a *group* rather than individually. They were also told that the group would contain one person who was completely ignorant as to the fact that the rest of the members of the group were stooges.

On certain *critical* trials, which Asch would indicate to the stooges by means of a secret signal, *all* were required to say out loud the same *wrong answer*. In Asch's original experiment, the stooges (usually 7–9 of them) and the naive participant were seated either in a straight line or round a table (see Figure 8.4) The situation was rigged so that the naive participant was always the last or last but one to say the answer out loud.

On the first two trials, all of the stooges gave the correct answer. However, on the third trial they unanimously gave a wrong answer. In all, this happened a further 11 times in the experiment, with four additional 'neutral' trials (in which all stooges responded with the correct answer) taking place between the critical trials.

Table 8.1   The findings from Asch's original experiment

Number of conforming responses made	Number of people making those responses
0	13
1	4
2	5
3	6
4	3
5	4
6	1
7	2
8	5
9	3
10	3
11	1
12	0

In the Asch paradigm, the important measurement is whether the naive participant conforms and gives the same wrong answer as the stooges have unanimously done, or is independent and gives the obviously correct answer. The behaviour of one participant on a critical trial and the findings from Asch's original experiment are shown in Figure 8.4 and Table 8.1.

Figure 8.4   A naive participant (number 6), having heard five stooges give the same incorrect answer, offers his own judgement as to which of three comparison lines matches a stimulus line.

Asch found a *mean* conformity rate of 32 per cent, that is, participants agreed with the incorrect majority answer on about one-third of the critical trials. If the *median* is used as the measure of central tendency, the conformity rate is 25 per cent. However, and as Table 8.1 shows, there are wide individual differences. Thus, no one conformed on all the critical trials and 13 of the 50 participants tested (26 per cent) never conformed at all. As we can see, though, one person conformed on

11 of the 12 critical trials and around three-quarters of participants conformed at least once. Given that Asch's pilot study had shown that the task was simple and unambiguous, such findings indicate a high level of conformity. As van Avermaet (1996) has remarked:

'the results reveal the tremendous impact of an "obviously" incorrect but unanimous majority on the judgements of a lone individual'.

How did the naive participants explain their behaviour?

After the experiment, the participants were interviewed about their behaviour. The interviews revealed a number of specific reasons as to why conformity had occurred. For example, some participants claimed that they wanted to act in accordance with what they imagined were the experimenter's wishes, and convey a favourable impression of themselves by 'not upsetting the experiment' (which they believed they would have done by disagreeing with the majority).

Others, who had no reason to believe that there was anything wrong with their eyesight, claimed that they genuinely doubted the validity of their own judgements by wondering if they were suffering from eye strain, or if the chairs had been moved so that they could not see the task material properly. Yet others denied being aware of having given incorrect answers – they had unwittingly used the stooges as 'marker posts' (Smith, 1995). Some participants said that they 'didn't want to appear different', or 'didn't want to be made to look a fool' or 'inferior'. For these participants, there was

clearly a discrepancy between the answer they gave in the group and what they *privately believed*. Whilst they knew the answer they had given was wrong, they nonetheless went along with the views of the group.

That participants were justified in fearing potential ridicule by group members was shown in an experiment in which 16 naive participants and a *single stooge* were tested (van Avermaet, 1996). When the stooge gave a wrong answer on the critical trials, the naive participants reacted with sarcasm and laughter. In other research, Asch (1952) showed that when the stooges gave their answers out loud, but the naive participant *wrote down* the answers, conformity was significantly reduced. This indicates that it must have been *group pressure*, rather than anything else, that produced conformity.

There is also evidence to suggest that participants in Asch-type experiments experience some degree of *stress*. For example, Bogdonoff *et al.* (1961) showed that plasma-free fatty acid levels (a measure of arousal) increased in naive participants as they heard the stooges giving wrong answers. When the naive participant responded, the levels decreased if a conforming response was made, but continued to increase if a non-conforming response was given.

FACTORS AFFECTING CONFORMITY

Using the Asch paradigm, researchers have manipulated particular variables in order to see if they increase or decrease the amount of conformity compared with that observed in the original experiment. Some important factors affecting conformity are shown in Box 8.2.

Box 8.2   Some factors affecting conformity

Group size: With one stooge and the naive participant, conformity is very low (at around 3 per cent), presumably because it is a simple case of the participant's 'word' against the stooge's. With two stooges, conformity rises to around 14 per cent. With three stooges, it reaches the figure of 32 per cent that Asch found in his original experiment. Thereafter, however, further increases in group size do not lead to increases in conformity, and with very large groups conformity may drop dramatically (Asch, 1955). According to Wilder (1977), this is because participants begin (quite rightly) to suspect *collusion*.

Unanimity: Conformity is most likely to occur when the stooges are unanimous in the answer

---

they give. When one stooge does not go along with the majority judgement, conformity decreases (Asch, 1956). The stooge need not even share the naive participant's judgement (the stooge may, for example, appear to have a visual impairment as evidenced by the wearing of thick glasses). Thus, just breaking the unanimity of the majority is sufficient to reduce conformity (Allen and Levine, 1971). For Asch, unanimity is a more important factor than group size. In Asch's (1951) view:

'a unanimous majority of three is, under given conditions, far more effective [in producing conformity] than a majority of eight containing one dissenter'.

Additionally, when a stooge begins by giving the correct answer but then conforms to the majority incorrect answer, conformity increases.

Task difficulty, ambiguity, and familiarity with task demands: With difficult tasks, as when the comparison lines are all similar to the stimulus line, conformity increases (Asch, 1956). Ambiguous tasks, such as making judgements about the number of clicks produced by a fast metronome, also produce increased conformity (Shaw *et al.*, 1957). The more familiar we are with the demands of a task, the less likely we are to conform. For example, women are more likely to conform to group pressure on tasks involving the identification of tools (such as wrenches), whereas men are more likely to conform on tasks involving the identification of cooking utensils (Sistrunk and McDavid, 1971).

Gender and other individual differences: It has been reported that women conform more than men (Cooper, 1979), although this claim has been disputed (Eagly and Steffen, 1984). Eagly and Steffen found that men conform to group opinions as frequently as women do when their conformity or independence will be kept private. However, when conformity or independence will be made known to the group, men conform less than women, presumably because non-conformity is consistent with the masculine stereotype of independence. Conformity has been found to be higher amongst those who:

• have low self-esteem (Santee and Maslach, 1982);
• are especially concerned about social relationships (Mullen, 1983);

- have a strong need for social approval (Sears *et al.*, 1991);
- are attracted towards other group members (Wyer, 1966).

EVALUATING ASCH'S CONTRIBUTION TO THE STUDY OF CONFORMITY

One of the earliest criticisms made of Asch's work was that the Asch paradigm was both time-consuming (in terms of setting up the situation) and uneconomical (in the sense that only one naive participant at a time could be investigated). Crutchfield (1954) overcame both of these problems with what is known as the *Crutchfield device*. Crutchfield's research is described in Box 8.3.

Box 8.3   Crutchfield's research into conformity

In Crutchfield's procedure, naive participants are seated in a cubicle which has a panel with an array of lights and switches (the Crutchfield device). Questions can be projected on to a wall and, by pressing switches, the naive participant can answer them. The participant is told that the lights on the panel represent the responses given by other participants. In fact, this is not true, and the illumination of the lights is controlled by an experimenter who has a 'master panel' in another cubicle.

Of course, the participant does not know this, and the arrangement removes the need for stooges and also allows several participants in different cubicles to be tested at once. Using this arrangement, Crutchfield tested over 600 people. Amongst many findings were those indicating that college students agreed with statements which, in other circumstances, they would probably not agree with. These included statements like 'The life expectancy of American males is only 25 years', 'Americans sleep four to five hours per night and eat six meals a day' and 'Free speech being a privilege rather than a right, it is only proper for a society to suspend free speech when it feels itself threatened'.

The findings originally reported by Asch have stimulated much research. Twenty or so years after the original findings were published, Larsen (1974) found significantly lower rates of conformity among American students than were reported by Asch. Larsen explained the discrepancy in terms of a change in climate of opinion in America 'away from the stupefying effects of McCarthyism in the 1950s' towards 'a more sceptical and independent individual'. Five years later, however, Larsen *et al.* (1979) found that conformity rates were similar to those obtained by Asch, possibly suggesting a move *away* from independence and criticism in American students.

In research conducted in Britain, Perrin and Spencer (1981) found very low rates of conformity among university students. However, when they tested young offenders on probation, with probation officers as stooges, very similar rates of conformity to those reported by Asch were obtained. According to Perrin and Spencer, the rate of conformity obtained in studies is a useful indicator of the cultural expectations people bring to the experiment from their contemporary world, a view with which Asch agreed (Perrin and Spencer, 1980). However, as well as participants' expectations influencing the amount of conformity obtained in a study, it is possible that experimenters can exert an influence too. As Brown (1985) has noted, experimenters may also have changed over time. Perhaps their expectations of the amount of conformity that will occur in an experiment are unwittingly conveyed to the participants, who respond accordingly.

MAJORITY OR MINORITY INFLUENCE IN ASCH-TYPE EXPERIMENTS?

In reviewing the findings from Asch's studies, Turner (1991) observed that most concern has centred around

'the weakness of the individual in face of the group and the strength of spontaneous pressures for conformity inherent in the group context'.

However, and as Table 8.1 shows, most participants remained independent either most or all of the time, and so conformity was actually the *exception* to the rule rather than the rule.

Typically, the stooges in an Asch-type experiment are thought of as the majority and, in a numerical sense, they are. However, Moscovici and Faucheux (1972) have argued that it is much more profitable to think of the naive participant as the majority (in that he or she embodies the 'conventional', self-evident opinion of most of us) and the stooges as the minority (who reflect an unorthodox, unconventional, eccentric and even outrageous viewpoint). In Asch's experiments, this minority influenced the majority 32 per cent of the time, and it is those participants who remained independent who are actually the conformists!

If we consider Asch-type experiments from this perspective, then they offer us evidence related to the question of how new ideas come to be accepted rather than to the processes that operate to maintain the status quo (Tanford and Penrod, 1984). In Moscovici's (1976) view, a *conformity bias* exists in this area of research, such that all social influence serves the need to adapt to the status quo for the sake of uniformity and stability. Moscovici, however, argues that change is sometimes needed to adapt to changing circumstances, and that this is very difficult to explain given the presence of a conformity bias. What would seem to be necessary is an understanding of the dynamics of *active minorities*. If such minorities did not exert an influence, in any arena of human social and scientific activity, innovations would simply never happen (van Avermaet, 1996).

How do minorities exert an influence?

If the data from Asch's original experiments are reanalysed, conformity or non-conformity can be shown to be related to the *consistency* of the stooge's judgements (Moscovici, 1976). In a series of experiments, Moscovici and his colleagues were able to show that by giving consistent responses, minorities can change the majority's views. In one such experiment, Moscovici and Lage (1976) instructed a stooge minority of two to describe a blue–green colour as green. The results showed that the views of the majority changed to that of the minority and that this effect persisted when further judgements were asked for after the minority had withdrawn from the experiment. The reasons why consistency is so important are considered in Box 8.4

Box 8.4   The importance of consistency and other factors in minority influence

According to Hogg and Vaughan (1995), consistency has five main effects:

1 It disrupts the majority norm, and produces uncertainty and doubt.
2 It draws attention to itself as an entity.
3 It conveys the existence of an alternative, coherent point of view.
4 It demonstrates certainty and an unshakeable commitment to a particular point of view.
5 It shows that the only solution to the current conflict is the minority viewpoint.

Minorities are also more effective if they are seen to have made significant personal/material sacrifices (*investment*), are perceived as acting out of

---

principle rather than an ulterior motive (*autonomy*), and display a balance between being 'dogmatic' (*rigidity*) and 'inconsistent' (*flexibility*) (Nemeth and Wachtler, 1973; Papastamou, 1979; Wood *et al.*, 1994; Hogg and Vaughan, 1995). Minorities also have more influence if they are seen as being similar to the majority in terms of age, gender and social category (Clark and Maass, 1988), and particularly if minority members are categorised as part of the ingroup (see Chapter 3, page 27).

Why do people conform?

As Abrams *et al.* (1990) have noted:

'we know groups constrain and direct the actions of their members, but there is considerable controversy as to how, and under what conditions, various forms of influence operate'.

One early attempt to account for conformity was provided by Deutsch and Gerard (1955). They argued that in order to explain group influence, it was necessary to distinguish between *informational social influence* (ISI) and *normative social influence* (NSI).

INFORMATIONAL SOCIAL INFLUENCE

Festinger's (1954) *social comparison theory* states that people have a basic need to evaluate ideas and attitudes and, in turn, to confirm that these are correct. This can provide a reassuring sense of control over the world and a satisfying sense of competence. In situations which are novel or ambiguous, social reality is defined by the thoughts and behaviours of others. For example, if we are in a restaurant and are not clear about which piece of cutlery to use with a particular course, we look to others for 'guidance' and then conform to their behaviour. This is ISI.

As Turner (1991) has remarked, the less we can rely on our own direct perception and behavioural contact with the physical world, the more susceptible we should be to influence from other people. As mentioned earlier, some participants in Asch's experiment claimed that they believed the majority opinion to be correct and that their own perceptions were incorrect. Taken at face value, this would suggest that ISI occurs even in unambiguous situations. However, we should remember that such explanations may actually be *defensive* (or perhaps *self-serving*) *attributions* (see Chapter 1, page 9) given by participants to justify their submission to the influence of the majority (Berkowitz, 1986).

NORMATIVE SOCIAL INFLUENCE

Underlying NSI is the need to be accepted by other people and to make a favourable impression on them. We may conform in order to gain social approval and avoid rejection, and we may agree with others because of their power to reward, punish, accept, or reject us. As noted previously, in both Asch's and Crutchfield's experiments, most participants did not seem to be uncertain about the correct answer. However, in making their own judgement they risked rejection by the majority, and so for at least some participants, conformity probably occurred because of NSI.

The costs of non-conformity

Evidence that the fear that others will reject, dislike or mistreat us for holding different opinions is warranted was provided by Schachter (1951). Schachter's study is described in Box 8.5.

Box 8.5   Schachter's (1951) study

Groups of male university students read and discussed the case of a delinquent youth called 'Johnny Rocco'. Johnny was described as having grown up in an urban slum, experienced a difficult childhood, and often been in trouble. Participants were asked to recommend that Johnny receive a great deal of love and affection, harsh discipline and punishment, or some combination of the two.

Johnny's case notes were written sympathetically, and participants made lenient recommendations. Included in each group, however, was a stooge who sometimes agreed with the genuine participants and sometimes recommended that Johnny be given harsh discipline and punishment. When the stooge adopted the deviant opinion, he maintained and defended it as best he could.

Schachter found that participants immediately directed their comments to the stooge in an effort to get him to agree with their lenient recommendations. When the deviant failed to do this, communication dropped off sharply and the stooge was largely ignored. After the discussion, participants were asked to assign group members to various tasks, and to recommend who should be included in the group. When the stooge's opinion deviated from the group majority, he was

rejected. However, in groups where he took the majority opinion, he was viewed positively and not rejected. So, holding an unpopular opinion, even in a short group discussion, can lead to an individual being ostracised, and it seems reasonable to suggest that at least under some circumstances a fear of rejection for failing to conform is justified.

Internalisation and compliance

Related to NSI and ISI are two major *kinds* of conformity. *Internalisation* occurs when a private belief or opinion becomes consistent with a public belief or opinion. In internalisation, then, we say what we believe and believe what we say. Mann (1969) calls this *true conformity*, and it can be thought of as a conversion to other people's points of view. This probably explains the behaviour of participants in Sherif's experiment (see page 69). In Asch-type conformity experiments, however, people face a conflict and reach a compromise in the form of *compliance* in which the answer that is given publicly is *not* the one that is privately believed. In compliance, then, we say what we do not believe and what we believe we do not say.

Conformity and group belongingness

The distinction between NSI and ISI has been called the *dual process dependency model of social influence*. However, this approach underestimates the role of group 'belongingness'. One important feature of conformity is that we are influenced by a group because, psychologically, we feel that we belong to it. This is why a group's norms are relevant standards for our own attitudes and behaviour. The dual process dependency model emphasises the *interpersonal* aspects of conformity experiments, which could just as easily occur between individuals as group members.

Box 8.6   Referential social influence

Abrams *et al.* (1990) argue that we only experience uncertainty when we disagree with those with whom we expect to agree. This is especially likely to be the case when we regard those others as members of the same category or group as ourselves in respect to judgements made in a shared stimulus situation. Social influence occurs, then, when we see ourselves as belonging to a group and possessing the same characteristics and reactions as other group members. Turner (1991) refers to this self-categorisation, in which group membership is salient, as *referent informational influence*.

This approach argues that in Sherif's experiment, for example (see page 69), participants were influenced by their assumption that the autokinetic effect is actually real, and their expectation of agreement between themselves. In support of this, it has been shown that when participants discover that the autokinetic effect is an illusion, mutual influence and convergence cease because the need to agree at all is removed (Sperling, 1946).

If, however, we believe that there *is* a correct answer, and we are uncertain what it is, *only* those whom we categorise as belonging to 'our' group will influence our judgement. As Brown (1988) has remarked:

'there is more to conformity than simply "defining social reality"': it all depends on who is doing the defining'.

According to this self-categorisation approach, then, people conform because they are group members, and evidence indicates that conformity on Asch-type experiments is higher when participants see themselves as ingroup members (Abrams *et al.*, 1990). This implies that it is not the validation of physical reality or the avoidance of social disapproval that is important. Rather, it is the upholding of a group norm that is important, and *people* are the source of information about the appropriate ingroup norm.

Conformity: good or bad?

On some occasions, *dissent* is just an expression of disagreement, a refusal to 'go along with the crowd'. On other occasions, it is more creative, as when someone suggests a better solution to a problem (Maslach *et al.*, 1985). Our refusal to 'go along with the crowd' may be an attempt to remain independent as a matter of principle (which Willis, 1963 calls *anticonformity*) and may betray a basic fear of a loss of personal identity. Constructive dissent and independence, by contrast, are positive qualities.

In most circumstances, conformity serves a valuable social purpose in that it:

'lubricates the machinery of social interaction [and] enables us to structure our social behaviour and predict the reactions of others' (Zimbardo and Leippe, 1991).

For most people, though, the word 'conformity' has a negative connotation and is often used to convey undesirable behaviour. In laboratory research, conformity has most often been studied in terms of what Milgram (1965) calls 'the conspiratorial group' who 'limit, constrain, and distort the individual's response'.

As a result, it has been implicitly assumed that independence is 'good' and 'conformity' is bad, a value judgement made explicit by Asch (1952). However, conformity can be highly functional, helping us satisfy social and non-social needs, as well as being necessary (at least to a degree) for social life to proceed at all. Moreover, because each of us has a limited (and often biased) store of information on which to make our decisions, why should we not consider information from others, especially those who have more expertise than us? A conforming response, then, may be a *rational judgement* by a person who does not have sufficient information on which to make a decision and so relies on others for assistance. However, whilst dissent can create unpleasantness, and conformity can help preserve harmony,

'there are obvious dangers to conformity. Failure to speak our minds against dangerous trends or attitudes [for example, racism] can easily be interpreted as support' (Krebs and Blackman, 1988).

Conclusions

Quite clearly, there are some circumstances in which we conform as a result of either real or imagined pressure from others. Exactly why we sometimes conform and sometimes show independent behaviour has been the subject of much research, and several factors influencing conformity have been identified. Whilst conformity is usually viewed as the influence of a majority over a minority, minorities can, under certain circumstances, exert influence over majorities.

SUMMARY

- The essence of conformity is yielding to (real or imagined) **group pressure** in the absence of any direct request to comply with the group.
- The groups which exert this pressure include both **membership groups** (such as family or peers) and **reference groups.** Conformity does not imply adhering to any particular set of attitudes or values, and the group may have majority or minority status.
- One of the earliest experimental studies of conformity was Sherif's using the **autokinetic effect.** When participants first made their estimates privately, then in a group, their individual estimates converged, representing a **group norm**.
- Asch criticised Sherif on the grounds that his task was ambiguous. The best way to measure conformity is to assess people's tendency to agree with others who unanimously give the **wrong answer** on a task with an obvious correct answer, as in the **Asch paradigm**.
- In the Asch paradigm, one naive participant is placed among a group of stooges, who, on certain **critical** trials all give the same wrong answer.
- The crucial measurement is whether the naive participant gives the same wrong answer as the stooges on the critical trials. Asch found a **mean** conformity rate of 32 per cent (but 25 per cent using the **median**). However, there were wide individual differences: no one conformed on all the critical trials, 26 per cent never conformed, and about 75 per cent conformed at least once. Nevertheless, these results indicate the powerful influence of a majority over a lone individual.
- When interviewed after the experiment, participants gave several specific reasons for their conformity, including wanting to act in line with the experimenter's wishes and to convey a favourable impression of themselves. Some genuinely wondered if their eyesight was reliable or if they had been seated in disadvantageous positions. Others denied being aware of having given incorrect answers.
- Yet others said they did not want to appear different or be made to look a fool or inferior or to be ridiculed. For these participants, there was clearly a discrepancy between the answer they gave in the group and what they **privately believed**: they gave the answer that they knew was wrong.
- When Asch allowed the naive participants to **write down** their answers, conformity was significantly reduced, showing that **group pressure** must have been the crucial factor.
- Using the Asch paradigm, several factors have been shown to affect conformity. As far as **group size** is concerned, conformity increases as the number of stooges increases, but only up to three. With very large groups it may drop dramatically, possibly because participants suspect **collusion**.
- According to Asch, **unanimity** is more important than group size. Conformity drops when one stooge fails to go along with the majority judgement, even if this stooge does not agree with the naive participant. Also, when a stooge initially gives the correct answer but then agrees with the majority wrong answer, conformity increases.
- With **difficult** tasks (such as making the comparison lines more similar), conformity increases, as it does when the task is **ambiguous** (such as judging how many clicks a metronome makes). The more **familiar** we are with a task's demands, the less likely we are to conform.
- According to Eagly and Steffen, men conform as frequently as women do when their conformity or independence will be kept private, but less than women when these will be made known to the group. Conformity also tends to be higher amongst those who have low self-esteem, are especially concerned about social relationships, have a strong need for social approval, and are attracted towards other group members.
- The **Crutchfield device** overcomes the time-consuming and uneconomical nature of the Asch paradigm. It removes the need for stooges, and several participants in their separate cubicles can be tested at once. Crutchfield found that college students agreed with statements that they probably would not have agreed with in other circumstances.
- Larsen initially found significantly lower rates of conformity than Asch among American students 20 years after the original research. However, five years later these were very similar to Asch's, reflecting changes in the American social and political climate.
- Perrin and Spencer found very low rates of conformity among British university students, but young offenders on probation showed rates very similar to Asch's. Conformity rates seem to reflect both the cultural expectations that participants bring with them from their contemporary world, and the experimenter's expectations.

- Although Asch's findings usually cause concern about the weakness of the individual in the face of group pressure, in fact conformity was the **exception** to the rule.
- According to Moscovici and Faucheux, instead of seeing the stooges in an Asch-type experiment as the majority, it is much more useful to think of the naive participant as embodying the 'conventional', self-evident, majority view, whilst the stooges reflect an unorthodox, unconventional, minority opinion.
- From this perspective, the minority influenced the majority 32 per cent of the time and it is those participants who remained independent who are actually the conformists. This is relevant to understanding how new ideas come to be accepted.
- Moscovici believes that this area of research involves a **conformity bias**, making it very difficult to explain how change comes about. Without **active minorities** exerting an influence in social and scientific arenas, innovations would simply not happen.
- Moscovici re-analysed Asch's data and found the **consistency** of the stooges' judgements to be crucial. This was confirmed by Moscovici's own research, which showed that minorities can change the majority's views by giving consistent responses.
- According to Hogg and Vaughan, consistency disrupts the majority norm, draws attention to itself as an entity, conveys the existence of an alternative, coherent point of view, and demonstrates certainty and a commitment to a particular viewpoint, which represents the only solution to the current conflict.
- Minorities are also more effective if they display **investment**, **autonomy** and a balance between **rigidity** and **flexibility**. They also have more influence if they are perceived as similar to the majority in terms of age, gender and social category.
- An early attempt to account for conformity was Deutsch and Gerard's distinction between **informational social influence/ISI** and **normative social influence/NSI.**
- ISI is related to Festinger's **social comparison theory**, according to which social reality is defined by the thoughts and behaviours of others in novel or ambiguous situations. The fact that some participants in Asch's experiment said they believed the majority opinion was correct suggests that ISI can occur even in unambiguous situations, although the explanations of these participants may have been **defensive/self-serving attributions**.
- **NSI** is based on the need for social acceptance and approval. Most of the participants in both Asch's and Crutchfield's experiments recognised that the majority answer was wrong but feared being rejected if they gave the correct answer.
- Related to ISI is **internalisation** (we say what we believe and believe what we say), which Mann calls **true conformity**. It can be thought of a conversion to other people's points of view and is the kind of conformity involved in Sherif's experiment.
- Related to NSI is **compliance** (we say what we do not believe and what we believe we do not say). It represents a compromise to the conflict faced by participants in Asch-type experiments.
- The distinction between ISI and NSI has been called the **dual process dependency model of social influence**. This emphasises the **interpersonal** aspect of conformity experiments and underestimates the role of **group belongingness**. According to Abrams *et al.*, we only experience uncertainty when we disagree with those with whom we expect to agree, especially those we regard as belonging to the same category/ group and thus sharing certain characteristics and reactions (**referent informational influence**).
- Sperling showed that if participants discover that the autokinetic effect is an illusion, the need to agree is removed. However, if we believe that there is a correct answer but are unsure about it, **only** members of 'our' group will influence our judgement. According to this self-categorisation approach, what is important is the upholding of ingroup norms.
- **Dissent** may represent an attempt to remain independent as a matter of principle (**anticonformity**). Alternatively, it can be constructive and creative.
- Whilst conformity often serves a valuable social function, the term has a negative connotation for most people and it has been studied experimentally largely in terms of the 'conspiratorial group'. Asch explicitly stated that conformity is 'bad' and independence is 'good'.
- Conformity may be a **rational judgement** by someone who does not have sufficient information on which to make a decision, and so relies on others with greater expertise. However, failure to speak our minds against racism, for example, can be (mis-)interpreted as support.

OBEDIENCE

Introduction and overview

When people in authority tell us to do something, we tend to comply with their instructions. As one example of this, Cohen and Davis (1981, cited in Carlson, 1987) describe a case in which a physician prescribed ear drops for a patient with an ear infection with the instruction that the nurse should 'place in R ear'. However, the physician evidently did not leave a suitably big gap between the 'R' (which stood for right) and the word 'ear'. Neither the nurse nor the patient questioned a treatment for earache in which the medication was delivered rectally.

The much more serious *social* problems that obedience can cause have been described by Milgram (1974):

'From 1933 to 1945 millions of innocent persons were systematically slaughtered on command. Gas chambers were built, death camps were guarded, daily quotas of corpses were produced with the same efficiency as the manufacture of appliances. These inhuman policies may have originated in the mind of a single person, but they could only be carried out on a massive scale if a very large number of persons obeyed orders'.

Our aim in this chapter is to look at research into obedience, much of it conducted by Milgram, and consider what this research can tell us about why we are sometimes blindly obedient to others and how we might behave more independently.

Distinguishing between conformity and obedience

The previous chapter looked at some of the research that has been conducted into conformity. According to Milgram (1992), conformity and obedience are similar in that both involve the abdication of individual judgement in the face of some external pressure. However, there are at least three important differences between them. First, in conformity there is no *explicit* requirement to act in a certain way, whereas in obedience we are *ordered* or *instructed* to do something. Second, those who influence us when we conform are our *peers* (or *equals*) and the behaviour of people becomes more alike because it is affected by *example*. In obedience, there is a difference in status from the outset and, rather than there being mutual influence, obedience is affected by *direction*, with somebody in *higher authority* influencing behaviour.

Third, conformity has to do with the psychological 'need' for acceptance by others and involves going along with one's peers in a group situation. Obedience, by contrast, has to do with the social power and status of an authority figure in a hierarchical situation. Although we typically deny that we are conformist (because it detracts from a sense of individuality), we usually deny responsibility for our behaviour in the case of obedience. As a result, behaviours occur because 'I was only following orders' (an explanation given by Adolf Eichmann, Director of the Nazi deportation of Jews to concentration camps) or because 'if the Commander in Chief tells this lieutenant colonel to go and stand in the corner and sit on his head, I will do so' (a response given by Oliver North in the Iran–Contra hearings of 1987).

Experimental studies: Milgram's research

The original purpose of a series of experiments conducted by Milgram (1963, 1964, 1974) was to test the 'Germans are different hypothesis'. This hypothesis has been used by historians to explain the systematic destruction of millions of Jews, Poles and others by the Nazis during the 1930s and 1940s (see above and also Chapter 3, page 22). The hypothesis maintains that Hitler could not have put his evil plans into operation without the co-operation of thousands of others, and that the Germans have a basic character defect (namely, a readiness to obey authority without question regardless of the acts demanded by the authority figure), which provided Hitler with the co-operation he needed. After carrying out his experiment in America, Milgram had originally planned to take it to Germany to test for the existence of this hypothesised character defect. As we shall see, though, the results Milgram obtained indicated that this was not necessary.

THE PARTICIPANTS

In his original experiments, Milgram advertised for volunteers to take part in a study of learning which was to be conducted at Yale University. The experiment would last about an hour and participants would be paid $4.50 for their involvement. The advertisement is shown in Figure 9.1. The first participants to be studied by Milgram were 20–50-year-old men who came from all walks of life.

THE BASIC PROCEDURE

When participants arrived at Yale University's psychology department, they were met by a young, crew-cut man in a grey laboratory coat who introduced himself as Jack Williams, the experimenter. Also present was a Mr Wallace, a mild and harmless looking, if a little overweight, accountant in his late fifties. In fact, neither the experimenter nor Mr Wallace was genuine, and everything else that followed in the procedure (apart from the genuine participants' behaviour) was carefully preplanned, staged and scripted.

The participant and Mr Wallace were told that the experiment would be concerned with the effects of punishment on learning, and that one of them would be the 'teacher' and the other the 'learner'. Their roles were determined by each drawing a piece of paper from a hat. In fact, both pieces of paper had 'teacher' written on them. Mr Wallace drew out the first and called out 'learner'. As a result, the real participant was always the 'teacher'. All three then went to an adjoining room where the learner was strapped into a chair with his arms attached to electrodes that would supposedly

---

Public Announcement

WE WILL PAY YOU $4.00 FOR ONE HOUR OF YOUR TIME

Persons Needed for a Study of Memory

*We will pay five hundred New Haven men to help us complete a scientific study of memory and learning. The study is being done at Yale University.

*Each person who participates will be paid $4.00 (plus 50c carfare) for approximately 1 hour's time. We need you for only one hour: there are no further obligations. You may choose the time you would like to come (evenings, weekdays, or weekends).

*No special training, education, or experience is needed. We want:

Factory workers	Businessmen	Construction workers
City employees	Clerks	Salespeople
Laborers	Professional people	White-collar workers
Barbers	Telephone workers	Others

All persons must be between the ages of 20 and 50. High school and college students cannot be used.

*If you meet these qualifications, fill out the coupon below and mail it now to Professor Stanley Milgram, Department of Psychology, Yale University, New Haven. You will be notified later of the specific time and place of the study. We reserve the right to decline any application.

*You will be paid $4.00 (plus 50c carfare) as soon as you arrive at the laboratory.

- -

TO:
PROF. STANLEY MILGRAM, DEPARTMENT OF PSYCHOLOGY, YALE UNIVERSITY, NEW HAVEN, CONN. I want to take part in this study of memory and learning. I am between the ages of 20 and 50. I will be paid $4.00 (plus 50c carfare) if I participate.

NAME (Please Print)............................

ADDRESS...................................

TELEPHONE NO. .... Best time to call you ....

AGE........ OCCUPATION.................... SEX......
CAN YOU COME:

WEEKDAYS .... EVENINGS ......WEEKENDS.........

Figure 9.1   The advertisement used by Milgram to recruit participants for his study (From Milgram, 1974)

---

deliver an electric shock from a shock generator in the adjacent room.

The teacher and experimenter then went into the adjacent room. The teacher was shown the generator, which had a number of switches on it, each clearly marked with voltage levels and verbal descriptions. The shocks began at 15-volts and went up in 15-volt increments to 450 volts, as shown in Figure 9.2. The teacher was then given a 45-volt shock to convince him that the generator was real. However, and unknown to the teacher, this would be the only *actual* electric shock that would be delivered during the whole experiment.

The task involved the teacher reading out a list of word

(a)

(b)

(c)

Figure 9.2   (a) The 'electric shock generator' used by Milgram (above) and a schematic representation of its front panel showing the voltages and verbal labels (below). In (b) the 'learner' is strapped into his chair, and in (c), the 'teacher' receives a shock of 45 volts (From Milgram, 1974)

pairs (such as 'blue–girl' and 'fat–neck'). After this, the first word of a pair was read out followed by a number of other words, one of which was the word it had been paired with. The learner had to choose the correct word by pressing one of four switches which turned on a light on a panel in the teacher's room. Each time the learner made a mistake, the teacher had to deliver a shock, with each successive mistake being punished by a shock 15 volts higher than the previous one.

In Milgram's first experiment (which is known as the *remote victim variation*), the learner was scripted to pound loudly on the wall at 300 volts and, after 315 volts, to stop pounding on the wall *and* give no further answers. In the second experiment (the *voice feedback variation*), the teacher heard a tape-recorded series of verbal responses that were Mr Wallace's 'spontaneous reactions' to the increasing shock levels. These verbal behaviours are shown in Box 9.1.

Box 9.1   Mr Wallace's 'spontaneous reactions' to increasing shock levels administered by the teacher

75, 90 and 105 volts: Makes a little grunt.

120 volts: Tells the experimenter that the shocks are becoming painful.

150 volts: Cries out 'Experimenter, get me out of here! I won't be in the experiment any more! I refuse to go on!'

180 volts: Shouts out 'I can't stand the pain'.

270 volts: Lets out an agonised scream and continues to insist on being released.

300 volts: Desperately shouts out that he will no longer provide answers.

315 volts. Lets out a violent scream and reaffirms vehemently that he will no longer provide answers.

330 volts: There is an ominous silence.

The scripted behaviours were, of course, dependent upon a participant actually continuing with the experiment up to that shock level. When Milgram asked his students what they thought would happen in the experiment, a few thought that some people would continue all the way to 450 volts, but that most would stop early or in the middle of the shock range. Psychiatrists asked to predict the teacher's behaviour suggested that less than 1 per cent would administer the highest voltage, and that most would stop around 120 volts (Milgram, 1974).

The teacher had been instructed to treat a non-response from Mr Wallace (which, as Box 9.1 shows, occurred at 330 volts) as an incorrect response, so that shocks should continue to be given. Milgram found that participants showed reluctance to administer the shocks. Whenever this happened, the experimenter gave a series of scripted 'verbal prods'. These were 'please continue' (or 'please go on'), 'the experiment requires that you continue', 'it is absolutely essential that you continue' and, finally, 'you have no other choice, you *must* go on'. The experimenter was also scripted to say 'although the shocks may be painful, there is no permanent tissue damage' in order to reassure the teacher that no permanent harm was being done. The experiment was terminated either when the participant refused to continue (see Figure 9.3) or when the maximum 450-volt shock had been administered four times.

Figure 9.3   A participant refuses to continue any further with the experiment (From Milgram, 1974)

THE RESULTS

The participants displayed great anguish, verbally attacked the experimenter, twitched nervously, or broke out into nervous laughter. Many were observed to

'sweat, stutter, tremble, groan, bite their lips and dig their nails into their flesh. Full-blown, uncontrollable seizures were observed for three [participants]' (Milgram, 1974).

Indeed, one experiment had to be stopped because the participant had a violent convulsive seizure. It is quite astonishing, then, that in the remote victim variation every teacher administered at least 300 volts and 65 per cent administered 450 volts. In the voice feedback variation, 62.5 per cent continued all the way up to 450 volts.

In order to determine why the level of obedience was so high in these two variations, Milgram conducted a number of variations to the basic experiment using the voice feedback condition as his baseline measure of obedience. In all, a further 16 experimental variations were conducted. The percentage administering 450 volts in each of the variations used by Milgram is shown in Figure 9.4. A description of what happened in some of the variations is presented in Box 9.2.

Box 9.2   Some of the variations on Milgram's basic procedure

Institutional context (variation 10): In post-experimental interviews, many participants said that they continued administering shocks because the experiment was being conducted at Yale University, a highly prestigious institution. However, when Milgram transferred the experiment to a rundown office in downtown Bridgeport, the 450 volt obedience rate was 47.5 per cent. This suggests that whilst the institutional context played a role, it was not a crucial factor.

Proximity and touch proximity (variations 3 and 4): In the original variations, the teacher and learner were in adjacent rooms and could not see one another. However, when they were in the same room (about 1.5 feet (46 cm) apart), the 450 volt obedience rate dropped to 40 per cent (variation 3). When the teacher was required to force the learner's hand down onto a shock plate (variation 4), the 450 volt obedience rate dropped to 30 per cent. Whilst seeing the effects of the shock on the participant reduces obedience, the figures observed are still very high.

Remote authority (variation 7): When the experimenter left the room, having given the essential instructions, 450 volt obedience dropped to 20.5 per cent when subsequent instructions were issued by telephone. Indeed, participants often pretended to administer a shock or administered a shock lower than they were supposed to. This suggests they were trying to compromise between their conscience and the experimenter's instructions. In his absence, it was easier to follow their conscience.

Two peers rebel (variation 17): In this variation, the teacher was paired with two other (actor) teachers. The actor teachers read out the list of word-pairs and informed the learner if the response was correct. The real participant administered the shocks. At 150 volts, the first teacher refused to continue and moved to another part of the room. At 210 volts, the second teacher did likewise. The experimenter ordered the real teacher to continue. Only 10 per cent of participants continued to 450 volts. Most stopped obeying when the first or second teacher refused to continue. According to Milgram (1965):

'the effects of peer rebellion are most impressive in undercutting the experimenter's authority'.

A peer administers the shocks (variation 18): When the teacher was paired with another teacher (in fact an actor) and had only to read out the word-pairs, rather than administer the shock, 450 volt obedience rose to 92.5 per cent. This shows that it is easier for the participants to shift responsibility from themselves to the other teacher.

EXPLAINING THE RESULTS OF MILGRAM'S OBEDIENCE STUDIES

According to Milgram (1974),

'the most fundamental lesson of our study is that ordinary people, simply doing their jobs, and without any particular hostility on their part, can become agents in a terrible destructive process'.

A number of explanations as to why people obey have been proposed.

The credibility of the set-up

It has been suggested that participants did not believe the experimental set-up they found themselves in, and that they knew the learner was not really being given electric shocks. A study which excludes this possibility was conducted by Sheridan and King (1972). They had students train a puppy to learn a discrimination task by punishing it with increasingly severe and *real* electric shocks each time it made an error. Although the puppy received only a small shock, it could be seen and its squeals heard by the participants.

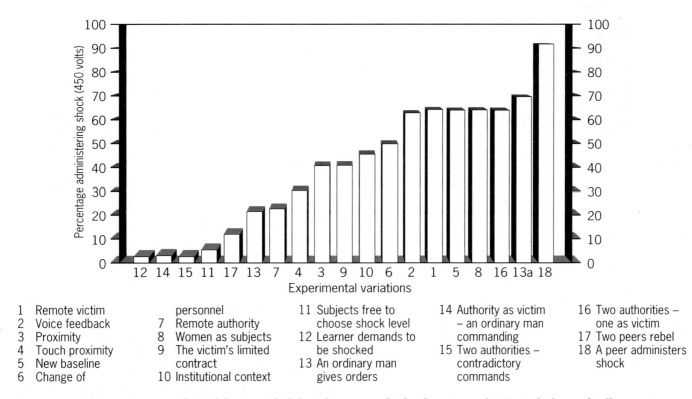

1	Remote victim		personnel	11	Subjects free to	14	Authority as victim	16	Two authorities –
2	Voice feedback	7	Remote authority		choose shock level		– an ordinary man		one as victim
3	Proximity	8	Women as subjects	12	Learner demands to		commanding	17	Two peers rebel
4	Touch proximity	9	The victim's limited		be shocked	15	Two authorities –	18	A peer administers
5	New baseline		contract	13	An ordinary man		contradictory		shock
6	Change of	10	Institutional context		gives orders		commands		

Figure 9.4   The percentage of participants administering 450-volt shocks across the 18 variations of Milgram's original experiment. Note that one experiment has two variations (13 and 13a) (From Zimbardo and Weber, 1994)

After a certain time, an odourless anaesthetic was released into the puppy's cage which caused it to fall asleep. Although participants complained about the procedure (and some even cried), they were reminded that failure to respond was a punishable error and that shocks should continue to be given. The results showed that 75 per cent of participants delivered the maximum shock possible. Clearly, then, it seems unlikely that the Milgram procedure leads participants to the belief that the learner is not really being harmed, and so the experiment has what Orne and Holland (1968) call *experimental realism*.

Demand characteristics

Another possibility is that the cues in the experimental setting influenced the participants' perceptions of what was required of them. According to this explanation, the obedience shown by the participants was simply a response to the demands of the unusual experimental setting (Zimbardo and Weber, 1994). Naturalistic studies of obedience, however, dispute this explanation, and suggest that Milgram's study also has *mundane realism* (Orne and Holland, 1968) in that the results from it extend beyond the laboratory setting. For example, Hofling *et al.*, (1966) showed that when nurses were instructed by telephone to administer twice the maximum dosage of a drug (actually a harmless tablet) to a patient, 21 out of 22 did so. Even when there are good reasons to defy authority, then, it is hard to resist it (Zimbardo and Weber, 1994).

Personal responsibility

Many participants in Milgram's studies raised the issue of responsibility should harm befall the learner. Although the experimenter did not always discuss responsibility, when he did say 'I'm responsible for what goes on here', participants showed visible relief. Indeed, when participants are told that *they* are responsible for what happens, obedience is sharply reduced (Hamilton, 1978). Milgram saw this *diffusion of responsibility* (see also Chapter 12, page 114) as being crucial to understanding the Nazi atrocities shown by people like Eichmann and his defence that he was 'just carrying out orders'. It can also explain the behaviour of William Calley, an American soldier who was court-martialed for the 1968 massacre by troops under his command of several hundred Vietnam civilians at My Lai (Opton, 1973).

The perception of legitimate authority

As mentioned earlier (see page 81), many participants showed signs of distress and conflict in Milgram's experiments, and so the diffusion of responsibility explanation cannot tell the whole story. Perhaps, then, the experimenter was seen as a legitimate authority by participants, at least up until the point when he said 'you have no other choice, you *must* go on'. The most common mental adjustment in the obedient participant is to see him/herself as an agent of external authority (the *agentic state*). This state (which is the opposite of an *autonomous state*) is what allows us to function in an organised and hierarchical social system. For a group to function as a whole, individuals must give up responsibility and defer to others of higher status in the social hierarchy. Legitimate authority thus replaces a person's own self-regulation (Turner, 1991).

Authority figures often possess highly visible symbols of their power or status that make it difficult for us to refuse their commands. In Milgram's experiments, the experimenter always wore a grey laboratory coat to indicate his position as an authority figure. The impact of such 'visible symbols' has been demonstrated by Bickman (1974), who showed that when people are told by a person in a guard's uniform to pick up a paper bag or give a coin to a stranger, obedience is higher (80 per cent) than when the instruction is given by somebody in civilian clothes (40 per cent). For Milgram,

'a substantial proportion of people do what they are told to do, irrespective of the content of the act and without limitations of conscience, so long as they perceive that the command comes from a legitimate authority'.

An interesting example of this is presented in Box 9.3.

Box 9.3   Obedience to authority in a simulated prison

In a study conducted by Zimbardo *et al.* (1973), participants were recruited through advertisements placed in a newspaper which asked for student volunteers for a two-week study of prison life. After potential participants had been given clinical interviews, 25 of over 100 who volunteered were selected. They were all judged to be emotionally stable, physically healthy, 'normal to average' on the basis of personality tests, and law abiding.

Participants were told that they would be randomly assigned to the role of either 'prisoner' or 'guard' (although all had stated a preference for being a prisoner). At the beginning of the study, then, there were no differences between those selected to be prisoners and guards. They were a relatively homogeneous group of white, middle-class college students from all over America and Canada.

Zimbardo *et al.* converted the basement of the Stanford University psychology department into a 'mock prison'. It was made as much like a real prison as possible in an attempt to simulate functionally some of the significant features of the psychological state of imprisonment. The experiment began one Sunday morning, when those allocated to the 'prisoner' role were unexpectedly arrested by the local police. They were charged with a felony, read their rights, searched, hand-cuffed, and taken to the police station to be 'booked'. After being fingerprinted, and having forms prepared for their central information file, each prisoner was taken blindfold to the 'prison'.

Upon arrival at the prison, the prisoners were stripped naked, skin-searched, deloused, and issued a uniform and bedding. Prisoners wore a loose-fitting smock with an identification number on the front and back, plus a chain bolted around one ankle. They also wore a nylon stocking to cover their hair (in a real prison, their hair would have been shaved off). The prisoners were referred to by their number, and housed in 6 × 9-foot (1.8 × 2.7-metres) cells, three to a cell. The guards wore military-style khaki uniforms, silver reflector sunglasses (making eye contact with them impossible) and they carried clubs, whistles, handcuffs and keys to the cells and main gate. The guards were on duty 24 hours a day, in eight-hour shifts, and had complete control over the prisoners. The prisoners were imprisoned around the clock, and allowed out of their cells only for meals, exercise, toilet privileges, head counts and work.

After an initial 'rebellion' had been crushed, the prisoners began to react passively as the guards stepped up their aggression each day (by, for example, having a roll call in the middle of the night simply to disrupt the prisoners' sleep). This made the prisoners feel helpless, and no longer in control of their lives.

The guards began to enjoy the power they had. As one said, 'Acting authoritatively can be great fun. Power

can be a great pleasure'. After less than 36 hours, one prisoner had to be released because of uncontrolled crying, fits of rage, disorganised thinking and severe depression. Three other prisoners developed the same symptoms and had to be released on successive days. Another prisoner developed a rash over his whole body, which was triggered when his attempt to get 'parole' was rejected. The prisoners became demoralised and apathetic, and even began to refer to themselves and others by their prison numbers.

The whole experiment, planned to run for two weeks, was stopped after *six days* because of the pathological reactions of the prisoners who had originally been selected because they were emotionally stable. An outside observer, who had a long history of being incarcerated, reported that the mock prison and the behaviour of both the guards and prisoners were strikingly similar to real life. One conclusion which can be drawn from this study is that the distinction between role-playing and role enactment is a very fine one.

The 'foot in the door' and not knowing how to disobey

According to Gilbert (1981), participants in Milgram's experiments may have been 'sucked in' by the series of graduated demands, which began with seemingly innocuous orders that gradually escalated. It is possible that having begun the experiment, participants found it difficult to extricate themselves from it. They may even not have known *how* to disobey, since nothing they said had any effect on the experimenter (at least until they refused the final verbal 'prod' in which they were told they had no choice but to continue).

Socialisation

Despite our expressed ideal of independence, obedience is something we are socialised into from a very early age by significant others (including our parents and teachers). Obedience may be an *ingrained habit* (Brown, 1986) that is difficult for us to resist.

AN EVALUATION OF MILGRAM'S RESEARCH

As we might expect, Milgram's results caused much interest when they were published. Critics of his research have largely focused on three main areas, namely *methodological issues*, *issues of generalisation*, and *ethical issues*.

Methodological issues

One of the first methodological criticisms made of Milgram's research was that the sample he studied was *unrepresentative*. Such a criticism is hardly justified. Altogether, Milgram studied 636 participants, who represented a cross-section of the population of New Haven, thought to be a fairly typical small American town. However, Milgram did concede that those participants who continued administering shocks up to 450 volts were more likely to see the learner as being responsible for what happened to him rather than themselves. These participants seemed to have a stronger authoritarian character (see Chapter 3, page 23) and a less advanced level of moral development, although this was a matter of degree only. Indeed, people who volunteer for experiments (as, of course, Milgram's participants did) tend to be considerably *less* authoritarian than those who do not (Rosenthal and Rosnow, 1966).

Milgram was also criticised for using mainly male participants. Whilst true, such a criticism is fairly weak. Of the 40 females who did serve as participants (in variation 8), 65 per cent continued administering shocks up to 450 volts, a figure that is comparable to the obedience shown by their male counterparts. A further methodological criticism concerns the cross-cultural replicability of Milgram's findings. Studies conducted in a number of countries have produced various obedience rates ranging from 16 per cent (Kilham and Mann, 1974, using female Australian students) to 92 per cent (Meeus and Raaijmakers, 1986, using members of the general population of Holland).

Issues of generalisation

A number of researchers have argued that whilst Milgram's experiments had high *internal validity*, the results he obtained would not prevail in other circumstances. The charge here is that Milgram's findings lack *external* or *ecological validity* (or to use Orne and Holland's term, *mundane realism*: see page 84). According to Milgram, though, the essential process in complying with the demands of an authority figure is the same, whether the setting is the artificial one of the psychological laboratory or a naturally occurring one outside it, a point accepted by many researchers (Colman, 1987).

There are, of course, differences between laboratory studies of obedience and the obedience observed in

Nazi Germany. However, as Milgram (1974) has remarked in this context:

> '... differences in scale, numbers and political context may turn out to be relatively unimportant as long as certain essential features are retained. The essence of obedience consists in the fact that a person comes to view himself as the instrument for carrying out another person's wishes, and he, therefore, no longer regards himself as responsible for his actions. Once this critical shift of viewpoint has occurred in the person, all the essential features of obedience follow'.

The study conducted by Hofling *et al.* (1966), which showed that 95 per cent of those nurses studied complied with an instruction that involved them infringing both hospital regulations and medical ethics (see page 84), definitely indicates that obedience is not a phenomenon confined to the setting of Milgram's laboratory.

Unfortunately, the available data are not particularly helpful in allowing us to comment on cross-cultural similarities or differences in obedience. One reason for this is that the replications undertaken have only been *partial*, and have not completely duplicated Milgram's procedures. For example, in Kilham and Mann's (1974) study, the female participants were required to administer electric shocks to another *female*. In Milgram's experiments, however, the learner was always a *male* (Smith and Bond, 1993). Humphreys (1994) has pointed out other differences in cross-cultural studies of obedience. These include the use of a maximum shock value of 330 volts rather than 450 volts (Ancona and Pareyson, 1968), and the use of a long-haired student as the learner rather than a 'Mr Wallace'-type character (Kilham and Mann, 1974).

Ethical issues

One of the strongest critics of Milgram's research was Baumrind (1964), who argued that the rights and feelings of Milgram's participants had been abused, and that inadequate measures were taken to protect participants from the undoubted stress and emotional conflict they experienced. Whilst accepting that participants did experience stress and conflict, Milgram argued that Baumrind's criticism presupposes the outcome of the experiment was *expected*, which, of course, it was not (at least not by those students and psychiatrists asked to anticipate what might happen: see page 81).

The production of stress was not an intended and deliberate effect of the experimental procedure. As Milgram (1974) noted,

> 'understanding grows because we examine situations in which the end is unknown. An investigator unwilling to accept this degree of risk must give up the idea of scientific enquiry'.

An experimenter cannot, then, know what his or her results are going to be before the experiment begins.

Box 9.4   Deception

A further ethical issue surrounding Milgram's research concerns *deception*. According to Vitelli (1988), more than one-third of social psychological studies (and virtually all of those that investigate conformity and obedience) deceive participants over the purpose of the research, the accuracy of the information they are given, or the true identity of a person they believe to be another genuine participant (or experimenter).

In defence of his use of deception, Milgram pointed out that, after learning about the deception when they were extensively debriefed, 84 per cent of participants said that they were glad or very glad to have participated, whilst fewer than 2 per cent said they were sorry or very sorry to have participated. Moreover, 80 per cent said they felt that *more* experiments of this kind should be conducted, and 74 per cent felt that they had learned something of personal importance as a result of participating.

Other researchers (e.g. Aronson, 1988) have defended Milgram's use of deception on the grounds that without it he would have found results 'which simply do not reflect how people behave when they are led to believe they are in real situations'. In some circumstances, then, deception may be the best (and perhaps the only) way to get useful information about how people behave in complex and important situations. A more detailed discussion of the ethical issues surrounding Milgram's research can be found in Gross and McIlveen (1998).

WHAT DO MILGRAM'S STUDIES TELL US ABOUT OURSELVES?

Perhaps one of the reasons why Milgram's research received the criticisms it did is that it paints a picture of humans that is unacceptable to us. Thus, it is far easier for us to accept that a war criminal like Adolf Eichmann was an inhuman impostor than that 'ordinary people' can be destructively obedient. Yet atrocities, such as those committed in Rwanda and the former Yugoslavia, continue to occur. Perhaps, like the 51 per cent of those people questioned following the trial and conviction of William Calley (see page 84) who said they would behave in the same way if commanded, 'we do as we are told'. Perhaps, such actions may be seen as

> 'normal, even desirable because [people like Calley] performed them in obedience to legitimate authority' (Kelman and Lawrence, 1972).

Box 9.5   Genocide

Hirsch (1995) has noted that many of the greatest crimes against humanity are committed in the name of obedience. *Genocide*, a term coined in 1944, tends to occur under conditions created by three social processes. The first of these, *authorisation*, relates to what we earlier termed the 'agentic state' (see page 84), that is, obeying orders because of where they come from. The second, *routinisation*, refers to massacre becoming a matter of routine, or a mechanical and highly programmed operation. The third process is *dehumanisation*, in which the victims are reduced to something less than human, which allows us to suspend our usual moral prohibition on killing (see Humphreys, 1994).

These ingredients of genocide were personified by Eichmann who, at his trial after the Second World War, denied ever killing anybody but took great pride in the way he transported millions to their death 'with great zeal and meticulous care' (Arendt, 1965). The comments of an East German judge in 1992, when sentencing a former East German border guard for having shot a man trying (three years earlier) to escape to the West, echo the spirits of the Nuremberg Accords which followed the Nazi war crimes trials:

'Not everything that is legal is right . . . At the end of the twentieth century, no one has the right to turn off his conscience when it comes to killing people on the orders of authorities' (cited in Berkowitz, 1993).

As we have noted, it is difficult to disobey authority. However, it seems that we are most likely to rebel when we feel that social pressure is so strong our *freedom* is in danger of being lost. In one demonstration of this, Gamson *et al.* (1982) invited the citizens of a midwestern town to a hotel conference centre in order to discuss community standards. The researchers explained that a local petrol station manager had publicly opposed high petrol prices and that the petrol company was taking legal action against him.

The participants were led to believe that an oil company was videotaping the group discussion, and were asked to speak out against the petrol station manager and to allow their taped discussions to be used in court. The researchers then left the participants. The participants reacted strongly to this threat to their freedom (even citing Milgram's research to justify their behaviour!). They strongly defended the station manager and refused to give in to the oil company's demands. Some partici-

pants even made plans to report the company, whilst others decided to tell their story to the newspapers.

Milgram himself felt that by *educating* people about the dangers of blind obedience, encouraging them to *question authority*, and exposing them to the actions of *disobedient models*, obedience would be reduced. Other researchers have emphasised the importance of *reactance*. According to Brehm (1966), we need to believe that we have freedom of choice. When we believe that this is not the case, and when we believe that we are *entitled* to freedom, we experience reactance, an unpleasant emotional state. To reduce this state, and restore our sense of freedom, disobedience occurs.

Conclusions

As is apparent in this chapter, there are circumstances in which we can become what Milgram calls 'agents in a terrible destructive process'. However, we are not *always* blindly obedient. Social psychology's task is to continue uncovering those situations in which such destructive obedience occurs, and to look at ways that such obedience can be reduced.

SUMMARY

- According to Milgram, both conformity and obedience involve the abdication of individual judgement in the face of external pressure. But only in obedience is there an **explicit order/instruction** to act in a certain way, coming from someone in **higher authority.** Whilst conformity involves **peer** influence, such that people's behaviour becomes more alike through **example**, obedience is affected by **direction**.
- Conformity relates to the psychological need for social acceptance in the context of the peer group, whereas obedience relates to the social power and status of an authority figure in a hierarchical situation. Whilst people typically deny being influenced by their peers, they do acknowledge their obedience to authority figures.
- Milgram originally intended to test the 'Germans are different' hypothesis, according to which Hitler's plan to systematically destroy millions of Jews and others depended on the co-operation of thousands of people. However, results from the

American research soon showed the hypothesis to be invalid.
- The sample in Milgram's original study comprised 20–50-year-old men from various occupational backgrounds. Both the experimenter, who wore a grey lab. coat, and Mr Wallace, introduced as another participant, were actors, and everything that happened (apart from the real participants' behaviour) was staged and scripted.
- The experiment was presented as concerned with the effects of punishment on learning, and the choosing of roles was rigged, so that the real participant was always the teacher.
- Each time the learner made a mistake on a word-pair task, the teacher was to deliver a shock 15 volts higher than the one before, with the voltage levels on the shock generator clearly marked from 15 to 450 volts. The teacher was given a 45-volt shock to convince him the generator was real, but this was the only **actual** shock delivered during the entire experiment.

- In the **remote victim variation**, the learner pounded loudly on the adjoining wall at 300 volts; after 315 volts, the pounding stopped and no further answers were given.
- In the **voice feedback variation,** the teacher heard a tape-recorded series of increasingly desperate verbal responses, supposedly the learner's spontaneous reactions to the increasing shock levels. These responses continued up to 315 volts, and at 330 volts there was an ominous silence. Non-responses were to be treated as incorrect responses.
- Both Milgram's students and psychiatrists asked to predict the teachers' behaviour said that very few would continue all the way to 450 volts, with most stopping in the early or middle ranges.
- Whenever participants showed reluctance to carry on giving the shocks, the experimenter gave a series of predetermined verbal prods. He also reassured the teacher that the shocks, though painful, were not dangerous.
- Participants showed great anguish, verbally attacking the experimenter, twitching and nervously digging their nails into their flesh and biting their lips. Three had uncontrollable seizures, and one experiment had to be stopped due to a participant's violently convulsive seizure.
- In the remote victim condition, 65 per cent went all the way to 450 volts, with a full 100 per cent giving at least 300 volts. In the voice feedback condition, 62.5 per cent went all the way to 450 volts.
- Using the voice feedback condition as a baseline, Milgram conducted a further 16 variations in order to determine why the level of obedience in the first two experiments was so high.
- Changing the **institutional context** from Yale University to a rundown office reduced the obedience rate to 47.5 per cent. When the teacher and learner were in the same room (**proximity**), it dropped to 40 per cent. There was a further drop to 30 per cent when the teacher had to force the learner's hand down onto the shock plate (**touch proximity**)
- When the experimenter left the room and gave subsequent instructions by telephone (**remote authority**), the obedience rate fell to 20.5 per cent. When the real participant was paired with two other actor teachers, who refused to continue at either 150 or 210 volts, it fell to 10 per cent (**peer rebellion**).
- When the teacher was paired with another actor teacher who gave the shock, the obedience rate rose to 92.5 per cent (**peer administers the shocks**).

- Sheridan and King's study, in which students gave real and increasingly severe electric shocks to a puppy, suggests that Milgram's participants genuinely believed the learner was being shocked (Milgram's experimental procedure had **experimental realism**).
- According to the **demand characteristics** explanation, the obedience shown by Milgram's participants was simply a response to the demands of the unusual experimental setting. However, naturalistic studies, such as Hofling *et al.*'s study of nurses, suggest that Milgram's study has **mundane realism**.
- When participants are told that **they** are responsible for what happens, rather than the experimenter, obedience is sharply reduced. Milgram saw this **diffusion of responsibility** as crucial to understanding the behaviour of Eichmann in Nazi Germany and Calley in Vietnam.
- Participants' distress implies that diffusion of responsibility cannot fully account for their behaviour. Perhaps the experimenter was seen as a **legitimate authority**, at least until he told participants that they had no choice but to go on. The most common mental adjustment in the obedient participant is the **agentic state** (the opposite of an **autonomous state**).
- The experimenter in Milgram's experiment always wore a grey lab. coat as a visible symbol of his authority, making it difficult to refuse his command, as was demonstrated by Bickman.
- Zimbardo *et al.*'s prison simulation experiment also demonstrates people's tendency to obey the commands of anyone whom they perceive as a legitimate authority. The prisoners reacted passively as the guards became progressively more aggressive, and they were made to feel no longer in control of their lives, demoralised and apathetic. The behaviour of both prisoners and guards was strikingly similar to real life, implying that what begins as role playing can quickly become role enactment.
- Milgram's participants may have found it difficult to remove themselves from an experiment that began with such harmless orders which were then gradually stepped up ('**foot in the door**'). They may not have known how to disobey, especially as obedience is an **ingrained habit** acquired through early **socialisation.**
- The **methodological criticism** of Milgram's research concerning his **unrepresentative** sample seems unjustified, since he studied over 600 participants who were a cross-section of New Haven. Nevertheless, those who showed maximum obedience tended to be more authoritarian

and less morally advanced than those who did not, although not significantly so.

- Although Milgram's participants were predominantly male, the 40 females showed a similar obedience rate. Cross-cultural replications have produced a variety of maximum obedience rates, although many replications have been **partial**, as in Kilham and Mann's use of a female learner.
- Whilst having high **internal validity**, Milgram's experiments have been accused of lacking **external/ecological validity**. According to Milgram, whilst there are obvious differences between obedience observed in laboratory experiments and in Nazi Germany, the essential features are the same, namely seeing oneself as the instrument of another's wishes and denying responsibility for one's actions.
- Baumrind criticised Milgram for failing to protect his participants from emotional conflict. However, their distress could not have been anticipated. Milgram defended his use of **deception** by pointing out that participants were extensively de-briefed, during which 84 per cent said that they were glad/very glad to have participated, with only 2 per cent saying they were sorry/very sorry. Deception may sometimes be necessary if we are to obtain useful information about how people behave in complex and important situations.
- Milgram's studies paint an unacceptable picture of ordinary people capable of destructive obedience. According to Hirsch, many of the greatest crimes against humanity have been committed in the name of obedience. **Genocide** tends to occur under conditions created by **authorisation**, **routinisation** and **dehumanisation**.
- As difficult as it is to disobey authority, we are most likely to rebel when we feel that our **freedom** is being threatened. According to Brehm, disobedience can occur when we try to reduce **reactance** and restore our sense of freedom.
- Milgram believed that obedience can be reduced by **educating** people about the dangers of blind obedience, encouraging them to **question authority** and exposing them to **disobedient models**.

10

SOCIAL POWER: LEADERS AND LEADERSHIP

Introduction and overview

Hollander (1985) has defined a *leader* as the person who exercises the most influence in a group, and *leadership* as the exercise of influence or power over others. The earliest research in this area attempted to identify the individual qualities that result in some people rising to positions of power and authority. Thus, the concern was with whether leaders are born or made and what it is about leaders, compared with followers, that makes them leaders. This focus on the 'the leader' is often referred to as the *trait approach*.

Later research concentrated on identifying the conditions which influence the effectiveness of those who are appointed to a formal leadership role, and typically took place within large organisations (such as businesses). This is often referred to as the *situational approach*, since it acknowledges that leadership is a complex social process in which the leader depends on the group as well as the group depending on the leader. Our aim in this chapter is to review social psychological theory and research relating to the emergence of leaders, and the factors which affect their leadership once they have assumed a position of power and authority.

Leaders: traits, situations and transactions

TRAITS AND LEADER EMERGENCE

For many years, theorising on the emergence of leaders was dominated by the 'great person' or *trait theory* of leader emergence. According to this, leaders are extraordinary people who naturally rise to positions of power and authority because they possess certain personality traits which suit them for 'life at the top'. According to this theory:

'the fate of societies . . . is in the hands of key, powerful, idiosyncratic individuals who by the force of their personalities reach positions of influence from which they can direct and dominate the lives of others. Such men are simply born great and emerge to take power in any situation regardless of the social or historical context' (Huczynski and Buchanan, 1991).

In a review of a large number of studies, Stogdill (1974) looked at leadership in various contexts, including the military, nursery schools, and political parties. On the basis of his review, Stogdill concluded that leaders tend to be slightly more intelligent, sociable, achievement oriented, experienced, older and taller than their followers. Other studies have shown that people who emerge as leaders tend to score higher on measures of self-confidence and dominance (Costantini and Craik, 1980) and combine an orientation towards success with an orientation towards affiliating with other people (Sorrentino and Field, 1986).

Evidence of particular traits in leaders has, however, been mixed and, in general, leaders have not been shown to be consistently different from non-leaders in terms of their personality traits (Turner, 1991). Whilst claims continue to be made about the characteristics that separate leaders from non-leaders (e.g. Kirkpatrick and Locke, 1991), it is generally agreed that the trait approach is limited, and that the kinds of traits a leader needs will vary from group to group and problem to problem.

SITUATIONS AND LEADER EMERGENCE

The view that different kinds of traits are needed in different situations was examined by Bales (1950), who stressed the *functional demands* of the situation. According to this perspective, the person most likely to emerge as a leader is the one who is best equipped to help the group fulfil its objectives in a particular context. Thus, the person most likely to become leader in a given situation is the one whose *skills* and *competence* are those most useful to the group in a given setting. At another time, and in another situation, someone else may be more suited for the role of leader. A good example of this comes from Sherif *et al.'s* (1961) Robber's Cave field experiment (see Chapter 3, page 26), in which the researchers found that when competition between two groups of boys was increased, one of the groups replaced its leader with a physically much stronger boy.

Whilst there is evidence consistent with the view that the situation determines who will emerge as a leader, this approach assumes that under the appropriate conditions, *anyone* can become a leader. However, the evidence does not support this, and whilst personality factors may not be as crucial as the trait approach proposes, it seems that some people adopt the role of a leader more readily than others (Nydegger, 1975), and that people seem to be fairly well aware of their relative ability to assume a position of power and authority.

TRANSACTIONS AND LEADER EMERGENCE

In recent years, *transactional theory* (Shaw, 1981) has been applied to both the trait and situational approaches to the emergence of leaders. According to this theory, both the characteristics of people and the demands of the situation determine who will become a leader. This approach to leaders will be looked at more closely when we examine *leader effectiveness*.

Leadership style and behaviour

AUTOCRATIC, DEMOCRATIC AND LAISSEZ-FAIRE STYLES

An early study of leadership style was conducted by Lewin *et al.* (1939). They wanted to investigate the effects of three different kinds of adult behaviour on a group of 10-year-old boys attending after-school clubs. The clubs, which were concerned with model making, were led by adults who acted in one of the three ways described in Box 10.1.

The boys with an *autocratic leader* became aggressive towards each other when things went wrong, and were submissive in their approaches to the leaders (and these

---

Box 10.1   The behaviour of the adults in Lewin *et al.*'s study

Autocratic leaders told the boys what sort of models they would make and with whom they would work. They sometimes praised or blamed the boys for their work, but did not explain their comments and, although friendly, they were also aloof and impersonal.

Democratic leaders discussed various possible projects with the boys and allowed them to choose who they would work with and generally make their own decisions. The leaders explained their comments and joined in with group activities.

Laissez-faire leaders left the boys very much to their own devices, and only offered help when asked for it (which was not very often) and gave neither praise nor blame.

---

approaches were often attention-seeking). If the leader left the room, the boys stopped working and became either disruptive or apathetic. However, the models they made were comparable, in terms of both quantity and quality, to those produced by the boys with the democratic leader.

Whilst the boys with the *democratic leader* actually produced slightly less work than those with the autocratic leader, they got on much better with each other, and seemed to like each other much more than was the case with the boys who had the autocratic leader. Any approaches made to the leader tended to be task-related, and when the leader left the room, the boys carried on working and showed greater independence. They also co-operated when things went wrong.

Like the boys with the autocratic leader, those with the *laissez-faire leader* were aggressive towards each other (although the amount of aggression shown was slightly less than for the boys with the autocratic leader). The boys also got very little work done, whether the leader was present or not, and were easily discouraged from finding solutions when things did not go exactly right for them.

The leader was changed every seven weeks and instructed to adopt one of the other kinds of leadership style. Thus, each group of boys was exposed to only one leadership style which was enacted by three different leaders. This was meant to ensure that the boys' behaviour could be attributed to the leadership style they were exposed to, rather than the leader's personality traits. Interestingly, when two of the most aggressive boys from the autocratic group were switched to the democratic group, they quickly became co-operative and involved in the tasks.

The findings of Lewin *et al.*'s study strongly suggest that it is leadership style (which is not necessarily a fixed characteristic) that is important rather than the personality of the leader (which is a fixed characteristic). However, Brown (1985) has argued that people, their groups and leaders, can only really be understood in the context of the wider society of which they form a part. The democratic style is, implicitly, the most favourable and acceptable one of the three studied by Lewin *et al.* because that style was the prevalent one in American society during the 1930s.

The results of a number of experimental and survey studies looking at the effects of these styles of leadership in industrial settings were reviewed by Sayles (1966). Sayles found that no one style was consistently superior to any other in experimental studies of supervisors, but that survey studies showed the democratic style to be associated with greater productivity and to be more acceptable than an autocratic style. However, Sayles argued that the tasks used in the experimental studies were so boring and limited that people did not really get involved in them. As a result, differences in leadership style were not really given the opportunity to show up. Sayles also pointed out that democratic supervisors probably differ from autocratic supervisors in ways other than leadership style (such as their level of intelligence).

INITIATING STRUCTURE AND SHOWING CONSIDERATION

One of the largest-ever studies of leadership was conducted by Halpin and Winer (1952). They asked people in many different kinds of groups what they felt were the most important behaviours a leader should exhibit. Two major categories emerged. They called the first *initiating structure*, which means that leaders should define the goals of the group, plan how those goals should be achieved, indicate how each member of the group will be involved, and generally direct the action of the whole group. The second category was called *showing consideration*. This involves communi-

cating with individual members of the group, explaining why certain actions have been taken, and demonstrating positive regard for group members.

Initiating structure involves giving orders, telling people what to do, getting the task underway and, perhaps, ruffling a few feathers. Showing consideration involves listening and explaining to group members, making people feel better and, perhaps, smoothing feathers. These two behaviours can be difficult, though not impossible, for one person to show. This incompatibility, coupled with the finding that leaders have somewhat different traits in different situations, led researchers to try to identify leaders according to whether they primarily initiate structure or show consideration.

TASK SPECIALISTS AND SOCIOEMOTIONAL SPECIALISTS

Research into the leadership patterns that emerge in small, unstructured groups was undertaken by Bales and Slater (1955). They studied a group of college students who spent about five hours per day discussing and trying to find solutions for a number of labour-management conflicts. At the end of each day, the students were required to indicate which person in the group had come up with the best ideas, which had most effectively guided the group discussion, and how much they liked each group member. The results are described in Box 10.2.

> **Box 10.2   The results of Bales and Slater's study**
>
> Bales and Slater found that at the end of the first day, the person who was most liked was also the person who was rated as having the best ideas and as having made the greatest contribution to moving group discussion along towards a successful solution to the task. However, after the first day, the tendency for the best-liked person also to be the one rated as having the best ideas diminished rapidly. What seemed to happen on the following days was that two leaders emerged. One of these, the *task specialist*, made suggestions, provided information and expressed opinions. The other, the *socioemotional specialist*, helped other group members express themselves, cracked jokes, released tension, and expressed positive feelings for others.

The task specialist style identified by Bales and Slater corresponds to the 'initiating structure' behaviour identified by Halpin and Winer. Bales and Slater's socioemotional style corresponds to Halpin and Winer's 'showing consideration' behaviour. Bales and Slater believed that these styles were *inversely related* and that no one person could display both of them simultaneously. However, the results from the Ohio State Leadership studies (e.g. Stogdill, 1974) suggested that the two styles were *independent dimensions* and that the most effective leaders are those who score above average on both. Later studies have tended to confirm this. For example, Sorrentino and Field (1986) carried out detailed observations of 12 problem-solving groups over a five-week period. Those who scored high on both of Bales and Slater's styles were subsequently elected leaders by the group members.

Another interesting finding concerns the relationship enjoyed by the two types of leader. Whilst there is rivalry between them, they get along well and co-operate extensively (Crider *et al.*, 1989). However, and as Crider *et al.* note, the general tendency to split leadership in unstructured groups has one qualification. According to Bales and Slater, the split happens only *after* the task specialist is identified and agreed upon. Once it has been decided who will lead the group in pursuit of the task's goal, the group can afford the luxury of a socioemotional leader.

Fiedler's contingency model of leader effectiveness

In a review of the findings concerning leadership effectiveness, Shaw (1981) suggested that evidence indicated that both autocratic (or task specialist) and democratic (or socioemotional specialist) leaders can be effective. In terms of group dynamics, followers are clearly happier in groups with socioemotional leaders. In terms of productivity, though, task specialist leaders are, on average, more successful.

However, Shaw pointed out that there were important qualifications to these findings. For example, the productivity of groups with socioemotional leaders is highly variable, and both the most and the least productive groups can have socioemotional leaders. Because some evidence suggests task specialist leaders are more effective and some that socioemotional leaders are more effective, researchers have looked at the possibility that each style may be more advantageous in different situations.

The *contingency model of leader effectiveness,* first proposed by Fiedler (1964; see also Fiedler, 1981; Fiedler and Chemers, 1984), is mainly concerned with the fit or match between a leader's personal qualities or leadership style, and the requirements of the situation in which the group must operate. Fiedler began by measuring the extent to which leaders distinguished between their most and *least preferred co-workers* (LPC). Fiedler then developed a scale to produce a LPC score as shown in Box 10.3.

Box 10.3   Fiedler's LPC scale

With the LPC scale, a leader is asked to think of all those people (or subordinates) who have ever worked under him or her, and to select the one that was most difficult to work with. This person is then rated on 18 bipolar scales including 'pleasant'–'unpleasant', 'trustworthy'–'untrustworthy', and 'friendly'–'unfriendly'. The sum of the values on the 18 scales gives a LPC score. The LPC scale is arranged so that leaders with a high LPC score still see their least preferred co-worker in a relatively favourable light. Leaders with a low LPC score have a very negative attitude towards their least preferred co-worker. Those with a high LPC score tend to be more accepting, permissive, considerate and person oriented in their relationships with group members, and Fiedler calls them *relationship-oriented leaders*. Those with a low LPC score tend to be directive, controlling and dominant in relationships with group members. Fiedler calls them *task-oriented leaders*.

Fiedler then investigated the fit between the two styles of leadership identified in Box 10.3 and the situation in which the group must operate. The basic hypothesis is that a leader's effectiveness is contingent upon the fit between the leader's style and the degree of 'favourableness' of the situation, that is, the extent to which the situation allows the leader to exert his or her influence. The degree of favourableness of the situation is determined by three situational variables, each of which can have a high or low value. Fiedler sees the first of these as being the most important, and the third as the least important. The three variables are shown in Box 10.4.

Box 10.4   The three situational variables that influence a situation's degree of favourableness

Quality of leader–member relationships: This is the extent to which the leader has the loyalty and confidence of the group members, and the general psychological atmosphere of the group.

Task structure: This is the clarity and complexity of the task and the number of possible solutions. The more unstructured the task is, the more the leader must motivate and inspire members to find solutions.

Position-power: This is the power inherent in the leader's role, such as the rewards and punishments at his or her disposal, and the organisational support from superiors.

The way in which the combinations of these factors (according to whether they are high or low) covary to produce conditions which are favourable or unfavourable to the leader is shown in Figure 10.1. Fiedler hypothesised that task-oriented leaders will be most effective in situations which are either highly favourable (the values of the three situational variables are high) or highly unfavourable (the values are low). Relationship-oriented leaders will be more effective when the degree of favourableness is neither very high nor very low.

The rationale for these hypotheses is that when the situation is very favourable, task-oriented leaders do not have to waste time worrying about the morale of the group members, and an emphasis on interpersonal relations is not only unnecessary but may even prove irritating to the group. In highly unfavourable situations, a task-oriented style is necessary since, without an emphasis on production, the group may fall apart. When conditions are moderately favourable or unfavourable, a relationship-oriented style may be able to smooth over differences of opinion in the group and improve co-operation enough to compensate for an ill-defined task and a lack of authority (Brown, 1988).

AN EVALUATION OF FIEDLER'S MODEL

According to Fiedler (1967),

'except perhaps for the unusual case, it is simply not meaningful to speak of an effective or an ineffective leader; we can only speak of a leader who tends to be effective in one situation and ineffective in another'.

Fiedler has studied leadership in a wide range of groups including store managers, research chemists, basketball players, furnace workers, and bomber crews, and reported data consistent with the predictions made by his model. Other researchers, too, agree that there is considerable empirical support for it (e.g. Hogg and Vaughan, 1995), although the support is stronger from laboratory than field studies.

Perhaps one reason why the data have not always offered strong support for the model concerns some of the assumptions it makes. For example, Fiedler claims that leadership style is a relatively fixed characteristic of the leader (that is, it is part of the leader's personality). As a result, leaders would be expected to find it difficult to modify their leadership style. However, the test–retest reliability of LPC scores has been found to be low (Rice, 1978), suggesting that leadership style can change.

Another criticism concerns Fiedler's assumption that the most important of the three situational variables is

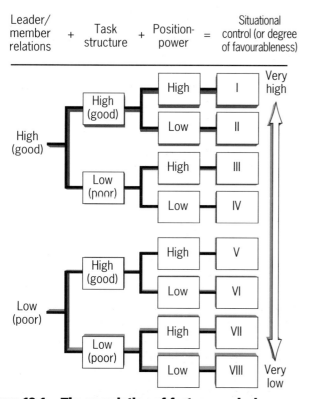

Figure 10.1   The covariation of factors producing varying degrees of favourability for a leader (From Gross, 1996)

the quality of the leader–follower relationship, and the least important the leader's legitimate power (see Box 10.4). It is not clear on what basis this assumption has been made, and the relative importance of the three situational variables could be a function of contextual factors (Hogg and Vaughan, 1995).

Hogg and Vaughan also argue that the contingency model ignores the group processes responsible for the rise and fall of leaders and the situational complexity of leadership. Despite these criticisms, though, there is little doubt that Fiedler's model has been useful in helping us begin to understand leadership effectiveness and, as additional leadership qualities (such as intelligence and prior experience) are incorporated into the model, so a more complete picture will emerge (Smith, 1995).

Leadership as a process

Leadership involves leaders *and* followers in various role relationships, and there are several paths to becoming validated as a leader. The issue of *validation* concerns how a leader comes to occupy the role, that is, how he or she achieves *legitimacy*. In a formal group structure, the leader is assigned by an external authority and is imposed on the group. Such a person is an *appointed leader*. In an informal group, however, the leader achieves his or her authority from the group members (who may withdraw their support just as they gave it). A person who achieves authority in this way is called an *emergent leader*. Note, though, that even in formal groups there are emergent (or 'informal') leaders, who exert influence among their peers by virtue of their personal qualities, especially how verbal they are.

Even in the case of appointed leaders, leadership is a complex social process involving an exchange (or transaction) between group members. The leader is dependent on the group for liking and approval, and their attitudes towards the leader will influence the leadership process. It is easy to overlook the fact that leaders are actually members of the groups they lead. At one and the same time, they represent and embody the group's norms and also act as agents of change, steering the group in new directions. A leader, then, is both a conformist (because he or she embodies the group's norms) and a deviant (because he or she can change prevailing norms).

However, the right to bring about change must be 'earned' by building up what Hollander (1958) calls *idiosyncrasy credit*. This can be earned by initially conforming closely to established norms, showing the necessary competence to fulfil the group's objectives, identifying with the group's ideals and aspirations, and so on. In one study supportive of this, Merei (1949) brought older children who had previously shown evidence of leadership potential into small groups of younger children in a Hungarian nursery. Merei found that the most successful leaders were those who initially conformed to the existing group practices and gradually introduced minor changes. Whilst this approach to leadership is a dynamic one, like Fiedler's it neglects the two features of the leader's interactions with others identified in Box 10.5.

> **Box 10.5 Two features of a leader's interactions with others**
>
> - The focus of leadership research has been on the links between leaders and their immediate subordinates. In practice, though, leaders devote substantial time to their own superiors, relevant colleagues, and many others inside (and sometimes outside) the organisation in which they work. According to Likert (1961), leaders play a crucial role as 'linking pins' between various groups within a large institution. This idea has been developed in those theories which have reformulated the concept of leadership to emphasise how leader effectiveness can be thought of as the successful management of the conflicting needs and demands of the leader's *role set* (that is, those that make demands on the occupant of a particular role: Smith and Peterson, 1988). Taking this broader view of a leader's interactions implies that the leader uses different leadership styles, or forms of influence, with different members of the role set (Smith, 1995).
> - Leaders not only lead their groups but, in varying ways, lead them against other groups. This is illustrated well by the familiar tactic of political leaders who are unpopular at home pursuing an aggressive foreign policy. Examples would be Margaret Thatcher's policy in the Falklands conflict (1982) and George Bush's in the Gulf War (1991). This *intergroup dimension* of leadership is usually overlooked in theory and research (Hogg and Vaughan, 1995).

Leadership and power

Clearly, leadership and power are closely related concepts. However, just as there are different kinds of leader (such as appointed and emergent), so there are different kinds of power. One classification of the different types of power that exist has been proposed by French and Raven (1959), who identify five types as shown in Box 10.6.

Box 10.6   The five kinds of power identified by French and Raven (1959)

Legitimate power is the formal power invested in a particular role regardless of the personality of the role occupant. Examples of people holding legitimate power include the Prime Minister and the head teacher of a school.

Reward power refers to control over valued resources (or 'rewards') such as money, food, love, respect and co-operation. Holders of this sort of power include employers, store owners, parents, friends and work colleagues.

Coercive power is the control over feared consequences ('punishments'), such as the withdrawal of rewards, demotion and loss of love. In both coercive power and reward power, power is largely inherent in the role itself, although personality can play some part.

Expert power is the possession of special knowledge, skills and expertise. Holders of this sort of power include doctors, teachers and car mechanics. This is related to *informational power*, which is to do with access to important sources of information such as the Internet.

Referent power consists of personal qualities, such as charm and the ability to persuade and 'win' people over. The *charismatic leader* (see, for example, Greenberg and Baron, 1995) has great referent power which often exceeds his or her legitimate power. However, parents, teachers and so on may also have referent power in addition to their other forms of power.

Possibly, one characteristic which is consistently displayed by every leader is the *lust after power*. If we accept Adler's (1927) claim that each of us has a 'will to power', by which he means a tendency in each of us to overcome our fundamental feeling of inferiority, then perhaps leadership is how leaders satisfy this. According to Gergen and Gergen (1981), however, such a view is mistaken. They argue that whilst leadership does imply power, it would be a mistake to assume that everybody who possesses power is highly motivated to achieve it. In Gergen and Gergen's view, many political leaders, for example, are recruited and encouraged by others who promote them to powerful positions. If anything, the need for affiliation may be far stronger than the need for power in such people.

Figure 10.2   Hitler can be regarded as embodying the 'will to power'. His lust for control of Germany's fate influenced the course of world history

Conclusions

This chapter has reviewed several theories concerning the emergence of leaders and the factors that influence leadership effectiveness once a position of power has been attained. Several theoretical positions exist with respect to both leader emergence and leader effectiveness, although the very complexity of this area of concern rules out the uncritical acceptance of one position over others.

SUMMARY

- Hollander makes the important distinction between a **leader** and **leadership**. The earliest research in this area concerned whether leaders are born or made and what it is that makes them leaders (the **trait approach**).
- The **situational approach** focuses on factors influencing the effectiveness of appointed/formal leaders, especially in large organisations. It acknowledges that leadership is a complex social process in which the leader and the group are interdependent.
- According to the 'great person' or **trait theory** of **leader emergence,** leaders are exceptional people whose personality traits make them suitable for positions of power and authority.
- There is some evidence that leaders tend to be slightly more intelligent, sociable, achievement oriented, experienced, self-confident and dominant than non-leaders. They also combine an orientation towards success with one towards affiliation. However, such differences have not been found consistently and it is now generally agreed that the kinds of traits a leader needs will vary from group to group and problem to problem.
- Bales stressed the **functional demands** of the situation, according to which the person most likely to emerge as a leader is the one whose **skills** and **competence** are most useful to the group in a given setting. This approach assumes that **anyone** can become a leader under the appropriate conditions, but this view is not supported by evidence.
- Both the trait and situational approaches have been replaced by **transactional theory**, which proposed that both traits and situational demands determine who will become a leader. This relates mainly to **leader effectiveness**.
- Lewin *et al.* identified three types of **leadership style**. **Autocratic leaders** tell followers what to do and with whom they will work. They are friendly, but also aloof and impersonal. **Democratic leaders** discuss options with their followers, allowing them to make their own decisions. They also join in with group activities. **Laissez faire leaders** leave followers to their own devices, neither praising nor blaming and only offering help when asked.
- Lewin *et al.* found that aggressiveness, co-operativeness, and the ability to work independently, were affected in characteristic ways by leadership style, rather than personality traits.
- Groups and leaders can only be properly understood in the context of their wider society. The democratic style is, implicitly, the most favoured of the three leadership styles, and was the most prevalent in 1930s America.
- According to Sayles, no one style is superior to any other in experimental studies of supervisors in industry, although this may reflect the nature of the tasks used. By contrast, survey studies show that democratic leaders are preferred to autocratic leaders and associated with higher productivity.
- Halpin and Winer identified **initiating structure** and **showing consideration** as the two most important behaviours that leaders should display. Initiating structure involves giving orders, telling people what to do and getting the task started. Showing consideration involves listening and explaining to group members and making people feel better.
- Bales and Slater found that, initially, the most popular person in small unstructured groups was also the one rated as having the best ideas in relation to solving the problems under discussion. Subsequently, two leaders emerged, a **task specialist** and a **socioemotional specialist.** Bales and Slater believed that these two styles were **inversely related**, but Sorrentino and Field suggested that they are **independent dimensions** and that the most effective leaders are those who display both types of behaviour. However, it seems that the socioemotional specialist emerges only **after** the task specialist has been identified and agreed upon.
- According to Shaw, followers are clearly happier in groups with democratic leaders/socioemotional specialists, whilst productivity is generally greater in groups with autocratic leaders/task specialists. However, the productivity of groups with socioemotional specialists is highly variable, suggesting that each leadership style may be more effective in different situations.
- Fiedler's **contingency model of leader effectiveness** is mainly concerned with the match between a leader's personal qualities/leadership style and the requirements of the group situation. **Relationship-oriented leaders** have a high LPC score and are more accepting, permissive, consid-

erate and person oriented than **task-oriented leaders**, who have a low LPC score and tend to be directive, controlling and dominant.

- The model predicts that a leader's effectiveness is contingent upon the fit between the leader's style and the degree of 'favourableness' of the situation, which is determined by the **quality of leader–member relationships, task structure,** and **position–power**, each of which can have a high or low value. Task-oriented leaders will be most effective when the situation is either highly favourable or highly unfavourable, whilst relationship-oriented leaders will be more effective when the situation is neither very favourable nor very unfavourable.
- Fiedlers's predictions are supported by data from studies of a wide range of groups, although the evidence from laboratory studies is stronger than that from field studies.
- The model's assumption that leadership style is part of the leader's personality is not supported by the low test–retest reliability of LPC scores, suggesting that leaders can change their leadership style. Also, the basis of the assumptions regarding the relative importance of the three situational variables is unclear and may be a function of contextual factors.
- Although the model fails to take account of group processes responsible for the rise and fall of leaders and the situational complexity of leadership, it has contributed to our understanding of leadership effectiveness.
- **Validation** refers to how a leader achieves **legitimacy**. In a formal group structure, the leader is **appointed** by an external authority and imposed on the group. In an informal group, the leader achieves authority from the group members themselves and is an **emergent leader**.
- Even with appointed leaders, leadership is a complex social **process**, involving a transaction between group members. Leaders are members of the group they lead and the group's liking and approval will influence the leadership process. The leader is simultaneously both a conformist (embodying the group's norms) and a deviant (capable of changing those norms).
- Leaders must earn **idiosyncrasy credit** if they are to bring about change, but this can only be achieved after initially conforming closely to established norms and helping the group to reach its goals.
- Both this approach and Fiedler's model overlook the leaders' interactions with their own superiors and relevant colleagues. Likert's view of leaders as 'linking pins' between various groups within large institutions has been adopted by theories which see leader effectiveness in terms of successful management of the leader's **role set.** This broader view implies that the leader adopts different styles with different members of the role set.
- Leaders not only lead their groups but lead them against other groups, a tactic used by political leaders at times of domestic unpopularity. This **intergroup dimension** is usually overlooked in both theory and research.
- French and Raven identify five kinds of **power**: **legitimate, reward, coercive, expert** (related to **informational power**) and **referent** (as displayed by the **charismatic leader**).
- What all leaders might have in common is a **lust after power**, which may be their way of overcoming the fundamental feeling of inferiority faced by each of us. However, whilst leadership implies power, not everyone who possesses it is highly motivated to achieve it. Many political leaders may have a greater need for affiliation than for power itself.

COLLECTIVE BEHAVIOUR

Introduction and overview

Milgram and Toch (1969) have defined collective behaviour as

'behaviour which originates spontaneously, is relatively unorganised, fairly unpredictable and planless in its course of development, and which depends upon interstimulation among participants'.

As we will see shortly, a number of phenomena can be identified as examples of collective behaviour, all of which could be included in this chapter. However, two types of collective behaviour will form the focus of our attention, these being crowds and mobs. Our aim in this chapter is to consider explanations and research evidence into these extensively investigated aspects of collective behaviour.

Types of collective behaviour

On the definition given by Milgram and Toch (see above), a number of phenomena can be identified as examples of collective behaviour. Box 11.1 identifies some of these.

Box 11.1 Some examples of collective behaviour

Panic: Panic is a form of action in which a crowd, excited by a belief in some imminent threat, may engage in uncontrolled and therefore dangerous collective flight. The action of the panicky crowd is not wholly irrational. Each individual acts to escape a perceived threat. However, the unco-ordinated

and uncontrolled action, and the response based on emotional contagion (see page 102), give panic an irrational character.

Fads: A fad is a trivial, short-lived variation in speech, decoration or behaviour. One example of a fad was that for 'streaking', which first emerged in the mid-1970s during the summer months, but died out as winter approached.

Fashions: These are similar to fads, but are less trivial and change less rapidly. Long hair in men has been in and out of fashion several times, as has the length of women's dresses.

Crazes: Whereas a panic is a rush away from a perceived threat, a craze is a rush towards some satisfaction. Crazes differ from fads in that they become an obsession for their followers.

Propaganda: Propaganda includes all efforts to persuade people to a point of view upon an issue. The distinction between education and propaganda is that the former cultivates the ability to make discriminating judgements, whereas the latter seeks to persuade people to the undiscriminating acceptance of a ready-made judgement.

Public opinion: Public opinion can be defined as (1) an opinion held by a substantial number of people, or (2) the dominant opinion among a population. The first use allows for many public opinions, whereas the second refers to public consensus on some issue.

Social movements: A social movement is a 'collectivity' acting with some continuity to promote or resist a change in the society or group of which it is a part.

Revolutions: A revolution is a sudden, usually violent, and relatively complete change in a social system.

(Based on Turner and Killian, 1957; Smelser, 1963; Horton and Hunt, 1976.)

Two examples of collective behaviour that could also have appeared in Box 11.1 are *crowds* and *mobs*. It is to psychological interest in them that we now turn.

Crowds and mobs

A *crowd* can be defined as a collection of people gathered around a centre or point of common attention (Young, 1946). Several types of crowd may be distinguished (Brown, 1965). For example, a *casual crowd* is one in which the members rarely know one another and whose forms of behaviour are mostly unstructured. In times of social unrest or tension, casual crowds may be transformed into *acting crowds* or *mobs*. Broom and Selznick (1977) define a mob as

> 'a crowd bent upon an aggressive act such as lynching, looting, or the destruction of property. The term refers to a crowd that is fairly unified and single-minded in its aggressive intent. Mob action is not usually randomly destructive but tends to be focused on a single target'.

Two examples of the grotesque behaviours of mobs are described in Box 11.2.

Box 11.2   Mob behaviour

Colonel Charles Lynch provided a name for a particularly barbaric and unofficial method of dealing with crime. Lynch's 'courts' against those who opposed the revolutionary cause in America in the 1700s did not exact the death penalty. However, they 'filled a gap left by the inadequacies of the official courts' (Sprott, 1958). Two examples of what Cantril (1941) calls *proletariat lynchings*, in which the victim is in a minority and the object is persecution, are those of James Irwin and Arthur Stevens.

- Raper (1933) reports the case of James Irwin, a black man who was chained to a tree in front of around 1000 people. These people watched as members of the mob cut off his fingers and toes joint by joint, pulled out his teeth with wire pliers, castrated him, and 'hung his mangled but living body . . . on a tree by the arms'. The mob then set fire to him, and shot him.
- In their book *Social Learning and Imitation*, Miller and Dollard (1941) describe the lynching

in the southern states of America of a black man called Arthur Stevens. Stevens confessed to murdering his lover, who was white, when she told him she wanted to end their relationship. Because the arresting sheriff feared violence, Stevens was moved 200 miles during the night of his arrest. However, over 100 people stormed the gaol and returned Stevens to the scene of his crime. There, he was tortured, emasculated and murdered. After dragging his body through the town, the mob went on the rampage, chasing and beating other black people. Their behaviour was brought to an end only by the intervention of troops.

Figure 11.1   The Heysel Stadium football disaster: a casual crowd became an acting crowd or mob

Theoretical approaches to collective behaviour

Turner and Killian (1972) identify several broad theoretical approaches to collective behaviour which have been specifically applied to crowds and mobs. The three most important of these are *contagion theories*, *convergence theories*, and *emergent norm theories*.

CONTAGION THEORIES

One early theory of crowd behaviour was proposed by Le Bon (1879) in his book *The Crowd: A Study of the Popular Mind*. According to Le Bon,

'isolated, a man may be a cultured individual; in a crowd he is a barbarian'.

For Le Bon, crowd behaviour is an

'irrational and uncritical response to the psychological temptations of the crowd situation'.

In Le Bon's view, the major question that needed answering was why crowds act in ways that are uncharacteristic of the individuals that comprise them, and in ways contrary to their everyday norms. Le Bon identified several situational determinants of behaviour which come into operation when a crowd is assembled, these being *suggestibility*, *social contagion*, *impersonality* and *anonymity*. The first three will be reviewed briefly, but more detailed consideration will be given to the fourth, since it is the factor which has been the subject of most research interest.

Suggestibility

In the absence of a leader or recognised behaviour patterns for members of a crowd to carry out, a situation may be chaotic and confused. Suggestion, if made in an authoritative manner, may lead people to react readily and uncritically (Lang and Lang, 1961). Le Bon believed that, in such circumstances, what he called the 'conscious personality' vanished, and the 'racial unconscious' took over.

Whilst few of today's psychologists would agree with this view, Freud (1921) suggested that crowds permit the expression of behaviour that would otherwise be *repressed*. For Freud, we possess a need, derived from our relationships with our fathers, to submit to more powerful forces, whether embodied in authorities or groups. Whilst some (e.g. Couch, 1968) believe that the role played by suggestibility has been overemphasised, heightened suggestibility does make *rumour* an important part of collective behaviour (see Box 11.3).

Social contagion

Social contagion (or *interactional amplification*) is the process whereby the members of a crowd stimulate and respond to one another and thereby increase their emotional intensity and responsiveness (Horton and Hunt, 1976). When so aroused, a crowd needs emotional

Box 11.3   Rumour

According to Shibutani (1966), heightened suggestibility makes rumour important in situations of collective excitement. A rumour is an unconfirmed, but not necessarily false, communication. Usually it is transmitted by word of mouth in a situation of anxiety or stress. Rumours occur in unstructured situations when information is needed but reliable channels do not exist.

Rumours tend to be passed rapidly from person to person and tend to distort or falsify the facts. This is because they are often coloured by emotions. A rumour may begin as an inaccurate report because of the narrowing of perception that occurs in emotionally charged situations. It may become progressively more distorted because *all* oral communication is subject to distortion. Even in the absence of emotional elements, factual reports tend to become shorter and simpler as they are passed on. The distortion of details typically occurs in accordance with personal or cultural predispositions or 'sets'. This relates to Bartlett's theory of reconstructive memory (see Gross and McIlveen, 1997).

(Adapted from Broom and Selznick, 1977.)

release, and it may act on the first suggested action which accords with its impulses (Lang and Lang, 1961). Thus, when an intended black victim of a lynching was protected by the town's mayor, the mob attempted to lynch the mayor and very nearly succeeded (Horton and Hunt, 1976).

Impersonality

Consider the account of a shooting reported by Lee and Humphrey (1943), which is given in Box 11.4.

Box 11.4   An impersonal attack

We drove around for a long time. We saw a lot of coloured people, but they were in bunches. We didn't want any of that. We wanted some guy all by himself. We saw one at Mack Avenue.

Aldo drove past him and then said 'Gimme that gun.' I handed it over to him and he turned around and came back. We were about 15 feet from the man when Aldo pulled up, almost stopped and shot. The man fell and we blew.

> We didn't know him. He wasn't bothering us. But other people were fighting and killing and we felt like it, too.
>
> (From Lee and Humphrey, 1943.)

The description given in Box 11.4 shows *impersonality*. In the case of a *riot* (see page 107), the impersonality of crowd behaviour is illustrated by treating one member of the 'enemy' as being as bad as another (which accounts for why innocent passersby are often the victims of a riot).

Anonymity

Le Bon believed that the more anonymous the crowd, the greater was its potential for extreme action, because anonymity removes the sense of *individuality* from members. When a person does not feel that he or she is being singled out as an individual, and when attention is not paid to others as individuals, restraints on behaviour are removed and a person is 'free' to indulge in behaviour that would ordinarily be controlled. The reason for this is that moral responsibility has been shifted from the individual person to the group of which he or she is a member.

As mentioned earlier, Le Bon wanted to know why people in crowds act in ways that are uncharacteristic for them and contrary to their everyday norms. Fromm (1941), however, was more concerned with the *motives* that lead some people to hide their individuality in crowds. Le Bon and Fromm's concerns were combined by Festinger *et al.* (1952) who proposed the concept of *deindividuation*. Festinger *et al.* defined deindividuation as

> 'a state of affairs in a group where members do not pay attention to other individuals *qua* individuals and, correspondingly, the members do not feel they are being singled out by others'.

According to Festinger *et al.*, membership of a group not only provides us with a sense of identity and *belongingness* (see Chapter 3, page 27), but allows us to merge with the group, forego our individuality, and become anonymous. This may lead to a reduction of our inner constraints and inhibitions. A field experiment demonstrating the effects of anonymity was reported by Zimbardo (1969). Zimbardo reasoned that a big city is a more anonymous place than a small town because people are more likely to know one another in a small town. For the big city, Zimbardo chose the Bronx area of New York. The little town was the Stanford area of Palo Alto, California.

In each location, a similar car was parked in a street adjoining a university campus. The car's number plates were removed and its bonnet raised in order to make it appear that it had been abandoned. Research assistants photographed the car and filmed people's behaviour from hidden locations. Zimbardo found that in New York, the car's battery and radiator were removed within ten minutes of it being parked. Within a day, just about everything else that could be removed was removed.

Within three days, there was little left of the car, a result of 23 incidents of 'destructive contact'. The 'destructive contacts' were nearly always observed by a passerby, who occasionally stopped to chat with the perpetrator. Moreover, the incidents took place in daylight by well-dressed, clean-cut whites who, argued Zimbardo, were the very people who would protest against such behaviour and demand a greater police presence! By contrast, the car in Palo Alto was left alone for seven days. Indeed, on the day it rained, a passer-by lowered the car's bonnet in order to protect its engine! Some other examples of research showing the effects of deindividuation are presented in Box 11.5.

Box 11.5   Some research showing the effects of deindividuation

- Defining deindividuation as 'a subjective state in which people lose their sense of self-consciousness', Singer *et al.* (1965) found that lessened individuality within a group was associated with a greater liking for the group and a larger number of obscene comments being made in a discussion of pornography. In a follow-up study, Singer *et al.* found that although deindividuated participants liked their group more, they conformed to it less.
- In one of several studies conducted by Zimbardo (1969), female undergraduates were required to deliver electric shocks to another student as 'an aid to learning'. Half of the participants wore bulky laboratory coats and hoods that hid their faces. They were spoken to in groups of four and never referred to by name. The other half wore their normal clothes, were given large name tags to wear,

---

and introduced to each other by name. They could also see each other dimly whilst giving the shocks.

Both sets of participants could see the student supposedly receiving the shocks, who pretended to be in extreme discomfort. Zimbardo found that the hooded participants gave twice as much shock as the other group. Moreover, the amount of shock given by the hooded participants did not depend on whether they were told that the student receiving the shocks was 'honest, sincere and warm' or 'conceited and critical'. For the other participants, however, the amount of shock given was related to the student's supposed characteristics. In Zimbardo's words:

'These sweet, mild-mannered college girls shocked another girl almost every time they had the opportunity to do so, sometimes for as long as they were allowed, and it did not matter whether or not that fellow student was a nice girl who didn't deserve to be hurt'.

- Watson (1973) conducted a study in which 23 different cultures were investigated. He found that those warriors who depersonalised themselves with face paints or masks were significantly more likely than those with exposed faces to kill, torture or mutilate captured enemies.
- Diener *et al.* (1976) observed 1300 'trick-or-treating' American children one Halloween night. When the children were anonymous, as a result of wearing costumes which prevented them from being recognised, and went from house to house in large groups, they were most likely to steal money and candy.

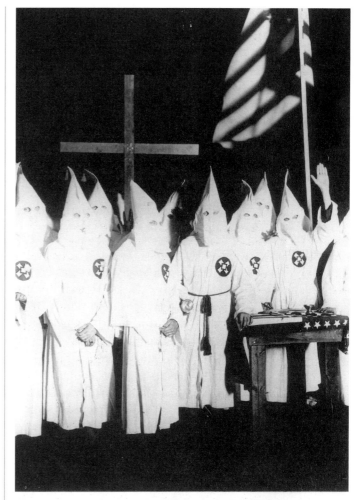

Figure 11.2   The Ku Klux Klan: deindividuated individuals but an easily identifiable group

Diener's theory of deindividuation

One theory of why deindividuation occurs was proposed by Diener (1979, 1980). According to Diener,

'a deindividuated person is prevented by situational factors in a group from becoming *self-aware*. Deindividuated persons are blocked from an awareness of themselves as separate individuals and from monitoring their own behaviour'.

Diener argues that in everyday life, we are frequently not aware of our individual identities or of ourselves as separate persons. Indeed, when we perform well-learned behaviours, express well-thought-out cognitions, or enact culturally scripted behaviour, we are not consciously aware. In some circumstances, such as when we are evaluated by others or when a behaviour does not produce an expected outcome, self-awareness and the self-regulation of behaviour are initiated. In other circumstances, such as when we are immersed in a group, self-awareness and individual self-conception are blocked, and it is this which Diener believes leads to deindividuation. When deindividuation occurs, certain self-regulatory capacities are lost. These include a weakening of normal restraints against impulsive behaviour, a lack of concern about what others will think of our behaviour, and a reduced capability to engage in rational thinking.

Prentice-Dunn and Rogers' theory of deindividuation

An alternative to Diener's model was advanced by Prentice-Dunn and Rogers (1982, 1983). According to them, it is possible to distinguish between two types of self-awareness. *Public self-awareness* refers to a concern about the impression we are giving others who will hold us accountable for our behaviour. *Private self-awareness* refers to the attention we pay our own thoughts and feelings.

Public self-awareness can be reduced by three factors. For example, in a crowd we would be difficult to identify and this would make us feel anonymous. If other members of the crowd were behaving anti-socially, a diffusion of responsibility (see Chapter 12, page 114) would also occur because one person alone could not be blamed for the group's actions. Finally, the behaviour of other group members would set some sort of standard or *norm* for behaviour and supply models to imitate (see also page 107 and emergent norm theory).

Private self-awareness can also be reduced by a number of factors. For example, in a crowd attending a rock concert, our attention would be directed outward, towards what was going on, and we might become so engrossed in what was going on (we might, for example, be singing, dancing, and/or drinking alcohol) that we would 'forget' who we are. Prentice-Dunn and Rogers argue that deviant behaviour can occur through a loss of either of these forms of self-awareness although, as Figure 11.3 shows, this occurs through different routes.

When we are publicly self-aware, we engage in rational calculations as to the likelihood of punishment being given for deviant behaviour. A state of deindividuation, however, is an *irrational state of altered consciousness*. As Figure 11.3 illustrates, Prentice-Dunn and Rogers' model does not see reductions in public or private self-awareness as causing deviant behaviour by themselves. Rather, both factors make us susceptible to *behavioural cues*, one of which is the behaviour of other people in a crowd.

The data presented in Box 11.5 are consistent with the two theories described above. Moreover, these theories may also help to explain other phenomena, such as that of the 'baiting crowd' in cases of threatened suicide. For example, in an analysis of 21 incidents of potential suicides threatening to jump from buildings, Mann

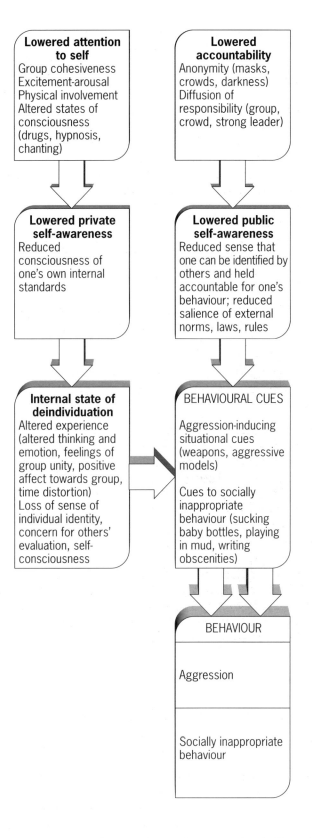

Figure 11.3   Prentice-Dunn and Rogers' theory sees deviant behaviour as occurring through two different paths, namely lowered attention to self and lowered accountability (From Prentice-Dunn and Rogers, 1983)

(1981) found that in 10 of the cases, people were more likely to shout 'Jump!' when they were part of a large crowd, it was dark, and the victim and crowd were distant from one another (as is the case when the victim threatens to jump from a tall building). Baiting was also found to be linked to other behavioural cues (see above), such as high temperatures and the long duration of the episode.

An evaluation of deindividuation research

Although there is a large body of experimental support for the concept of deindividuation, several cautions should be exercised. First, participants in the Zimbardo (1969) study outlined in Box 11.5 wore clothing that actually resembled the attire worn by the Ku Klux Klan, an American racist group (see Figure 11.2). Johnson and Downing (1979) have argued that this uniform may have acted as a *demand characteristic*, in that it might have led American participants to believe that more extreme behaviour was expected of them. In support of this, Johnson and Downing found that when participants wore surgical masks and gowns, they delivered significantly *less* electric shock than those participants whose names and identities were emphasised. This suggests that the clothing worn by the participants, rather than deindividuation, may have led to differences in their behaviour.

Similarly, Brown (1985) has pointed out that in another of the studies reported by Zimbardo (1969), the participants were Belgian soldiers rather than the female undergraduates investigated in the study described in Box 11.5. When these soldiers wore the hoods, they did *not* behave more aggressively. Instead, they became self-conscious, suspicious and anxious. Their apparently *individuated* counterparts, who wore their army-issue uniform, retained their 'normal' level of deindividuation resulting from their status as *uniformed soldiers*. As Brown points out, one of the functions of uniforms in the 'real world' is to *reduce* individuality and hence, at least indirectly, to increase deindividuation. Indeed, dispossessing someone of the clothes they normally wear is a major technique of depersonalising them in what Goffman (1968, 1971) calls 'total institutions' such as prisons and psychiatric hospitals.

A further point made by Brown is that whilst the anonymity produced by wearing, say, police or military uniform, may increase the likelihood of deindividuated behaviour, such anonymity may make the wearers of

these uniforms appear less human and affects the perceptions and attitudes of others, as shown in Box 11.6.

> ### Box 11.6 Do crowds resent the anonymity of their opponents?
>
> In a disturbance in the Notting Hill area of London in 1982, 100 police officers were sent to the scene wearing special flameproof suits. According to *The Times* newspaper:
>
> [The] uniform, combined with a hard helmet and visor, does not include a police serial number, making it difficult for anyone who wishes to identify and complain against an individual officer to pursue a grievance. A middle-aged West Indian, who was in [a] restaurant when it was raided, said yesterday: 'When they came through the door they looked like zombies, dressed in full black with headgear. All they had was one white stripe saying 'police' on it. We could not know in the world who they were, their faces were covered and they had helmets.'
>
> (Taken from Brown, 1985.)

A final point worth making is that deindividuation does not necessarily produce anti-social behaviour. A study by Gergen *et al.* (1973) showed that in some circumstances when people cannot be identified, more *affiliative* behaviours can occur. In their study, groups of six men and six women were placed in either a normally lit room (control group) or a completely dark room (experimental group). The participants, who had never met one another, were told that there was nothing special the experimenters wanted them to do. The experimenters left the participants for one hour, tape-recorded what they said and, when the experiment was over, asked them what had happened.

The results showed that during the first 15 minutes, the experimental group participants mainly explored the room and chatted idly to one another. In the following 30 minutes, the conversation turned to more serious matters. In the final 15 minutes, the participants began to get physical in that half of them hugged one another. Some of them became quite intimate, and 80 per cent reported feeling sexually aroused! It seems that we can become uninhibited in the dark where the norms of intimacy no longer prevail. We feel less accountable for our behaviour in such situations, but this state of deindividuation can be to the mutual benefit of all (Gergen and Gergen, 1981).

CONVERGENCE THEORY

Convergence theory (e.g. Shellow and Roemer, 1966) argues that crowd behaviour arises from the gathering together of a number of people who share the same needs, impulses, dislikes and purposes. According to Durkheim (1898), 'controlled emotional contagion' (as occurs in a peaceful crowd) can serve a useful social function. For example, it may allow people to release emotions and tensions that they cannot ordinarily express (consider, for instance, the behaviour of some types of spectators at wrestling bouts), and stimulate feelings that enhance group solidarity.

Organised gatherings of many kinds (such as mass meetings and religious services) provide settings that integrate crowd behaviour into the social structure (Broom and Selznick, 1977). In a study supportive of this, Benewick and Holton (1987) interviewed members of the 80 000-strong crowd that gathered at Wembley Stadium for an open air-mass given by the Pope during his visit to Britain in 1982. Interviewees reported that they found the event powerful and meaningful and experienced strong feelings of unity with the others present.

EMERGENT NORM THEORY

One weakness of contagion theory is that it does not explain why a crowd takes one course of action rather than another (Turner and Killian, 1957; Turner, 1964). According to emergent norm theorists, contagion theorists are guilty of exaggerating the irrational and purposeless components of crowd behaviour. In support of this, consider social psychological analyses of certain *riots*.

Smelser (1963) defines a riot as a form of civil disorder marked by violent mob action. Smelser views a riot as a 'hostile outburst' of resentment or rebelliousness. Prior to the 1960s, the dominant view of riots was what is known as *riffraff theory*. As applied to race riots, this says that only a small percentage of people take part in riots, those that do are criminals, drug addicts, drifters, leaders of youth gangs, and welfare cheaters, and that a riot is an isolated event that receives little or no support from the community (Sears and McConahay, 1969).

Analyses conducted in the 1960s, however, showed that there was little if any truth in the riffraff theory of

riots. For example, Orum (1972) found that participants in American race riots were relatively representative cross-sections of the categories of people involved. Moreover, they were motivated by genuine group grievances rather than by personal instabilities.

Orum found that the burning and looting which accompanied race riots was *not* indiscriminate. Whilst stores and offices which were perceived as exploitative were looted and burned, private homes, public buildings, and agencies serving the needs of the people were usually spared. Of course, not all riots are alike, but according to emergent norm theory the perceptions and grievances of a group, fed by the contagion process, lead to the emergence of a norm which justifies and sets limits to the behaviour of the crowd (Horton and Hunt, 1976).

An analysis of why 'ordinary people' can turn into looters and rioters has been attempted by Brown (1954). According to Brown, there are varying *thresholds for participation* in physical action. These are shown in Box 11.7.

> **Box 11.7   Brown's thresholds for participation**
>
> 1 **The lawless**: These are impulsive people, usually men and often with criminal records, who need little provocation before they try to retaliate. The lawless have little understanding of or concern for the consequences of their actions.
> 2 **The suggestible**: These are people who are easily influenced by an impulsive leader. They only need 'a little push' to follow an example, although it is unlikely that they would initiate action on their own.
> 3 **The cautious**: These are people with strong interests in the kinds of action initiated by others, but who would not act because of a fear of the law. If this constraint is lifted, they take action in pursuit of their own interests.
> 4 **The yielders**: These are people who are easily persuaded that everybody is engaged in a particular behaviour. Yielders act when a sufficient number of people are acting because they do not want to be left out, and see an action as being right because others are engaged in it.
> 5 **The supportive**: Whilst the supportive cannot be 'stampeded' into action, they do not actively oppose it. They may watch or shout encouragement. They are not violent, but they do not stand out against violence in others.

> **6 The resisters**: These are people whose values are opposed to mob action, and who will not support it even passively. Because of this, they are in danger of their lives if they speak up at the wrong time.
>
> (Based on Brown, 1954.)

In an extension of emergent norm theory, Reicher (1984) has proposed a model of collective behaviour which is based on *social identity* (see Chapter 3, page 28). Reicher argues that a crowd is

'a form of social group, in the sense of a set of individuals who perceive themselves as members of a common social category, or, to put it another way, adopt a common *social* identification'.

Reicher analysed the riots that occurred in the St Paul's area of Bristol in 1980. Following a tip-off about illegal drinking, police raided a cafe and arrested two men. However, as they tried to leave, bricks were thrown at them. Police reinforcements subsequently arrived, and were attacked by a crowd of several thousand who overturned cars and set them alight.

Reicher's analysis showed that the crowd did not behave in a random and unpredictable manner. For example, they did not damage any vehicles other than police cars and those suspected of being unmarked police cars, and did minimal damage to property. The crowd also confined their behaviour to the St Paul's district and prevented any other forms of violence from taking place. In Reicher's view, the crowd saw the police as an illegitimate presence. The community members (the *ingroup*) behaved in a way they perceived as being legitimate given the police's presence.

Unfortunately, Reicher's view is weakened by the finding that crowds do not always behave in a like-minded way. For example, during the riot that took place in the Watts district of Los Angeles in 1965, looting and burning occurred at different times and in different areas. As Brown (1985) has noted, whether these actions, occurring in different locations and at varying times, are the expression of common social identity is difficult to answer unless considerable first-hand experience of riots is gained.

Conclusions

This chapter has reviewed explanations and research evidence concerning crowds and mobs, two important examples of collective behaviour. A number of theoretical accounts have been advanced to explain the behaviour of crowds and mobs. However, whilst these are supported to some extent by evidence, none offers a completely adequate account.

SUMMARY

- Several phenomena can be identified as examples of collective behaviour, including panic, fads, fashions, crazes, propaganda, public opinion, social movements and revolutions. The most extensively researched examples are **crowds** and **mobs**.
- A **crowd** is a collection of people gathered around some point of common attention. A **casual crowd** can be transformed into an **acting crowd** or **mob** at times of social unrest, the latter being a crowd bent upon an aggressive act such as lynching, looting, or the destruction of property.
- Mobs are also fairly unified and single-minded in their aggressive intent and tend to be focused on a single target. This can be seen in **proletariat lynchings**, in which the victim belongs to a minority group and the object is persecution.
- The three most important theoretical approaches to collective behaviour which apply specifically to crowds and mobs are **contagion, convergence** and **emergent norm theories**.
- One early **contagion theory** was that of Le Bon, who tried to explain why crowds act in ways that are uncharacteristic of the individuals who compose them and contrary to everyday norms. He identified several situational influences on crowd behaviour, namely **suggestibility, social contagion, impersonality** and **anonymity**.
- A crowd may be **suggestible** in the absence of a

leader, especially if the suggestion is made in an authoritative way, such that a chaotic and confused situation is replaced by a ready and uncritical reaction. For Le Bon, in these circumstances the 'conscious personality' is taken over by the 'racial unconscious'.

- Not dissimilar is Freud's claim that crowds permit the expression of otherwise **repressed** behaviour. Groups can satisfy our need to submit to a more powerful force, deriving from our relationship with our father.

- Although the role of suggestibility may have been exaggerated, heightened suggestibility makes **rumour** an important part of collective behaviour. It is usually transmitted in stressful or anxiety-provoking situations that are also unstructured, where reliable channels of information are lacking.

- Rumours tend to distort or falsify the facts because they are often coloured by emotions, which narrow perception, making an inaccurate report progressively more distorted. This applies to **all** oral communication. The distortion occurs in line with personal or cultural sets.

- **Social contagion/interactional amplification** refers to the stimulation and response process between members of a crowd which increases their emotional intensity and responsiveness. This produces a need for emotional release, making it likely that the crowd will act on the first suggested action that accords with its impulses, such as violence.

- In the case of a **riot,** the **impersonality** of crowd behaviour is demonstrated by treating one member of the 'enemy' as being as bad as another: they become interchangeable.

- According to Le Bon, the more **anonymous** the crowd, the greater its potential for extreme action, since members lose their sense of **individuality**. This, combined with a failure to perceive others as individuals, removes restraints on behaviour, freeing the person to indulge in behaviour that is ordinarily controlled. Moral responsibility is shifted from the individual to the group.

- Fromm was concerned with people's **motives** for hiding their individuality in crowds. Festinger *et al.* combined this with Le Bon's concern for the uncharacteristic behaviour of individuals when in a crowd through the concept of **deindividuation.**

- According to Festinger *et al.*, groups provide a sense of identity and belongingness, and an opportunity to merge with the group, thus foregoing individuality and becoming anonymous. This may reduce inner constraints and inhibitions.

- Singer *et al.* found that a reduced sense of self-consciousness within a group was associated with a greater liking for, but less conformity with, the group, and a larger number of obscene comments in a discussion of pornography.

- Zimbardo's female undergraduates, who wore bulky lab. coats and hoods that hid their faces and were never referred to by name, gave twice as much shock to another student, whose discomfort they could see, as participants who wore their normal clothes, plus large name tags, and who were introduced by name.

- Watson's study of 23 cultures showed that those warriors who depersonalised themselves with face paints or masks were significantly more likely to kill, torture, or mutilate captured enemies. Similarly, Diener *et al.'s* study of trick-or-treating American children found that those who could not be recognised were most likely to steal money and candy.

- According to Diener, **deindividuated** individuals are prevented from an awareness of themselves as separate individuals and from monitoring their own behaviour. This occurs when we are immersed in a group, resulting in loss of certain self-regulatory capacities, such as restraints against impulsive behaviour, concern about what others will think of our behaviour, and rational thinking.

- Prentice-Dunn and Rogers distinguish between **public self-awareness** (concern about the impression we are giving others) and **private self-awareness** (the attention we pay to our own thoughts and feelings).

- **Public self-awareness** can be reduced by being in a crowd, where we would be difficult to identify, thus making us feel anonymous. There is also likely to be a diffusion of responsibilty for anti-social behaviour on the part of any group members, who set a standard or **norm** for behaviour and provide models to imitate.

- **Private self-awareness** can also be reduced by being in a crowd, as when attendance at a rock concert involves directing our attention at what is going on around us to such a degree that we 'forget' who we are.

- According to Prentice-Dunn and Rogers, deviant behaviour can occur through a loss of either type of self-awareness. But this happens indirectly, either through inducing an internal state of deindividuation (an **irrational state of altered consciousness**) in the case of reduced self-awareness, or making us more susceptible to **behavioural cues**, including the behaviour of other people in a crowd (in the case of reduced public self-awareness).

- Whilst there is considerable experimental support for the concept of deindividuation, some findings are open to alternative interpretations. For example, the clothing worn by Zimbardo's participants resembled that of the Ku Klux Klan and so may have acted as a **demand characteristic.** This was supported by Johnson and Downing's finding that participants who wore surgical masks and gowns delivered significantly **less** shock than those whose identities were stressed.
- In another of Zimbardo's experiments, Belgian soldiers who wore bulky coats and hoods (supposedly deindividuated) became self-conscious, suspicious and anxious, whilst others who wore their army uniform (supposedly **individuated**) retained their normal level of deindividuation associated with being **uniformed soldiers**.
- One function of uniforms in the real world is to **reduce** individuality and so, indirectly, to increase deindividuation. Dispossessing someone of their everyday clothes is a means of depersonalising them in total institutions, such as prisons and psychiatric hospitals.
- Police and military uniforms may also serve to make their wearers appear less human, thus affecting how they are perceived and treated by others, such as rioting crowds.
- Gergen *et al.'s* 'dark room' experiment showed that, under certain circumstances, deindividuation can increase **affiliative** behaviours. In the dark, the usual norms of intimacy no longer prevail and the resulting reduction in accountability can be mutually beneficial.
- According to **convergence theory**, crowd behaviour is the result of the gathering together of people who share the same needs, impulses, dislikes and goals. What Durkheim called 'controlled emotional contagion' can be socially useful, as when people release tension at a sports event, or when group solidarity is increased. Many kinds of organised gatherings, such as mass rallies and religious services, provide settings that integrate crowd behaviour into the social structure.
- According to **emergent norm theory**, contagion theories overemphasise the irrational and purposeless components of crowd behaviour. For example, prior to the 1960s, the dominant view of **riots** was **riffraff theory**, which was shown to be false by analyses of American race riots.
- Rather than being driven by personal instabilities, the participants were motivated by genuine group grievances and a fairly representative cross-section of the groups was involved. Burning and looting was not indiscriminate.
- Whilst not all riots are alike, emergent norm theory claims that the perceptions and grievances of a group, fed by contagion, lead to the emergence of a norm which justifies and sets limits to the crowd's behaviour.
- Brown has attempted to explain why ordinary people can become looters and rioters by identifying **thresholds for participation** in physical action. These are presented as six groups: the **lawless, suggestible, cautious, yielders, supporters** and **resisters**.
- Reicher's extension of emergent norm theory, based on his analysis of the St Paul's riots in Bristol, claims that a crowd is a set of individuals who adopt a common **social identity**. The crowd did not behave randomly and unpredictably but was selective in the damage it caused and where the violence took place. The **ingroup** behaved towards the police in a way it saw as being legitimate.
- However, crowds do not always behave in a like-minded way, as in the 1965 Los Angeles riot, where looting and burning occurred at different locations and at varying times.

PART 4
Pro- and anti-social behaviour

BYSTANDER BEHAVIOUR AND ALTRUISM

Introduction and overview

In April, 1994, under the heading 'Violent Britain', *The Sun* newspaper published the photograph shown in Figure 12.1. In the text accompanying the photograph, the journalist wrote:

'These are the appalling injuries six thugs inflicted on brave cop Gary Boughen as 30 people just stood and watched. The sergeant was battered

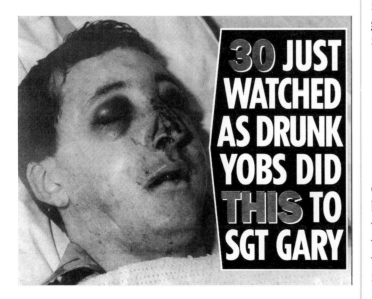

Figure 12.1   One of the consequences of bystander apathy

senseless after he asked the drunken teenagers to stop swearing outside a village chip shop at 11.30 p.m. . . . Det. Sgt. John Hope said "What's so worrying is that the officer approached the men politely and simply asked them to go home. It was a routine situation – yet these men resorted to dreadful violence. He could have died. Thirty people saw the attack. One woman comforted the officer afterwards but it seems the others did nothing. None of them have come forward to give us assistance and I would ask them to contact us"' (Sharpe, 1994).

Similarly, a man received serious injuries to his head, inflicted by a bottle and wire cutters, when he saved a girl from 'sex bullies'. According to the newspaper report of the incident:

'Twenty passengers just watched as 27-year-old Mark Maynard was dragged off a bus and punched and kicked in the street. Last night as he recovered with a broken cheekbone, nose and ribs, he said: "I'd do it again if I had to. But I'm disgusted with the people who stood by"' (*The Daily Sport*, 1995).

Contrast the above with a newspaper report in which a book-dealer on a business trip from Bristol to London was taken 194 miles to York after he helped to carry a woman's luggage on to her train; and was trapped when the doors locked automatically. As the passenger remarked:

'Nobody was helping this poor woman, so I gave her a hand. I couldn't believe my eyes when the automatic doors closed and a few seconds later the train started moving ... I only stopped at the station for a cup of coffee and I ended up at the other end of the country' (reported in O'Neill, 1996).

Finally, consider the praise given by a magistrate to a group of bus passengers who pursued a thief on foot and by taxi after he snatched a woman's purse. In the magistrate's words:

'"I have never heard of a case with so many Good Samaritans coming forward to help". The thief stole a purse on a bus and was chased by two passengers. When the thief hailed a taxi, one of the pursuants did the same and, after finding a police officer, an arrest occurred' (Curphey, 1995).

The accounts given above are, we suspect, just the tip of an iceberg of incidents that actually find their way into our national newspapers. We may be appalled at the behaviour of people in the first two and greatly admire the behaviour of those in the last two. Would you have intervened to prevent the attackers of Gary Boughen or Mark Maynard, and would you want to end up in York when you should have been in London, or hotfoot it through London 'following that cab' when you did not even know the person whose purse had been stolen? The conditions under which bystanders behave or do not behave *pro-socially* or *altruistically* has been the subject of much social psychological research. Our aim in this chapter is to review research into bystander behaviour and altruism.

The tragic case of Kitty Genovese

At 3.20 a.m. on March 23rd, 1964, 28-year-old Kitty Genovese was fatally wounded by a knife-wielding stalker close to her apartment in the Queens district of New York. Miss Genovese's screams of 'Oh, my God, he stabbed me' and 'please help me' woke up 38 of her neighbours in the apartment block. Their lights went on, and they opened their windows to see what was happening. One of her neighbours even turned *out* his light and pulled a chair to the window to get a better view of the disturbance. As Miss Genovese lay dying, her attacker fled, only to return to sexually assault her and stab her again. Despite her shouts for help, it was not until 3.50 a.m., half an hour after the attack had begun, that the police were made aware as a result of a telephone call from one of her neighbours. When police questioned the witnesses sometime later, they were unable to explain their inaction.

Explaining 'bystander apathy': the decision model of bystander intervention

According to Milgram (whose research into obedience was considered in Chapter 9), the murder of Kitty Genovese

'touched on a fundamental issue of the human social condition. If we need help, will those around us stand around and let us be destroyed, or will they come to our aid?' (cited in Dowd, 1984).

At the time of Miss Genovese's murder, commentators in America attributed her neighbour's indifference to her plight to a cold and apathetic (urban) society:

'It can be assumed ... that their apathy was indeed one of the big-city variety. It is almost a matter of psychological survival, if one is surrounded and pressed by millions of people, to prevent them from constantly impinging on you, and the only way to do this is to ignore them as often as possible. Indifference to one's neighbour and his troubles is a conditioned reflex in New York as it is in other big cities' (Rosenthal, 1964).

That the reasons for Miss Genovese's neighbours' apathy were *not* quite as straightforward as this was shown in a series of experiments conducted by Latané and Darley and their colleagues. As a result of this extensive research (the findings from some of which are described below), Latané and Darley proposed a five-step decision model of bystander intervention. The five steps are shown in Figure 12.2.

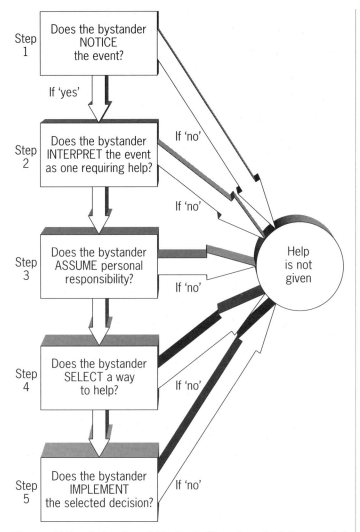

Figure 12.2   Latané and Darley's five-step decision model of bystander intervention and non-intervention (Based on Schroeder *et al.*, 1995)

As Figure 12.2 illustrates, the model proposes that before a person helps a stranger, five decisions must be made. First, a situation requiring help must be *noticed*. If a situation has not been noticed, then intervention cannot possibly occur. Second, the event that has been noticed must be *defined* by the observer as a situation in which help is needed. If the decision that help is needed is made, then, in the third step, the potential helper must *assume personal responsibility* for helping. If personal responsibility is assumed, the potential helper must then *select a way to help*. If this fourth decision is successfully made, the potential helper must make a fifth decision, that being whether to *implement* the selected way. The decision model of bystander inter-

vention represents a logical sequence of steps, such that a negative decision at any step results in the bystander not intervening, with help only being given when a positive decision has been made for all five steps.

DEFINING THE SITUATION AS ONE IN WHICH HELP IS NEEDED

In a number of studies, Latané and Darley have shown that we are less likely to define a situation as being dangerous if other people are present, a phenomenon they called *pluralistic ignorance*. Some examples of pluralistic ignorance are given in Box 12.1.

Box 12.1   Some demonstrations of pluralistic ignorance

Latané and Darley (1968): Participants were taken to a room to fill out a questionnaire, either alone or with other people present. After a while, steam, which resembled smoke, began to pour out through a vent in the wall. Participants reacted most quickly to this when they were alone. With others present, participants often failed to react, even though the steam was so thick it was difficult to see the questionnaire! In Latané and Darley's words, the participants

'continued doggedly working on the questionnaire and waving the fumes away from their faces. They coughed, rubbed their eyes, and opened the window – but they did not report the smoke'.

Latané and Rodin (1969): Participants sitting in a room waiting to be called for an experiment heard a voice from an adjoining room (actually the voice of a female experimenter) cry out and moan for nearly a minute. Participants were significantly slower to respond and offer help when they were with other people in the room than when they were alone.

Clark and Word (1974): In a similar experiment to that conducted by Latané and Rodin, a 'workman' carried a ladder and venetian blinds past a room in which participants were sitting. Shortly afterwards, a loud crash was heard. Again, the more people there were in the room, the less likely help was to be given, *unless* the workman made it clear what had happened.

Interviews conducted with participants after the experiments described in Box 12.1 suggested that one of the reasons for people's failure to help was *social influence*. Many of the participants indicated that they had looked at, and tended to follow, the reactions of others. Since these others were trying (and evidently succeeding) to appear calm, participants defined the situation as 'safe'. Thus, each participant influenced others into thinking there was no cause for alarm.

Another reason for failing to help is the potential *embarrassment* that might be caused by incorrectly defining a situation. The snatching of money by one person from another *might* be a potential 'mugging', but what if the behaviour is the result of a harmless bet between two friends? The fear of making a social blunder and being subject to ridicule if a situation is ambiguous also deters people from helping (Shotland and Straw, 1976; Pantin and Carver, 1982).

Interestingly, Latané and Rodin (1969) found that when two friends were placed in an ambiguous situation, their response to a potential emergency was just as quick as when either was alone, and much quicker than when two strangers were together or when a naive participant was with a 'stooge' who had been instructed *not* to respond. Presumably, with people we do not expect to see again, we are deterred from acting because we will not have the opportunity to explain ourselves if our interpretation is incorrect (Shotland and Heinold, 1985).

However, we should note that some evidence suggests that when an emergency *clearly* requires bystander intervention, help is much more likely to be given, even when a large number of people witness the emergency (see below). For example, Clark and Word (1974) staged a realistic 'accident' (in which a 'technician' supposedly received a severe electric shock) in a room next to one in which individual participants or participants in groups of two or five were answering a questionnaire. All the groups of participants responded and went to the 'technician's' assistance.

ASSUMING PERSONAL RESPONSIBILITY OR DIFFUSING RESPONSIBILITY?

Whilst some of the witnesses to Kitty Genovese's murder claimed that they believed the attack to be a 'lover's tiff', it is doubtful if pluralistic ignorance was operating, since her screams when the attacker returned

would have made the situation unambiguous (if, after the first attack, it was not already).

In a laboratory simulation of an emergency, Darley and Latané (1968) led students, who were in separate cubicles, to believe they were participating in a group discussion of the problems of living in a high-pressure urban environment. In order to avoid any embarrassment and preserve anonymity, the students were told that the discussion would take place over an intercom system, and that only the person whose microphone was switched on could be heard. The students were also told that each would talk for two minutes and then comment on what the others had said.

Some of the students were told that there were five others in the discussion group, some that there were two others, and some that there was only one other. In actual fact, the other 'participants' were pre-recorded tapes played through the intercom system. Early on in the 'discussion', one of the 'participants' hesitantly admitted that he had epilepsy and that the anxiety and stress of urban living made him prone to seizures. Later on, the 'participant' had a 'seizure', began to speak incoherently, and stammered out a request for help before lapsing into silence. The results are shown in Figure 12.3.

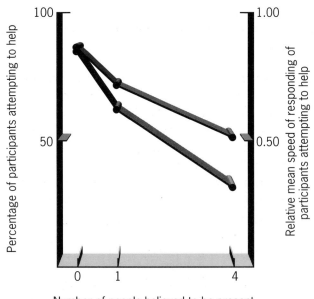

Figure 12.3   Percentage of participants attempting to help as a function of the number of others believed to be present, and the relative mean speed of responding of participants attempting to help (Adapted from Darley and Latané, 1968)

As Figure 12.3 shows, almost all (85 per cent) of the participants left the room to offer help when they believed themselves to be the only other person. However, when participants believed there were witnesses other than themselves, they were much less likely to leave the room, and the likelihood of helping lessened the more witnesses there were. Also, and as Figure 12.3 shows, participants responded more quickly when they believed themselves to be the only other person present.

Latané and Darley called the phenomenon they observed in this experiment a *diffusion of responsibility*, suggesting that, as probably happened in the Kitty Genovese murder, people reason that somebody else should, and probably will, offer assistance. The consequence of no one person feeling responsible for helping is that the victim is not helped, and the more people that are present, the less likely it is that any one of them will give assistance (and this has been called the *inverse law of helping behaviour*).

When the participants in Darley and Latané's (1968) experiment were interviewed about their behaviour, they were *not* actually indifferent, callous or apathetic to the plight of the student. Indeed, Latané and Darley reported that

> 'if anything they seemed more emotionally aroused than did the [participants] who reported the emergency',

and the participants typically asked the experimenter who entered the room whether the victim was being taken care of. Latané and Darley's explanation for the participants' behaviour was that they were caught in a *conflict* between a fear of making fools of themselves and ruining the experiment by over-reacting (the anonymous nature of the experiment had previously been stressed as important by the experimenter) and their own guilt and shame at doing nothing.

Piliavin *et al.* (1981) have pointed out that what Darley and Latané's experiment actually shows is a *dissolution* rather than a *diffusion* of responsibility. In Darley and Latané's experiment, participants could not observe the behaviour of others and 'reasoned' that someone must have intervened. In other situations, responsibility is *accepted* by the participant but *shared* by all witnesses. The term diffusion best applies in these circumstances, whilst dissolution is a better

descriptor for what happened in Darley and Latané's experiment.

Whether this distinction is an important one or not is debatable. What is important is the reliability with which the inhibitory effects of the presence of others on helping behaviour has been found. Latané *et al.* (1981) reviewed over 50 studies, conducted in both the laboratory and the natural environment, in which a variety of 'emergencies' were staged. In almost all of them (but see below), the so-called *bystander effect* was observed.

CHOOSING A WAY TO HELP: THE ROLE OF COMPETENCE

Related to diffusion of responsibility, and something which may interact with it, is the *competence* of a bystander to intervene and offer help (Huston and Korte, 1976). When bystanders have the *necessary skills* (such as a knowledge of first aid: 'let me through I'm a doctor') helping is more likely. However, in the presence of others, one or more of whom we believe to be better equipped to help, a diffusion of responsibility will be increased (Huston *et al.*, 1981). Thus, the inhibiting effects of other people may not necessarily indicate bystander apathy – non-helpers may sincerely believe that someone else is more likely, or better qualified in some way, to help (Schroeder *et al.*, 1995). Evidence for this comes from a study conducted by Bickman (1971), which is described in Box 12.2.

Box 12.2   Proximity and competence

Bickman (1971) replicated Darley and Latané's (1968) 'seizure' experiment, but manipulated the participants' belief about their proximity to the victim. Those who believed that another person was as close to the victim as they were (that is, in the same building) and equally capable of helping, showed diffusion of responsibility and were less likely to help than those who believed they were alone. However, when participants believed that the other person was in another building, and therefore less able to help, they helped as much as those who believed they were alone.

AN EVALUATION OF THE DECISION MODEL

Schroeder *et al.* (1995) argue that Latané and Darley's model provides a valuable framework for understanding why bystander non-intervention occurs. Moreover, whilst the model was originally designed to explain intervention in emergency situations, it has been successfully applied in other situations, ranging from preventing someone from drinking and driving to deciding whether to donate a kidney to a relative. However, the model does not tell us *why* 'no' decisions are taken at any of the five steps, particularly once the situation has been defined as an emergency. Additionally, the model focuses on why people *don't* help and pays much less attention to why they *do*.

It is also important to note that whilst the presence of others is a powerful and well-established factor influencing the likelihood of help being given in an emergency, other factors have been shown to increase or decrease helping behaviour. Two early studies in this respect were conducted by Piliavin *et al.* (1969) and Piliavin and Piliavin (1972). In Piliavin *et al.*'s study, a confederate of the experimenter pretended to collapse in a subway carriage. Sometimes the confederate carried a cane, and on other occasions carried a bottle in a brown paper bag and wore a jacket which smelled strongly of alcohol. Help was much more likely to be given to the 'victim' with the cane (who was helped 90 per cent of the time within 70 seconds, compared with 20 per cent of the time within 70 seconds for the other victim).

In one of Piliavin and Piliavin's (1972) experiments, the 'victim' who 'collapsed' bit off a capsule of red dye resembling blood and let it run down his chin. This reduced the helping rate to 60 per cent, with those who witnessed the event being likely to get others they believed to be more competent to help. In another experiment, Piliavin and Piliavin looked at the effect of the victim having an ugly facial birthmark. They found that helping dropped from 86 per cent when the victim was not disfigured to 61 per cent when he was. A number of other factors which have been shown to influence helping behaviour are presented in Box 12.3 (see opposite).

The research of Piliavin and his colleagues is also interesting in terms of the operation of a diffusion of responsibility. Earlier (see page 115), we noted that in *almost* all of the studies looking at the effects of the

Box 12.3 Some situational factors and individual differences in bystander behaviour

According to Amato (1983), help is less likely to be given in *urban* than in *rural* environments. This is because the conditions that discourage bystander intervention (e.g. the ambiguity of the situation) are more likely to be met in cities than in rural areas. Amato studied 55 cities and towns in Australia which were selected on the basis of their size and geographical isolation. Using various measures of helping behaviour, Amato found that city size was negatively correlated with all but one measure of helping (the measure not correlated, picking up a fallen envelope, was considered to be an insensitive measure of helping since it was infrequently observed in all towns and cities studied). A population of about 20000 was the point at which helping behaviour was inhibited. If the findings from these Australian cities and towns generalise to Britain, then helping behaviour would be expected to be an infrequently occurring phenomenon even in some smaller towns.

No matter how people are put in a good *mood*, they are more likely to help than is the case when mood is neutral or negative (Brown and Smart, 1991). In Europe and America, *husband and wife disputes* are considered to be private affairs. In Mediterranean and Latin cultures, however, a dispute between *any* two people can be intervened in (Wade and Tavris, 1993). People who feel a *moral obligation* to a victim, have deeply held *moral values* or personal feelings for the victim, and/or *empathy* with the victim are more likely to act as helpers (Dovidio *et al.*, 1990). People with a *high need for approval* from others are more likely to help than people low on this need (Deutsch and Lamberti, 1986). People who score high on measures of *fear of being embarrassed* in social situations are less likely to offer help (McGovern, 1976).

Women are more likely than men to *receive* help (Eagly and Crowley, 1986), and victims who are similar in appearance to the potential helper are more likely to receive help than victims dissimilar in appearance (Hensley, 1981). Interestingly, most victims themselves do not actually like to ask for help and feel they will be viewed as being less competent if they accept it (De Paulo and Fisher, 1981). In a *reverse bystander effect*, victims are generally less likely to seek help as the number of potential helpers increases (Williams and Williams, 1983).

presence of others on helping behaviour, an inhibitory effect has been found. Piliavin *et al.* (1969) found that help was just as likely to be given on a crowded subway as on a relatively empty one. In an attempt to account for this, Piliavin offered an alternative model of the conditions under which help is and is not likely to be given. It is to this model that we now turn.

The arousal:cost–reward model

Although originally proposed as an explanation for the results obtained in their 'subway studies', Piliavin and his colleagues (1981; Dovidio *et al.*, 1991) subsequently revised and expanded their model to cover both emergency *and* non-emergency helping behaviour. The model is shown in Figure 12.4.

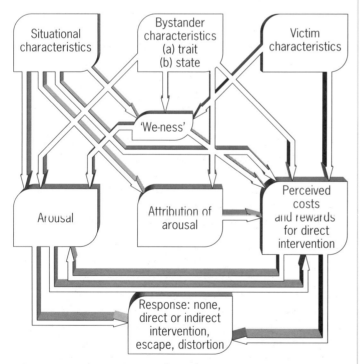

Figure 12.4   Piliavin *et al.*'s alternative to the decision model proposed by Latané and Darley. The model emphasises the interaction between the potential helper, the situation and the victim, and the cognitive and affective reactions of the potential helper (From Piliavin *et al.*, 1981)

The model emphasises the interaction between two sets of factors. The first are situational, bystander and victim characteristics, along with what Piliavin *et al.* call 'we-ness'. The second are cognitive and affective reactions. Situational characteristics include things like a victim asking, rather than not asking, for help. Bystander characteristics include both *trait* factors (such as the potential helper being an empathic person) and *state* factors (such as the potential helper being in a positive or negative mood). Victim characteristics include things like the victim's appearance and other factors identified in Box 12.3. 'We-ness' refers to what Piliavin *et al.* call

> 'a sense of connectedness or the categorisation of another person as a member of one's own group'

These characteristics produce certain *levels of arousal*. Whether or not helping behaviour occurs depends on *how* the arousal is interpreted or *attributed*. For example, if the arousal can be attributed to the distress of the victim rather than to other factors, then helping is more likely to occur, because the arousal is unpleasant and the bystander is motivated to reduce it (Batson and Coke, 1981). However, the exact way in which arousal is reduced depends upon the *rewards and costs* involved in helping and not helping. Piliavin *et al.* suggest that bystanders weigh the costs and benefits of intervening, and that the result of this *hedonic calculus* determines whether or not they help.

In the case of helping, rewards include enhanced self-esteem, praise from others, and even financial reward. In the case of not helping, rewards include time and the freedom to go about our normal business (Darley and Batson, 1973; Bierhoff and Klein, 1988). Costs for helping include lost time, effort, physical danger, embarrassment, the disruption of ongoing activities, and psychological aversion (as in the case of a victim who is bleeding or drunk). The costs of not helping include guilt, the disapproval of others, and cognitive and/or emotional discomfort associated with knowing that a person is suffering.

When the costs of helping are low and the costs of not helping are low, the model predicts that the likelihood of intervention will be fairly high, although the behaviour of bystanders will vary according to individual differences and how they perceive the norms that operate in a particular situation. Box 12.4 illustrates the predictions made by a simple application of this model to some of the data obtained by Piliavin *et al.* (1969) and Piliavin and Piliavin (1972).

Box 12.4   The application of Piliavin, *et al.'s* model to some of the data reported by Piliavin, *et al.* (1969) and Piliavin and Piliavin (1972)

- **Circumstances**: The costs of helping are low (e.g. there is little danger to the self) and the costs of not helping are high (e.g. one may receive criticism for not helping).
  Prediction: Direct intervention and helping are very likely.
  Finding: A person carrying a cane who collapses is helped 90 per cent of the time within 70 seconds.
- **Circumstances**: The costs of helping are high (e.g. the situation is dangerous or the person seems very strange) and the costs of not helping are high (something needs to be done).
  Prediction: Indirect helping, such as calling for an ambulance, will be fairly likely to occur.
  Finding: People are more likely to get somebody else to help when they see a person who collapses with 'blood' running down his chin.
- **Circumstances**: The costs of helping are high (e.g. the person could be violent) and the costs of not helping are low ('who would blame me if I didn't help?').
  Prediction: The likelihood of helping is very low.
  Finding: People are less likely to help a 'victim' who collapses smelling of alcohol and carrying a bottle in a brown paper bag.

Whilst arousal and helping are often only correlated, the model clearly sees the former as *causing* the latter and, according to Dovidio *et al.* (1991), the evidence does indicate that emotional reactions to the distress of others play an important role in motivating helping. The model proposes that bystanders will choose the response that most rapidly and completely reduces the arousal, incurring as few costs as possible. So, the emotional component provides the motivation to do *something*, whilst the cognitive component determines what the most effective response will be. As far as costs are concerned, it is clearly the case that what is high cost for one person might be low cost for another, and costs may even differ for the same person from one situation to another or from one occasion to another.

Piliavin *et al.'s* original model was subsequently elabo-

rated to take into account the role played by a variety of other factors, such as bystander personality and mood, the clarity of the situation, characteristics of the victim, the relationship between the victim and potential helpers, and attributions made by potential helpers of the victim's deservingness. Not surprisingly, many of these variables interact and contribute to how aroused the bystander is and the perceived costs and rewards for direct intervention.

THE 'PERSONAL COSTS' VERSUS 'EMPATHY COSTS' DISTINCTION

Two kinds of costs associated with not helping are personal costs (such as self-blame and public disapproval) and empathy costs (such as knowing that the victim is continuing to suffer). According to Dovidio *et al.* (1991),

> 'in general ... costs for *not* helping affect intervention primarily when the costs for helping are low'.

Although *indirect helping* becomes more likely as the costs for helping increase (as is the case in serious emergencies), indirect helping is relatively infrequent, possibly because it is difficult for bystanders to 'pull away' from such situations in order to seek other people to assist (Schroeder *et al.*, 1995).

Box 12.5   Cognitive reinterpretation and bystander intervention

The most common (and positively effective) way of resolving the high-cost-for-helping/high-cost-for-not-helping dilemma (as shown in (2) in Box 12.4) is *cognitive reinterpretation*. This can take one of three forms, namely redefining the situation as one *not* requiring help, diffusing responsibility, or denigrating (blaming) the victim. Each of these has the effect of reducing the perceived costs of not helping. However, and as Schroeder *et al.* (1995) have noted, cognitive reinterpretation does *not* mean that bystanders are uncaring. Rather, it is the fact that they do care that creates the dilemma in the first place.

IMPULSIVE HELPING

Piliavin *et al.'s* model suggests that help is least likely to be given in high-cost (that is, life-threatening) situations. In some situations, however, people act in an

almost reflex way, irrespective of the personal consequences and number of others present (Anderson,
1974). Such examples of *impulsive helping* appear to
occur in (but are not limited to) situations which are
clear and realistic, and in which the potential helper has
some sort of prior involvement with the victim (see
Figure 12.5).

**Figure 12.5   When Hurricane Hortense hit Puerto Rico in
1996, at least eight people were killed in flash floods and
mudslides. Here, Jose Louis de Leon and Miguel Rodiguez
brave the floods to attach a rope to the home of the
Gomez family and bring one-year-old Cassandra, her
three brothers and sisters and father to the safety of dry
land**

As Piliavin *et al.* (1981) have noted,

> 'not coincidentally, (these) factors . . . have also
> been demonstrated to be related to greater levels
> of bystander arousal'.

Piliavin *et al.* argue that when people encounter an
emergency situation they cannot avoid, they become
'flooded' with intense arousal and this produces a narrowing of attention which is directed towards the victim's plight. In their view, cost considerations become
peripheral and not attended to and, more speculatively,

> 'there may be an evolutionary basis for . . . impul-
> sive helping' (see page 120).

Bystander behaviour: universal egoism or empathy–altruism?

One conclusion that might be drawn from the various
studies on bystander behaviour reviewed in this chapter
is that we are an essentially selfish species that is motivated to minimise our costs and behave in a way that
causes us least displeasure. An *altruistic act* is one which
is performed to benefit others and which has no expectation of benefit or gain for the benefactor, and may
even involve some degree of cost to the benefactor. So,
is the behaviour of a responsive bystander ever motivated by a *genuine* wish to benefit others?

Universal egoism is the view that people are fundamentally selfish, a view that has been dominant in the social
sciences and which sees altruism as an impossibility
(Dovidio, 1995). There are many examples of apparently altruistic behaviour in the animal kingdom. For
example, in certain songbirds an individual which
detects a predator signals this by making a vocal 'alarm
call' which causes those in the immediate vicinity to
form a flock (for other examples of such apparent altruism see Clamp and Russell, 1998).

Box 12.6   The paradox of altruism

From a Darwinian perspective, altruistic behaviour is not *adaptive*, because it reduces the likelihood of an individual who raises an alarm
surviving (the reason being that the predator is
likely to be attracted to the source from which
the signal emanated). According to sociobiologists, this *'paradox of altruism'* can be resolved if
apparently altruistic behaviour is viewed as *selfish*
behaviour 'in disguise'. Sociobiologists argue that
an individual animal should be seen as a *set of
genes* rather than a separate 'bounded organism',
and that these *'selfish genes'* (Dawkins, 1976) aim
to secure their own survival. For a detailed
account of the ways in which this can be achieved
– notable examples include Hamilton's, 1964, *kin
selection theory* and Trivers', 1971, *delayed reciprocal altruism theory* – see Clamp and Russell,
1998).

The theories that explain the apparently altruistic behaviour of non-human animals can, at least as far as sociobiologists are concerned, be applied to humans (Wilson, 1978). The model proposed by Piliavin *et al.* is clearly one form of universal egoism, in that it sees decision-making about probable rewards and costs as ultimately concerned with choosing a course of action that is really directed towards the goal of *self-benefit*.

The *empathy–altruism hypothesis* accepts that much of what we do is egoistic, including much that we do for others. However, this hypothesis argues that at least in some circumstances we feel *empathic concern* when people are in difficulty, and we help in order to relieve the distress of *others*, rather than to relieve our own emotional distress. The emotions associated with empathic concern include sympathy, compassion and tenderness, and can be distinguished from the more self-oriented emotions of discomfort, anxiety and upset (and this corresponds to the distinction between personal and empathic costs for not helping: see page 118). Whilst personal distress produces an egoistic desire to reduce *our own* distress, empathic concern produces an altruistic desire to reduce *others'* distress, and these are *qualitatively* different.

According to Darley (1991), who is clearly a universal (or at least a Western capitalist) egoist:

'In the United States and perhaps in all advanced capitalistic societies, it is generally accepted that the true and basic motive for human action is self-interest. It is the primary motivation, and is the one from which other motives derive. Thus it is the only 'real' motivation, a fact that some bemoan but most accept ... To suggest that human actions could arise for other purposes is to court accusations of naivety or insufficiently deep or realistic analysis'.

Biological and psychological altruism

Whilst there is some degree of plausibility in sociobiological accounts of altruism, it is important to note that sociobiologists have failed to make the distinction between *biological* (or what Sober, 1992, calls *evolutionary*) *altruism* and *psychological* (or *vernacular*) *altruism*.

Biological altruism is the kind displayed by, for example, birds and rabbits when they give alarm signals. We would not normally attribute the behaviour of birds and rabbits to an altruistic 'motive' or 'intention' (it would be anthropomorphic to do so). Rather, such behaviour is better seen as part of the animal's biologically determined behavioural repertoire.

Psychological altruism is displayed by the higher mammals, in particular primates and especially humans. Whether humans are capable of biological altruism has been the subject of much debate. For some,

'human altruism goes beyond the confines of Darwinism because human evolution is not only biological in nature but also cultural and, indeed, in recent times primarily cultural' (Brown, 1986).

However, biological altruism *may* be triggered under very specific conditions. As mentioned earlier, in the case of impulsive helping, people react in a rapid and almost reflexive way in certain conditions (an example being a natural disaster such as an earthquake or a flood: see Figure 12.5).

Piliavin *et al.* argue that impulsive helping is generally unaffected by social context or the potential costs of intervention. In clear and realistic situations, especially those involving friends or acquaintances, the bystander is (as noted earlier) most concerned with the costs for the victim of receiving no help. This is very close to Sober's definition of evolutionary altruism, and it seems that our ability to carry out sophisticated reasoning (as in psychological altruism), along with more primitive, non-cognitive, biological mechanisms, may permit us to perform a range of altruistic behaviours well beyond those of other species (Schroeder *et al.*, 1995).

Conclusions

Research into bystander behaviour and altruism has told us much about the conditions under which we are likely to behave pro-socially towards others. Thirty years after the brutal murder of Kitty Genovese, we seem to be closer to understanding why we behave (or do not behave) pro-socially towards others. According to sociobiologists and those who believe in universal egoism, pro-social behaviour is always selfish behaviour in disguise, motivated by benefit to the helper rather than the one being helped.

SUMMARY

- Latané and Darley were the first researchers to systematically investigate the circumstances under which bystanders are/are not likely to intervene to help others.

- At the time of the murder of Kitty Genovese, American commentators attributed the failure of 38 of her neighbours to intervene to **bystander apathy**, reflecting a cold and apathetic urban society. Indifference to other people's plight was seen as a way of surviving in big cities. However, a series of experiments by Latané and Darley showed that the reasons for not helping are more complex than simply apathy.

- Latané and Darley proposed a five-step **decision model** of bystander intervention, according to which (i) a situation requiring help must first be **noticed** before (ii) it can be **defined** as one requiring help; (iii) the potential helper must then **assume personal responsibility** and (iv) **select a way to help** before (v) **implementing** the selected way. This represents a logical sequence of steps, such that a negative decision at any step results in non-intervention.

- Several experiments have shown that, in the presence of other people, we are less likely to define a situation as being dangerous (**pluralistic ignorance**).

- Post-experimental interviews from such experiments revealed that, apart form pluralistic ignorance, which represents a form of **social influence**, participants failed to help because of the potential **embarrassment** that might be caused by incorrectly defining a situation. Also, the fear of being ridiculed for making a social blunder in an ambiguous situation deters people from helping.

- Latané and Rodin found that two friends placed in an ambiguous situation responded as quickly to a potential emergency as when either was alone, and much quicker than two strangers together or a naive participant with a non-responsive confederate. This is presumably because, in the latter cases, we do not expect to be able to explain ourselves if we make an incorrect interpretation.

- However, when an emergency **clearly** requires bystander intervention, help is much more likely to be given when a large number of witnesses are present.

- Darley and Latané's 'epileptic student' experiment showed that the greater the number of other witnesses the participants believed there were, the less likely they were to try to help and the longer it took them to do so. The consequence of this **diffusion of responsibility** is that the victim is not helped, and the more people present, the less likely any one of them is to offer assistance (the **inverse law of helping behaviour**).

- Far from being indifferent or apathetic, Darley and Latané's participants who failed to respond to the epileptic student were more aroused than those who did. They seemed to be in **conflict** between a fear of making fools of themselves/ruining the experiment through over-reacting, and guilt and shame at doing nothing.

- According to Piliavin *et al.*, this experiment actually shows a **dissolution of responsibility**, since the participants reasoned that someone else must have intervened and denied personal responsibility. **Diffusion of responsibility**, on the other hand, involves witnesses **accepting** and **sharing** responsibility.

- Latané *et al.* found the **bystander effect** to be very reliable, based on a review of over 50 laboratory and naturalistic studies, involving a variety of emergencies.

- A bystander's **competence** to intervene and offer help may interact with diffusion of responsibility. When they have the **necessary skills** (such as first aid), bystanders are more likely to respond. However, if they believe that others are better qualified to help, diffusion of responsibility increases.

- According to Schroeder *et al.*, the decision model, which has successfully been extended to non-emergency situations, fails to explain **why** 'no' decisions are taken, especially once the situation has been defined as an emergency. It also concentrates on why people **do not** help rather than why they **do**.

- In Piliavin *et al.'s* 'subway' experiment, a cane-carrying stooge who collapsed was much more likely to be helped than one who appeared to be drunk. Later studies showed that victims who appeared to be bleeding from the mouth or were facially disfigured were much less likely to receive help.

- Amato's research in Australia found that help is less likely to be given in **urban** than in **rural** environments. In the former, conditions that discourage intervention, such as the ambiguity of the situation, are more commonplace.

- People in a good **mood** are more likely to help, as they are if they live in cultures where it is thought appropriate to intervene in any dispute, including those between husband and wife. People who feel a **moral obligation** to a victim, have deeply held **moral values**/personal feelings for the victim, and/or **empathy** with the victim, are more likely to get involved.

- People with a **high need for approval** from others are more likely to help, whilst those with a high **fear of being embarrassed** in social stuations are less likely to help.

- **Women** are more likely than men to **receive** help, as are victims similar in appearance to the potential helper. Most victims do not like to ask for help, and are even more reluctant to do so as the number of potential helpers increases (**reverse bystander effect**).

- Piliavin *et al.'s* 'subway' experiment found no evidence of a diffusion of responsibility, which they accounted for in terms of their **arousal:cost-reward model**. This emphasises the interaction between (a) situational, bystander and victim characteristics, plus 'we-ness', and (b) cognitive and affective reactions.

- These various characteristics produce certain **levels of arousal. How** the arousal is **attributed** will determine whether or not helping occurs. The exact way in which arousal is reduced depends on the outcome of a **hedonic calculus** of the **rewards and costs** for helping/not helping.

- Rewards for helping may include enhanced self-esteem and praise from others, whilst not helping brings rewards such as time and being free to do what one would normally do. Costs of helping include lost time, effort, physical danger, embarrassment and psychological aversion, whilst the costs of not helping include guilt, others' disapproval, and the discomfort of knowing that someone is suffering.

- The model predicts the likelihood and nature of helping, depend on the combination of costs for helping and not helping. For example, when the costs are **low** in both cases, intervention should be quite likely, although there will be individual differences between potential helpers. When the costs are **high** in both cases, indirect helping is quite likely, as when people are more likely to get someone else to help when the victim is bleeding.

- The model clearly sees arousal as **motivating/causing** helping behaviour. Bystanders will choose the response that most rapidly and completely reduces the arousal, at the lowest possible cost.

- Two kinds of costs associated with not helping are **personal** and **empathy costs**. These tend to become more relevant when the costs of helping are low. As the costs of helping increase, so **indirect helping** becomes more likely, but remains relatively infrequent.

- The most common way of resolving the high-cost-for-helping/high-cost-for-not-helping dilemma is **cognitive reinrepretation**. This can take the form of redefining the situation as one **not** requiring help, diffusing responsibility, or blaming the victim, all of which reduce the costs of not helping. The dilemma only arises at all because bystanders are caring.

- The model suggests that help is least likely in high-cost (life-threatening) situations. However **impulsive helping** sometimes occurs regardless of personal consequences and the presence of other helpers, especially when the situation is clear and realistic and there is some prior involvement with the victim.

- Unavoidable emergencies induce intense arousal in the people who witness them, narrowing attention towards the victim's plight. Considerations of cost become peripheral.

- According to **universal egoism**, people are fundamentally selfish, and it is impossible for anyone to perform a truly **altruistic act**. From a Darwinian perspective, altruistic behaviour is not **adaptive**, but according to sociobiologists, the **paradox of altruism** can be resolved by viewing all apparently altruistic behaviour as really selfish behaviour in disguise. An individual animal is a **set of genes** which selfishly aim to secure their own survival.

- Piliavin *et al.'s* model is a form of universal egoism, since the cost/reward analysis is ultimately concerned with **self-benefit.** By contrast, the **empathy–altruism hypothesis**, whilst not denying our egoistic behaviour, acknowledges that we sometimes also feel **empathic concern** for **others'** distress.

- Sociobiologists fail to distinguish between **biological/evolutionary altruism** and **psychological/vernacular altruism**. Whilst the former is seen in various non-human species and is best viewed as part of an animals's biologically determined behavioural repertoire, the latter is displayed by higher mammals, in particular primates and especially humans.

- Whilst non-humans are limited to biological altruism, humans sometimes engage in impulsive helping (which is very similar to evolutionary altruism), as well as displaying altruistic motives and intentions (psychological altruism).

THEORIES OF AGGRESSION AND THE REDUCTION AND CONTROL OF AGGRESSIVE BEHAVIOUR

Introduction and overview

Baron and Richardson (1994) define anti-social behaviours as those 'which show a lack of feeling and concern for the welfare of others'. One type of anti-social behaviour is aggression. Used as a noun, the word aggression usually refers to some behaviour that is intended to harm or destroy another person who is motivated to avoid such treatment. Penrod (1983) calls this *anti-social aggression* to distinguish it from those instances when, for example, a person defends him or herself from attack (*sanctioned aggression*) or when, for example, an aircraft hijacker is shot and killed by security agents (*pro-social aggression*). When used as an adjective, the word aggressive sometimes conveys an action carried out with energy and persistence, and may even be regarded as socially desirable (Lloyd *et al.*, 1984).

Moyer (1976) and Berkowitz (1993) see aggression as always involving some sort of behaviour, either physical or symbolic, that is carried out with the intention of harming someone. They reserve the word *violence* to describe an extreme form of aggression in which a deliberate attempt is made to inflict serious physical injury on another person or damage to property. One long-standing issue in social psychology concerns the causes of interpersonal aggression. For many years, debate has centred around the nature versus nurture controversy, that is, whether aggression, as a characteristic of human beings, is biologically determined (nature) or the product of learning and various environmental influences (nurture).

Our first aim in this chapter is to review the claims made by the various theories that have been advanced to explain the occurrence of interpersonal aggression,

and to consider the evidence relating to them. Given the occurrence of aggression within society, our second aim in this chapter is to look at some of the proposals that have been made concerning the reduction and control of aggressive behaviour.

'Instinct' theories

According to the seventeenth century political philosopher Thomas Hobbes (1651), people are naturally competitive and hostile, interested only in their own power and gaining advantage over others. Hobbes argued that in order to prevent conflict and mutual destruction, people needed government. Two theories which share Hobbes' pessimistic views about the nature of people are those proposed by Sigmund Freud and Konrad Lorenz.

FREUD'S PSYCHOANALYTIC APPROACH

According to Freud, the purpose of all instincts is to reduce tension or excitation to a minimum and, ultimately, to totally eliminate them. Much of Freud's early writing emphasised what he called *Eros*, the human drive for pleasure and self-preservation. After the loss of millions of lives in the First World War, however, Freud (1920, 1923) proposed the existence of a second drive, *Thanatos*, directed towards self-destruction, death and the return to an inanimate, lifeless state (which Freud saw as the only way of achieving the idyllic state we enjoyed in the womb and at our mother's breast).

Freud thought that because these two instincts conflicted, the self-directed aggression of thanatos was satisfied by being turned *outward*, and that we must destroy some other thing or person if we are not to destroy ourselves. So, unless a more acceptable way to express thanatos could be achieved (through some sort of *cathartic activity* such as sport), people would act aggressively from time to time in order to dissipate or discharge the aggressive energy that had built up. For Freud, then, just as we need to eat, drink and express our sexual needs periodically, so too must our hostile and destructive impulses be expressed.

LORENZ'S ETHOLOGICAL APPROACH

Although Freud's and Lorenz's views are, in most respects, very different, Lorenz also saw aggression as being instinctive, with aggressive energy needing to be released periodically if it is not to build up to dangerously high levels. In his book *On Aggression*, Lorenz (1966) argued that aggression is instinctive in all species because it is *adaptive*, that is, it allows animals to adapt to their environment, survive in it, and successfully reproduce. Lorenz defined aggression as

'the fighting instinct in beast and man which is directed *against* members of the same species'.

Most animals have what Lorenz called 'built-in safety devices' which prevent them from killing members of their own species when they fight for territory or dominance. One such device is *ritualisation*, a way of discharging aggression in a fixed, stereotyped pattern, in which fights between members of the same species result in relatively little harm to either, but at the same time allow a victor to emerge. For example, a fight between two wolves will end with the loser exposing its jugular vein to indicate submission and end the conflict (see Figure 13.1).

Alternatively, a conflict may be avoided by means of an *appeasement ritual*, in which a particular gesture will prevent an attack even when one animal is on the verge of attacking another. Thus, in one species of jackdaw, the nape section of the bottom of the head is clearly marked off from the rest of the body by its plumage and colouring. A conflict is avoided when one bird 'offers' its nape to a potential attacker.

Lorenz felt that humans are biologically weaker, 'basically harmless', and lacking the strong compensating devices seen in non-humans. Whilst aggression is basically adaptive, for humans it is no longer under the control of rituals. This is not to say that human

appeasement gestures are not effective, because behaviours like cowering, cringing, and begging for mercy clearly are. However, Lorenz argued that once we acquired the ability to kill each other through our *weapons technology*, in which aggression can take place without eye contact (as with intercontinental ballistic missiles), our appeasement rituals became ineffective. As Lea (1984) has noted,

'we have developed a technology which enables our intentions to override our instincts'.

Figure 13.1   Unlike non-humans, human aggression is no longer under the control of rituals

An evaluation of instinct theories

Some support for instinct theories of aggression has been claimed by Megargee (1966) in his study of people who had committed brutally aggressive crimes. Megargee found that such crimes were often committed by *overcontrolled individuals*. These people repress their anger and, over a period of time, the pressure to be aggressive builds up. Often, a seemingly trivial event provokes an aggressive outburst and, when the aggression has been released, the aggressor returns to a passive state in which he or she is seemingly incapable of violence (Megargee and Mendelsohn, 1962).

There are, however, many problems with instinct theories of aggression. Freud's theory, for example, is difficult to test empirically. As Mummendey (1996) has noted,

'the essential concepts such as that of destructive energy are so global and inexact that one can derive no precise predictions or hypotheses that can then be tested. The psychoanalytic approach is really only able to attempt an explanation of events or behaviour that have already taken place'.

As far as Lorenz's theory is concerned, there is a large body of evidence to dispute his claims. For example, Lea (1984) cites several examples of non-human aggression resulting in the death of the loser, and Lea believes that Lorenz's claim that aggression always stops before one of the animals is killed to be little more than a myth. Lorenz has also been criticised for failing to take account of how the *goals* of behaviour influence the degree of ritual. For example, whilst antelopes are more likely to engage in ritualised aggression when fighting over territory, they are less likely to do this when competing for a sexual partner. Finally, Lorenz's view of aggression as being spontaneous rather than reactive has also been questioned.

Like Freud, Lorenz believed that aggression does not occur in response to environmental stimuli, but occurs spontaneously when aggressive energy builds up (the so-called *hydraulic model*). Siann (1985) has observed that Lorenz's evidence for this is actually very sparse, amounting to the male cichlid fish (which attacks its female mate) and an anecdote about Lorenz's maiden aunt! The view that aggression is inevitable because aggressive energy builds up, and is unrelated to external events, has been attacked by many biologists and ethologists (e.g. Hinde, 1974). In their view, aggression in non-humans is reactive and modifiable by a variety of internal and external conditions.

The frustration–aggression hypothesis

Unlike his ideas on sexuality, Freud's ideas on aggression had little impact until the publication of *Frustration and Aggression* by Dollard *et al.* (1939). Intended partly to 'translate' Freudian psychoanalytic concepts into learning theory terms, the frustration–aggression hypothesis proposes that

'aggression is always a consequence of frustration and, contrariwise . . . the existence of frustration always leads to some form of aggression'.

In everyday language, we use the word frustration to refer to an unpleasant feeling produced by an unfulfilled desire. Dollard *et al.*, however, defined frustration as

'an interference with the occurrence of an instigated goal-response at its proper time in the behaviour sequence'.

Put another way, frustration prevents the occurrence of an *expected reinforcer*.

Whilst Dollard *et al.* agreed that aggression was an innate response, they argued that it would only be elicited in specific situations. Thus, whenever an important need was thwarted, the resulting frustration would produce an aggressive response. This does not mean that aggression is always directed towards the object of the frustration. According to Dollard *et al.*, aggression may be delayed, disguised or displaced from its most obvious source to a more accessible target. One example of such displacement behaviour is *scapegoating* which, as was seen in Chapter 3 (see page 24), is one way of accounting for prejudice and discrimination.

Research conducted shortly after the publication of Dollard *et al.*'s theory obtained results consistent with it. For example, in a study conducted by Barker *et al.* (1941), young children were shown an attractive set of toys but prevented from playing with them. When the children were eventually allowed access to the toys, they threw them, stomped on them, and smashed them. These behaviours did not occur in a comparison group of children who were not frustrated. Despite this support, however, the original version of the frustration–aggression hypothesis has attracted much criticism. Some of the major criticisms are summarised in Box 13.1.

> **Box 13.1   Some criticisms of the original frustration–aggression hypothesis**
>
> According to Miller (1941), frustration is an instigator of aggression, but situational factors (such as learned inhibition or the fear of retaliation) may prevent actual aggression from occurring. So, whilst frustration may make aggression more likely, it is far from being a *sufficient* cause of aggressive behaviour. Miller also suggested that frustration can produce a number of possible responses, of which aggression is only one. These include withdrawal, apathy, hopelessness, depression, and sometimes an increased effort to achieve the goal.
>
> Other research has shown that frustration can produce different responses in different people in different situations (Kulik and Brown, 1979). Miell (1990) and Berkowitz (1993) have suggested that aggression is most likely to occur when a person is close to achieving a goal or the frustrator is perceived as being arbitrary or illegitimate. So, we are not usually bothered by a failure to reach a goal unless we believe that the frustrator intentionally or improperly interfered with our efforts.
>
> This *attribution of intention* perspective (Kulik and Brown, 1979) is consistent with the definition of aggression as the (perceived) intention to harm another person. If there are mitigating circumstances, the attribution made by the victim may change (Weiner, 1992; see also page 131). Interestingly, research indicates that children who display chronic aggression have a strong attributional bias towards seeing others as acting against them with hostile intent, especially in ambiguous situations. These biased attributions often lead to retaliatory aggression (Taylor *et al.*, 1994).

Berkowitz's cue-arousal (or aggressive cue) theory

Whilst research indicates that frustration and aggression are related, frustration does not (as shown in Box 13.1) always lead to aggression. Berkowitz (e.g. 1966, 1978, 1989) was the first to point out that aggression, like any other behaviour, can be reinforced. For example, a hired assassin kills people for *money*, and frustration does not play a causal role in an assassin's behaviour. Moreover, things other than frustration can produce aggressive behaviour. For example, if two animals are placed in a cage and receive electric shocks to their feet, they are likely to fight (Carlson, 1987).

Berkowitz suggested that frustration produces *anger* rather than aggression. However, frustration is psychologically painful, and anything that is psychologically (or, indeed, physically) painful can produce aggression. According to Berkowitz, there are two conditions which act together to produce aggression when frustration occurs. The first is a *readiness* to act aggressively and the second is the presence of *environmental cues* associated either with aggressive behaviour or with the frustrating person or object. In Berkowitz's view, then, whilst we might become angry as a response to frustration, aggressive behaviour will be elicited only when certain environmental cues are present. A number of studies in which participants are frustrated in the presence or absence of aggressive cues have been conducted. Three of these are described in Box 13.2.

> **Box 13.2   Three tests of Berkowitz's cue-arousal theory**
>
> • Geen and Berkowitz (1966) had a stooge who was introduced as either Kirk Anderson or Bob Anderson, insult and berate participants for failing to solve a jigsaw puzzle. The participants then watched a film in which the actor Kirk Douglas was brutally beaten. After the film, the participants were given the opportunity to administer supposed electric shocks to the stooge. Participants gave higher intensity 'shocks' to the stooge called Kirk. Geen and Berkowitz argued that because of its association with brutality in the film, the name Kirk served as a cue to aggressive behaviour.
> • In a parallel to the experiment described above, Berkowitz and Geen (1966) introduced the stooge as Bob Kelly, Bob Dunne or Bob Riley.

Dunne was the name of the victorious character in the film in which Kirk Douglas was brutally beaten. Douglas's character was called Kelly. The stooge received 'shocks' of greater intensity when he was called Kelly. Presumably, the character called Kelly was associated with an instance of successful aggression, and this makes it more likely that anger will be converted into aggression (Berkowitz, 1993).

- Berkowitz and LePage (1967) had participants perform a task which was then evaluated by a stooge. The evaluation consisted of the stooge delivering a number of electric shocks to participants. The number of shocks delivered generated different levels of anger in the participants. Later, the participants were required to evaluate the stooge, also by delivering electric shocks. The participant was taken to a 'control room' and shown the shock apparatus. For some participants, a shotgun and revolver had been placed on a nearby table. Sometimes, participants were told that these belonged to the stooge, and sometimes they were given no explanation for their presence. In two other conditions, there were either badminton rackets and shuttlecocks on the table or no objects at all.

As shown in Figure 13.2, angry participants delivered most shocks when the weapons present were associated with the stooge, and only slightly fewer shocks when the weapons were present but not associated with the stooge. The no objects and badminton rackets conditions

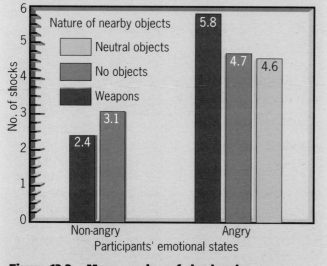

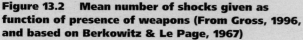

Figure 13.2   Mean number of shocks given as function of presence of weapons (From Gross, 1996, and based on Berkowitz & Le Page, 1967)

led to significantly fewer shocks being delivered. Berkowitz (1968) called this *the weapons effect* and, in his view,

> 'guns not only permit violence, they can stimulate it as well. The finger pulls the trigger, but the trigger may also be pulling the finger'.

Whilst a number of researchers have failed to replicate the weapons effect (see, for example, Mummendey, 1996), Berkowitz (1995) cites several examples of successful replications in a number of countries. Indeed, in a study conducted in Sweden, Frodi (1975) reported the weapons effect in high-school boys even when they had *not* been angered by means of receiving electric shocks.

From the results of Berkowitz's own experiments, and those conducted by other researchers, it would seem that frustration and pain are examples of *aversive stimuli*. Other aversive stimuli include noise (Donnerstein and Wilson, 1976), uncomfortably high temperature (Bell and Baron, 1974) and foul odours such as cigarette smoke (Berkowitz, 1983).

Zillman's excitation-transfer theory

According to Zillman (1982), arousal from one source can be transferred to, and energise, some other response. This is because arousal takes time to dissipate. In circumstances when we are aroused, aggression may be heightened, provided that the aroused person has some disposition to react aggressively, and provided that the arousal is incorrectly attributed to the aggression-provoking event rather than to the correct source.

In one test of this proposal, Zillman and Bryant (1974) created a state of arousal in participants by requiring them to ride bicycles. For some participants, a high level of arousal was induced, whilst for others a low level was induced. Then, the participants played a game during which they were verbally insulted by a confederate. When the participants were later given the opportunity to deliver a harsh noise in headphones worn by the confederate, significantly more noise was delivered by the highly aroused participants.

Excitation-transfer theorists have been particularly interested in the relationship between sexual arousal and aggression (see, for example, Zillman and Bryant, 1982). Unfortunately, the data reported have been inconsistent. It seems that 'soft' pornography either decreases or has no effect on aggression, whereas 'hard core' pornography can lead to an increase in aggressive behaviour (Donnerstein *et al.*, 1987). Also, sexual excitement, combined with the observation of aggressive behaviour in the sexually arousing material, has been shown to produce an increase in aggression (Donnerstein and Berkowitz, 1981). The effects of observing aggressive behaviour are considered briefly in the following section, and looked at in greater detail in the following chapter.

As Mummendey (1996) has noted, excitation-transfer theory sees the relationship between arousal and aggression as a *sequence*, in which arousal is generated and then, depending on its perceived causes, is labelled and leads to a specific emotion such as anger. Berkowitz (1990), however, disputes the existence of 'unspecific' or 'neutral' arousal. According to his *cognitive-neoassociationistic approach*, anger and aggression are *parallel* rather than sequential processes, because aversive events automatically lead to the instigation of aggression, depending on what situational cues are present (Mummendey, 1996).

Social learning theory

According to social learning theory (SLT), aggressive behaviours are learned through the *reinforcement* and *imitation* of aggressive 'models' (Bandura, 1965, 1973, 1994). Reinforcement of aggressive behaviour can occur in a number of ways. For example, a child who behaves aggressively in order to play with attractive toys will quickly learn to repeat the behaviour in the future. Non-tangible reinforcement, such as praise for 'being tough', can also increase the tendency to behave aggressively.

Imitation is the reproduction of learning through observation (*observational learning*), and involves observing other people who serve as models for behaviour.

In experiments conducted in the 1960s, Bandura *et al.* (1961, 1963) demonstrated how a child's aggressive tendencies can be strengthened through *vicarious reinforcement*, that is, seeing others being rewarded for behaving aggressively. The research is summarised in Box 13.4.

Bandura's basic experimental procedure involved 3-, 4- and 5-year-old children observing an adult model behaving aggressively towards an inflated plastic 'Bobo' doll. Later, the children were allowed to play with the doll themselves. Those who saw the adult model's aggressive behaviour being reinforced performed significantly more imitative aggressive acts than those who saw the model's behaviour being neither reinforced nor punished. Those who saw the model being punished for behaving aggressively made fewest imitative responses of all.

Figure 13.3   Spontaneous imitation of an aggressive model

However, Bandura and his colleagues pointed out that there is an important distinction between *learning* and *performance*. The fact that a child does not perform an imitative behaviour does not necessarily mean that the behaviour has not been learned. In other experiments, Bandura and his colleagues found that when children who had seen the model's behaviour being punished were themselves offered rewards for behaving aggressively, they had learned (or acquired) the model's aggressive behaviours just as well as those who saw these behaviours being reinforced.

Whilst there are a number of methodological concerns with Bandura and his colleagues' research which make it difficult to generalise their findings to the 'real world', SLT has received support from a number of quarters (Hollin and Howells, 1997). For example, children who are raised by aggressive and physically abusive parents often behave in the same way (Kaufman and Zigler, 1987). Indeed, for Straus *et al.* (1980), 'each generation learns to be violent by being a participant in a violent family'. SLT has also contributed to our understanding of the role played by the media in both pro-social and anti-social behaviour. This contribution is considered in the following chapter.

The social constructionist approach

The most recent theoretical approach to understanding aggression is social constructionism. Mummendey (1996) has proposed that whether or not a behaviour is aggressive or non-aggressive depends on whether the behaviour (or, in the case of failing to help someone, the non-behaviour) is *judged* to be aggressive either by an observer or by the performer him or herself. In Mummendey's view, the appraisal of a behaviour as aggressive involves going beyond a description of it to an evaluation of it. For Mummendey,

'when asking about the causes of aggression, more is of interest than simply the conditions for the occurrence of that behaviour. Of even greater importance are the conditions for judging the individual behaviour as "aggressive"'.

Mummendey's own research (Mummendey and Otten, 1989) and that of others (such as Mikula, 1994) suggests that the intention to harm, actual harm, and norm violation are the main criteria people use to label a behaviour as aggressive. In looking for the cause of aggressive behaviour, then,

'we should not concentrate on the conditions that energise individual drives or reduce the rational control of behaviour. Rather, we should look for the conditions (at least from the actor's point of view) which make intentionally harming another person seem both situationally appropriate and justified' (Mummendey, 1996).

The reduction and control of aggressive behaviour

CATHARSIS

Both the Freudian and ethological approaches to aggression propose that the most effective way of reducing aggression is through *catharsis* (which comes from the Greek word 'katharsis' meaning 'purge'). The view that giving people the opportunity to 'let off steam' through arousing but non-harmful actions can reduce aggression is not, however, strongly supported by experimental evidence. Thus, watching scenes of filmed or television violence (Williams, 1986: see Chapter 14) does not appear to be effective in reducing aggression, nor does attacking inanimate objects (Mallick and McCandless, 1966) or attending sporting events (Arms *et al.*, 1980). Indeed, there is evidence that aggression may actually be *increased* by such conditions (Baron and Byrne, 1994).

Similarly, acting out aggression has been shown to lead to even more aggression (Geen *et al.*, 1975). Possibly, the reduction of unpleasant feelings creates the conditions for *negative reinforcement*, which is achieved through the termination of an aversive stimulus. So, when a person behaves cathartically and feels better afterwards, the experience tends to increase rather than decrease the likelihood of aggressive behaviour occurring (Carlson, 1987).

129

PUNISHMENT

There is evidence to suggest that punishment can be effective in deterring aggression provided that it is prompt, of sufficient magnitude to be aversive, and highly probable following the behaviour (Bower and Hilgard, 1981). However, punishment does not tend to be used in this way in at least some societies, including our own. In Britain, many crimes (even those involving aggression) are not reported to the police, and the 'clear up' rate for the most frequent categories of anti-social behaviour (theft and robbery) is very low (Holdaway, 1988).

The weak association between committing an anti-social act and the probability of being caught and punished for it means that most criminals hardly think about incarceration at all when contemplating and committing anti-social acts (Giddens, 1993). The delay between committing an anti-social act and being punished for it can also be very long and, when punishment is administered, it can vary greatly. Additionally, being punished for behaving anti-socially does not teach new, positive behaviours (as, perhaps, is indicated by the fact that 60 per cent of offenders reoffend and are put back in prison within four years: Giddens, 1993).

Whilst common sense suggests that punishment is an effective way of deterring anti-social behaviour, then, psychological research findings suggest a more cautious view of its effectiveness should be taken. As well as the reasons identified above, punishment may be ineffective because the recipient sees it as being unjustified (particularly if it is not applied in the same way to others). Indeed, when this is the case, anti-social behaviour may be *more* likely to occur because of the recipient's desire for *revenge* (Baron and Byrne, 1994).

EXPOSURE TO NON-AGGRESSIVE MODELS

A further reason why punishment may not be effective in the reduction of anti-social behaviour is that those who deliver the punishment are seen as *aggressive models* by those who receive it. Similarly, in a study conducted by Bandura (1965), children who observed an adult being punished for behaving aggressively still behaved more aggressively than children who did not witness any aggression at all. As shown in the following chapter, exposure to aggressive behaviour as portrayed by the media can produce heightened aggression amongst at least some of those who observe it.

According to Deaux *et al.* (1993), it is impossible to eliminate all aggressive models from society. However, it may be possible to reduce aggression by adding more non-aggressive models to the environment. That seeing other people behaving non-aggressively, even in the face of extreme provocation, can reduce aggression has been demonstrated in a number of studies (e.g. Donnerstein and Donnerstein, 1976).

Given that, as noted on page 129, children who are raised by aggressive and physically abusive parents often behave in the same way, parents and other significant role models could reduce aggression by not engaging in those behaviours, either with their own children or with other adults. For Patterson (1986), encouraging children (by means of positive reinforcement) to develop socially positive traits such as nurturance and sensitivity, and at the same time discouraging inappropriate aggression (using, for example, consistent but non-physical punishment), can strengthen pro-social behaviours.

SOCIAL SKILLS TRAINING, COGNITIVE INTERVENTIONS, AND INCOMPATIBLE RESPONSES

In addition to the approaches considered above, Baron and Byrne (1994) suggest three others that might be effective in the reduction of aggression. These are social skills training, cognitive interventions, and incompatible responses.

Social skills training

People who lack the ability to communicate their wishes to others, often suffer repeated frustration and this can lead them to behave aggressively (Hollin and Howells, 1997). Those who lack essential *social skills* evidently account for a high proportion of the violence occurring in any given society (Toch, 1980). Toch's solution, therefore, is to train people in the essential social skills. A number of studies (e.g. Goldstein *et al.*, 1981; Schneider, 1991) suggest that such training can be effective in reducing the likelihood of a person being either the source or a target of aggressive behaviour.

Cognitive interventions

If, as seems likely, the way we explain a person's behaviour determines the likelihood of our behaving aggressively, it seems reasonable to propose that changing our attribution (see Chapter 1) for a particular behaviour might be effective in reducing aggression. Several studies (e.g. Kremer and Stephens, 1983) have found that when people are made aware of the *mitigating circum-*

stances for a person's potentially aggression-inducing behaviour, they are less likely to behave aggressively, provided that the information about the mitigating circumstances is given early enough and is believable.

Incompatible responses

According to the principle of *reciprocal inhibition* (Wolpe, 1958), it is impossible for us to experience two incompatible emotional responses simultaneously. A number of researchers (e.g. Baron, 1983) have applied this principle to the reduction of aggressive behaviour, and have shown that when emotional states incompatible with anger or actual aggression are induced in people, the tendency to react aggressively is reduced.

CLINICAL APPROACHES TO THE REDUCTION OF AGGRESSION

In the case of those people convicted of violent offences and referred by a probation officer to the forensic services, a variety of techniques drawn from mainstream clinical psychology may be used (Hollin and Howells, 1997). Box 13.5 shows how a 'multi-faceted intervention programme' was used with an aggressive adult offender.

> **Box 13.5   Using a multi-faceted intervention programme with an aggressive adult offender**
>
> John, aged 23 was described by his probation officer as 'a violent man who seems incapable of controlling his temper … he displays his anger verbally and physically … he describes himself as like a "fuse" ready to explode … he is very disturbed by his behaviour and … fears that he may hurt someone seriously'.

The four techniques used with John were:

1 **Desensitisation**, in which he imagined provoking stimuli and then used relaxation to bring about self-control over his angry thoughts and arousal.
2 **Active challenging** of his thoughts and the development of more realistic views of other people.
3 **Environmental control**, in that John was encouraged to remove himself from risky environments, such as nightclubs.
4 **Rehearsal and practice** of alternative ways of dealing with the escalating verbal exchanges that preceded violent incidents.

The success of the *anger management* interventions with John suggests that a knowledge of the individual person, the situation in which he or she behaves aggressively, and the complex interactions between cognition, emotion and behaviour can all be useful in reducing aggressive behaviour.

(From Hollin and Howells, 1997)

Conclusions

Several theories have been advanced to explain the occurrence of aggressive behaviour, some of which are better supported by experimental evidence than others. A number of approaches to the reduction and control of aggressive behaviour have also been advanced. As with the theories that seek to explain the occurrence of aggression, research findings support the effectiveness of some approaches to the reduction and control of aggression more than others.

SUMMARY

- Whilst aggression is a type of anti-social behaviour, there are different types of aggression, including **anti-social, sanctioned** and **pro-social**.
- According to Moyer and Berkowitz, aggression always involves some behaviour, either physical or symbolic, intended to harm another person. **Violence** denotes an extreme form of aggression involving an attempt to inflict serious physical injury or damage to property.
- A long-standing debate within social psychology concerns whether interpersonal aggression is biologically determined (nature) or the product of learning and environmental influences (nurture).
- According to the philosopher Hobbes, people are naturally competitive and hostile, and government is necessary for the prevention of conflict and mutual destruction. Both Freud and Lorenz share Hobbes' pessimistic view of human nature.
- Freud's **psychoanalytic approach** maintains that instincts are aimed at reducing and, ultimately, eliminating tension/excitation. Having initially stressed **eros**, the human drive for pleasure and self-preservation, he later proposed **thanatos**, directed towards self-destruction and death.
- Because these two instincts are in conflict, thanatos is satisfied by being turned **outward**. In the absence of some **cathartic activity** such as sport, people will periodically act aggressively towards other people or things in order to discharge the aggressive energy that builds up.
- Like Freud, Lorenz saw aggression as instinctive and needing to be released every so often if it is not to build up to dangerously high levels. According to his **ethological approach**, aggression is **adaptive** in all species, most of which have built-in safety devices that prevent them from killing members of their own species. These include **ritualisation** and **appeasement rituals**.
- In humans, certain appeasement gestures can be effective, but aggression is no longer under the control of rituals. The ability of humans to kill each other through **weapons technology** represents a way in which our intentions can override our instincts.
- Megargee's study of violent crimes committed by **overcontrolled individuals** lends support to instinct theories of aggression. However, Freud's theory is difficult to test empirically, and is better at explaining what has already taken place than at predicting what will happen.

- There is considerable evidence that contradicts Lorenz's claim that aggression between members of the same non-human species always stops before one of the animals is killed. Lorenz also failed to take into account how the **goals** of behaviour, such as fighting over territory or competing for a sexual partner, influence the degree of ritual.
- Like Freud, Lorenz believed that aggression occurs spontaneously when aggressive energy builds up (the **hydraulic model**). The evidence for this is extremely limited, and many biologists and ethologists consider that aggression in non-humans is reactive and modifiable by various internal and external conditions.
- Dollard *et al.*'s **frustration–aggression hypothesis** was intended to translate Freudian concepts into learning theory terms. It defined frustration as anything that prevents the occurrence of an **expected reinforcer**. Whilst agreeing that aggression was an innate response, they argued that it would only be triggered in specific situations.
- Whilst Dollard *et al.* claimed that frustration always produces an aggressive response, this is not always directed at the object of the frustration: it may be displaced on to a more accessible target, as illustrated in **scapegoating**.
- The original version of the frustration–aggression hypothesis has been criticised in a variety of ways. According to Miller, frustration makes aggression more likely but is not a **sufficient** cause of aggressive behaviour, since situational factors may prevent actual aggression from occurring. Aggression is also just one possible response to frustration.
- According to Miell and Berkowitz, aggression is most likely to occur when a person is close to achieving a goal or the frustrator is perceived as intentionally or improperly interfering with his or her efforts (i.e. an **attribution of intention** is made). Children who are chronically aggressive have a strong attributional bias towards seeing others as having hostile intent, which often leads to retaliatory aggression.
- According to Berkowitz, frustration produces **anger**, but this will only result in aggression if two conditions are met. There must be both a **readiness** to act aggressively and **environmental cues** associated either with aggressive behaviour or with the frustrating person or object.

- In experimental tests of Berkowitz's **cue-arousal/ aggressive-cue theory**, participants were frustrated in the presence/absence of aggressive cues. So, for example, angry participants displayed most aggression (as measured by electric shocks to the stooge) in the presence of a shotgun and revolver, especially if they supposedly belonged to the stooge, and least in the presence of a badminton racket or when no objects at all were present (**the weapons effect**).
- Frustration and pain are **aversive stimuli**. Other examples include noise, uncomfortably high temperature and foul odours.
- According to Zillman's **excitation-transfer theory**, arousal from one source can be transferred to, and energise, some other response. Because arousal takes time to dissipate, aggression may be heightened if the aroused person is disposed to react aggressively and provided the arousal is incorrectly attributed to the aggression-provoking event.
- Whilst 'soft' pornography either decreases aggression or has no effects, 'hard core' pornography can increase it, especially if sexual excitement is combined with aggression in the material itself.
- Whilst excitation-transfer theory sees the relationship between arousal and aggression as a **sequence**, Berkowitz rejects the existence of 'unspecific'/'neutral' arousal. According to his **cognitive-neoassociationistic approach,** anger and aggression are **parallel** processes.
- According to **social learning theory/SLT**, aggressive behaviours are learned through **reinforcement** and **imitation**, which is closely related to **observational learning**. Experiments conducted in the 1960s by Bandura *et al.* showed how a child's aggressive tendencies can be strengthened through **vicarious reinforcement.**
- Bandura's procedure involved 3–5-year-olds observing an adult model behaving aggressively towards a Bobo doll, which the children were later allowed to play with themselves. Reinforced models were imitated the most, punished models the least, with the control condition falling in between.
- When children who had seen the model punished were themselves offered rewards for imitating the model, they displayed as much imitative aggression (**performance**) as children in the model-rewarded condition, showing that both groups had acquired the model's behaviour to the same extent (**learning**).
- Whilst it is difficult generalising Bandura *et al.*'s findings to the 'real world', SLT has received support from various sources, including studies of children raised by aggressive and physically abusive parents.
- According to the **social constructionist approach**, behaviour is aggressive or non-aggressive as **judged** to be so, either by an observer or by the actor. According to Mummendey, calling behaviour aggressive involves an evaluation of the behaviour.
- Research suggests that the main criteria people use to label a behaviour as aggressive are the intention to harm, actual harm, and norm violation. Rather than focusing on the conditions that energise individual drives or reduce rational control of behaviour, we should look for the conditions which make aggression both situationally appropriate and justified.
- Both the Freudian and ethological approaches advocate **catharsis** as the most effective way of reducing aggression. However, there is little support for this and, indeed, aggression may actually be **increased** by watching filmed or television violence, attacking inanimate objects, attending sporting events or acting out aggression. This may be due to the **negative reinforcement** of aggressive behaviour through the reduction of unpleasant feelings.
- Whilst **punishment** can be effective in deterring aggressive behaviour if it is prompt, aversive and predictable, in practice this often does not happen. Also, there is often a long delay between committing a crime and being punished for it.
- Not only does punishment fail to teach new, positive behaviours, but the punished person may see it as unjustified, which may induce a desire for **revenge**. Also, the punisher is an **aggressive model**. Even when children see an aggressive model being punished, they behave more aggressively than children who see no aggression at all.
- It may be possible to reduce aggression by increasing the number of **non-aggressive models** in society, including parents, especially if they are seen resisting extreme provocation. Pro-social behaviours can be increased by combining positive reinforcement for socially positive traits with punishment for inappropriate aggression.
- People who lack essential **social skills** often suffer repeated frustration and account for much of the violence that occurs in any given society. Several studies suggest that **social skills training** can be effective in reducing aggression.
- **Cognitive interventions** involve changing people's attributions for a particular behaviour, such as making them aware of the **mitigating**

circumstances. This can make aggression less likely, provided the relevant information is given early and is believable.

- Based on the principle of **reciprocal inhibition**, it has been shown that the tendency to react aggressively can be reduced by inducing emotional states that are **incompatible** with anger or actual aggression.
- **Clinical approaches** to treating people convicted of violent crimes may include a range of techniques, including **desensitisation, active challenging, environmental control** and **rehearsal and practice.**
- According to Hollin and Howells, successful **anger management** suggests that knowledge of the indivdual, the situation in which he or she behaves aggressively, and the complex interactions between cognition, emotion and behaviour, can all help reduce aggressive behaviour.

MEDIA INFLUENCES ON PRO-SOCIAL AND ANTI-SOCIAL BEHAVIOUR

Introduction and overview

The previous two chapters have looked at social psychological theory and research relating to pro-social and anti-social behaviour. Our aim in this chapter is to look at the influence of the *media* on these two types of social behaviour. The media are

'the methods and organisations used by specialist groups to convey messages to large, socially mixed and widely dispersed audiences' (Trowler, 1988).

Most social psychological research has looked at the influence of the media (and in particular television) on anti-social behaviour. However, there has been a growing interest in the relationship between the media and pro-social behaviour. We look first at the media and anti-social behaviour and then turn our attention to pro-social behaviour.

How much aggressive behaviour is shown on television?

The basic method used by researchers to quantify the amount of violence shown on television involves simple counting techniques. Violence is defined objectively by researchers, who then code samples of television programmes for incidents which match those definitions. Probably the largest American study to look at the amount of televised violence is that conducted by Gerbner and his colleagues (Gerbner, 1972; Gerbner and Gross, 1976; Gerbner *et al.*, 1980, 1986). These researchers have monitored samples of all major network prime-time and weekend day-time programmes since 1967.

Defining violence as

'the overt expression of physical force against others or self, or the compelling of an action against one's will on pain of being hurt or killed',

the researchers found that since 1967 the percentage of television shows containing violent episodes has remained about the same, but the number of violent episodes per show has gradually increased. In 1986, Gerbner *et al.* reported an average of around five violent acts per hour on prime-time television. On children's weekend shows, mostly consisting of cartoons, about 20 violent acts per hour occurred. Interestingly, despite agreement in 1979 from the major networks to limit the amount of violence in cartoons, Cramer and Mechem (1982) found no actual decrease and, if anything, an increase.

It has been estimated that during their impressionable years, young viewers will witness some 13 000 murders on television. A fair proportion of these can be seen in the Sylvester Stallone film *Rambo 3*, which has 245 separate acts of violence and an astonishing 123 killings. Yet researchers in America have been at pains to point out that what the viewer sees is *not* an accurate depiction of real life. In a typical American 'TV cop' drama, a gun is fired at least once in every episode. In Chicago, a typical police officer will fire his gun once every 27 years (Radecki, 1989).

Gerbner *et al.'s* analysis of violence on television provided the framework for British research, which began with studies conducted by Halloran and Croll (1972) and the BBC's Audience Research Department. Both of these studies found that violence was a common feature of programming, although it was not as prevalent on British as on American television. Commissioned by the BBC, Cumberbatch (1987) analysed all programmes broadcast on the (then) four terrestrial channels in four separate weeks between May and September 1986. Cumberbatch's main findings are summarised in Box 14.1.

Box 14.1   The main findings from Cumberbatch's (1987) study

Cumberbatch found that 30 per cent of programmes contained some violence, the overall frequency being 1.14 violent acts per programme and 1.68 violent acts per hour. Each act lasted around 25 seconds, with the result that violence occupied just over 1 per cent of total television time. These figures were lower if boxing and wrestling were excluded, but higher (at 1.96 violent acts per hour) if verbal threats were included.

Death resulted from violent acts in 26 per cent of cases, but in 61 per cent of acts no injuries were shown and the victim was portrayed as being in pain or stunned. In 83 per cent of cases, no blood was shown as a result of a violent act, and considerable blood and gore occurred in only 0.2 per cent of cases. Perpetrators of violent acts were much more likely to be portrayed as 'baddies' than 'goodies', and violence occurred twice as frequently in a law-breaking than in a law-upholding context.

On the basis of his findings, Cumberbatch argued that whilst violence and concerns about violence had increased in society in the decade up to 1987, this was not reflected by a proportional increase on television, even in news broadcasts. He concluded that:

'while broadcasters may take some comfort from our data on trends in television violence, they must expect to be continually reminded of their responsibilities in this area and be obliged to acknowledge that a significant minority of people will remain concerned about what's on the box'.

More recently, the BBC and ITV commissioned a team at Sheffield University, headed by Barry Gunter and Jackie Harrison, to look at the frequency of violence on terrestrial and satellite channels (Frean, 1995; Armstrong, 1997). Some of the findings from the study are shown in Box 14.2.

Box 14.2   Some findings from the Sheffield University analysis of violence on British television

The Sheffield researchers monitored 2084 programmes on eight channels over four weeks in October 1994 and January/February 1995. The findings include:

- On BBC 1 and 2, ITV and Channel 4, 28 per cent of programmes contained violent acts, compared with 52 per cent on Sky One, UK Gold, Sky Movies and the Movie Channel.
- Violence occupied 0.61 per cent of time on the terrestrial channels and 1.53 per cent on the satellite stations.
- The greatest proportion of violent acts (70 per cent) occurred in dramas and films; 19 per cent occurred in children's programmes.
- Most violent acts occurred in contemporary settings in inner-city locations. The majority of perpetrators were young, white males.
- One per cent of programmes contained 19 per cent of all violent acts. *Double Impact*, shown on the Movie Channel, for example, contained 105 violent acts, as against an average of 9.7.
- The United States was the most common location for violence (47 per cent), followed by the United Kingdom (12 per cent). The third most likely location was a cartoon setting (7 per cent) and then science fiction locations (4 per cent).

(From Frean, 1995.)

On the basis of the finding that violent acts account for 1 per cent of the programme content on the four main terrestrial channels, and for less than 2 per cent on some satellite stations, and the fact that 1 per cent of programmes contained 19 per cent of all violent acts, Gunter and Harrison concluded that:

'The picture that emerges is not one of a television system permeated by violence, but rather one in which violence represents only a tiny part of the output and where it tends to be concentrated principally in a relatively small number of programmes' (cited in Frean, 1995).

As well as television, violent behaviour can also be seen at the *cinema* or on *video* (and what is shown may or may not be subsequently screened on television). There is some evidence to suggest that a large percentage of 9–11-year-olds have watched 18-rated videos, including the particularly violent *Nightmare on Elm Street*,

Figure 14.1   Jean-Claude van Damme performs another aggressive act in Double Impact

The Silence of the Lambs, and *Pulp Fiction* (Ball and Nuki, 1996; Wark and Ball, 1996: see Figure 14.1). The current controls used in Britain are shown in Box 14.3.

Box 14.3   Current controls in Britain

In the cinema, the film industry operates a voluntary system via the British Board of Film Classification (BBFC). Outside of certain areas where BBFC practice is to cut, matters of taste and decency are dealt with primarily through classification according to the categories below. Video recordings are covered by the Video Recordings Act (1984), which requires any video supplier to have been classified by the BBFC, which is required to give particular consideration to the likelihood of home viewing and the law, in particular the Obscene Publications Act. The classification system differs from films. The law makes it illegal to supply videos to anyone below the age of the classification restriction.

Film	Video	Meaning
U	U	Universal, suitable for all
–	Uc	Suitable for all, especially children
PG	PG	Parental guidance, general viewing but some scenes may be unsuitable for young children
12	–	Suitable only for persons 12 and over
15	15	Suitable only for persons 15 and over
18	18	Suitable only for persons 18 and over

On TV, the BBC Governors are responsible for relevant standards at the BBC, whilst commercial TV companies operate under the terms of licences from the ITC (or S4c). Both BBC and ITC have their own programming guidance which, under the Broadcasting Act (1990), must reflect the British Standards Council's (BSC) Code. Satellite TV which originates from the UK is covered by the same ITC code as terrestrial channels. Broadcasts from other EC countries are regulated under standards within the EC Broadcasting Directive (89/552/EEC).

(Taken from Briefing Note 44 of the Parliamentary Office of Science and Technology, 1993.)

The effects of television on children's behaviour

Research into the effects of television on children's behaviour began in America in the 1960s, following the publication of the results of Bandura *et al.*'s 'Bobo doll experiments' (see Chapter 13, page 128). These so-called 'first generation' (or 'phase one': Baron, 1977) studies into the effects of media violence involved filmed (or symbolic) models. Essentially, Bandura *et al.* showed that children can acquire new aggressive responses not previously in their behavioural repertoire merely through exposure to a filmed or televised model.

If children could learn new ways of harming others through such experience, then the implication was that mass media portrayals of violence might be contributing, at least to a degree, to increased levels of violence in society (Baron, 1977). However, Bandura (1965)

warned against such an interpretation in the light of his finding that the learning of aggressive responses does not necessarily mean that they will be displayed in the child's behaviour (see Chapter 13, page 129). Nevertheless, the *possibility* that such effects could occur was sufficient to focus considerable public attention on Bandura *et al.*'s research.

HOW MUCH TELEVISION DO PEOPLE WATCH?

American research conducted since 1965 suggests that the amount of time people in a typical household spend in front of the television has, in general, been steadily increasing (Burger, 1982; Liebert and Sprafkin, 1988). However, it is important to recognise that these data are typically derived from paper-and-pen surveys concerning viewing habits and that these may not be reliable. Indeed, evidence that such figures are not reliable comes from a study conducted by Anderson *et al.* (1986).

Anderson *et al.* installed automated time-lapse video recording equipment in the homes of 99 families consisting of 462 people aged between 1 and 62. The recordings began when the television was switched on and stopped when it was switched off. One video camera used a wide-angled lens to record people's behaviour in the room where the television was, whilst a second focused on the television screen itself. The main findings reported by Anderson *et al.* are shown in Box 14.4.

Box 14.4   The main findings from Anderson, *et al.'s* (1986) study

- No one actually watches the television for more than 75 per cent of the time it is on.
- Children spend an average of 12.8 hours per week with the television on. Of this, 9.14 hours are spent looking at it. Adults spend an average of 11.5 hours per week with the television on. Of this, 7.56 hours are spent looking at it.
- Adult females pay significantly less attention to television than do children. Adult males look at the television more than females but watch it less than school-aged children.
- The number of hours spent looking at television increases up until the age of 10, after which it decreases, levels off at about age 17, and continues around the same level (10 hours per week) into adulthood.

Exactly why people have the television on but do not watch it is an interesting question in its own right! But the findings reported by Anderson *et al.* suggest that data about how much television people *watch* should be treated with caution.

Figure 14.2   The fact that the TV is on does not necessarily mean that anyone is watching it

HOW DO VIEWERS PERCEIVE VIOLENCE?

Much of the concern about the effects of television has centred on children. Cumberbatch (1987) found that whilst violence was more likely after 9 p.m., and whilst violence in children's programmes was rare, a notable exception was *cartoons*. Whether children perceive cartoons as representing 'reality' is debatable. According to Gunter and McAleer (1990), viewers can be highly discriminating when it comes to portrayals of violence, and do not invariably read into television content the same meanings as do researchers. Thus, merely knowing how often certain pre-defined incidents occur in programmes does not tell us how significant these features are for viewers.

Viewers' perceptions of how violent television content is, then, may not agree with objective counts of violence in programmes. However, *realism* does appear to be an important element in viewers' perceptions of violence, since real-life incidents in news and documentary programmes are generally rated as being more violent than those shown in fictional settings. As far as children are concerned, research suggests that they are very similar to adults in terms of their judgements of the *amount* of violence. However, their *ratings* of violence do differ from those of researchers and, in the case of cartoons, something which has an objectively high number of violent acts may be subjectively perceived as hardly containing any. Subjective assessment of violence should, therefore, be incorporated into assessments of the amount of violence shown on television (Gunter and McAleer, 1990).

WHAT ARE THE EFFECTS OF WATCHING VIOLENT TELEVISION?

What Baron (1977) calls 'phase two' research, that is, research into the effects of media violence, has been conducted using a variety of methodological approaches. *Correlational studies* typically involve asking people which programmes they like best and which they watch most often. These data are then correlated with measures of aggression given by parents, teachers, self-reports, peers, and so on. Evidence from such studies has generally been inconsistent, but one finding that has emerged is that the overall amount of viewing is related to self-reports of aggressive behaviour. Of course, it is possible that those who watch violent television are *different* in some way from those who do not, and it is the inability to infer cause and effect in a correlational study which weakens this particular methodology (Freedman, 1984).

Laboratory studies are designed to enable a causal link to be shown between watching violent television and behaving aggressively (if one exists). In one study (Liebert and Baron, 1972), participants were randomly assigned to two groups. One watched '*The Untouchables*', a violent television programme, whilst the other watched an equally engaging and arousing, but non-violent, sports competition. Afterwards, the children were allowed to play, and the researchers found that those who had watched the violent programme behaved more aggressively than those who had watched the sports competition programme.

The problem with laboratory studies is that most use small and unrepresentative samples of people who are exposed to the independent variable under highly contrived and unnatural viewing conditions. The measures of television viewing and aggression tend to be so far removed from normal everyday behaviour that it is doubtful whether such studies have any relevance to the real world (Gunter and McAleer, 1990). Much more ecologically valid are *field experiments*. In these, children or teenagers are assigned to view violent or non-violent programmes for a period of a few days or weeks.

Measures of aggressive behaviour, fantasy, attitude and so on are taken before, during and after the period of controlled viewing. To ensure control over actual viewing, children in group or institutional settings are studied, mostly nursery schools, residential schools, or institutions for adolescent boys. In general, the results show that children who watch violent television are more aggressive than those who do not (Parke *et al.*, 1977).

The weakness of the field experiment is that the experimental setting cannot be as well controlled as the laboratory experiment. As a result, we cannot be certain that the *only* difference between the children is in terms of who watches violent and non-violent television. This is especially the case when participants are not assigned randomly to conditions. In Parke *et al.*'s study, for example, 'cottages' (or pre-existing *groups*), rather than individuals, were assigned to the viewing conditions. Also, and by definition, such participants (juvenile delinquent males in Parke *et al.*'s study) are not representative of children or adolescents in general.

Like experiments, but unlike correlational studies, *longitudinal panel studies* can say something about cause and effect *and* normally use representative samples. Their aim is to discover relationships that may exist or develop over time between television viewing and behaviour. Such studies are, then, concerned with the *cumulative* influence of television and whether or not attitudes and behaviour are linked with watching television.

A number of studies in both America (e.g. Lefkowitz *et al.*, 1972; Eron and Huesmann, 1985; Phillips, 1986) and Britain (e.g. Sims and Gray, 1993; Bailey, 1993) have shown that such a link exists. Sims and Bailey, for example, reported an extensive body of literature linking heavy exposure to media violence and subsequent aggressive behaviour. Similarly, Bailey's study of 40 adolescent murderers and 200 young sex offenders in

Britain showed repeated viewing of violent and pornographic videos to be 'a significant causal factor'. This was particularly important in the case of adolescents who abused while they were babysitting, where videos provided 'a potential source of immediate arousal for the subsequent act', including imitating violent images.

It is important to note, though, that at least some studies have failed to find such a link. Milavsky *et al.* (1982), for example, found that there were only small associations between exposure to violent programmes and verbal and physical aggression amongst 3200 elementary school children and adolescents. Variables such as family background, social environment, and school performance were actually much better predictors of aggressiveness (Gunter and McAleer, 1990).

One of the most useful kinds of study is the *natural experiment*, in which the researcher does not manipulate an independent variable, but takes advantage of a fortuitous and naturally occurring division. In one such study, Williams (1986) studied a community ('Notel') where television had only been recently introduced. This community was compared with one in which there was a single television channel and another with several channels. The major finding was that verbal and physical aggression in both male and female 6–11-year-olds increased over a two-year period following the introduction of television to 'Notel', but that no such increase occurred in the communities that already had television. An ongoing natural experiment looking at the effects of the introduction of television is described in Box 14.5.

Box 14.5   A natural experiment on the island of St Helena

In July 1994, a study began to look at the effects of the introduction of television to St Helena. This remote island in the south-east Atlantic, has a little under 6000 inhabitants, none of whom has ever seen live television. Of the 9–12-year-olds on the island, only 3.4 per cent have behavioural problems, compared with 14 per cent of children in London. Of the 3–4-year-olds, less than 7 per cent have behavioural problems, compared with 12 per cent in London. The figure of 3.4 per cent for the 9–12-year-olds is the lowest ever recorded for any age range anywhere in the world.

Prior to the introduction of several 24-hour channels (including BBC World Television, MNET, a South African commercial service, and the American satellite channel, CNN), the only access the islanders had to news was on short-wave radio from the BBC World Service. Whilst the island has three video libraries, it does not have a cinema.

The study's leader, Tony Charlton, is looking at the effects of the introduction of television on 59 pre-school children, who will be monitored until they are 13, and all 800 children on the island who are of first and middle-school age. According to Charlton,

'the children on the island represent a unique control group – it is extraordinarily difficult to find a group that doesn't have television'.

Prior to the study beginning, Charlton noted that

'it could be that excessive viewing interferes with the development of social skills and mental capacities which children need to acquire. But there could be enormous educational benefits'.

In the fourth year of the seven-year study, Charlton and his team found that *pro-social behaviour* (defined as helping others and playing amicably) had not only been maintained since the introduction of television, but had actually *improved* slightly.

(Based on Cooper, 1994; McIlroy, 1994; Frean, 1994; Lee, 1996; Midgley, 1998)

On the basis of the many studies that have been carried out, which have involved at least 100 000 participants (Hearold, 1986), a number of researchers have concluded that research has effectively established a link between television and aggressive behaviour in children and adolescents (Singer, 1989). Indeed, the American National Institute of Mental Health's (1982) review of 2500 studies led it to conclude that:

'the consensus amongst most of the research community is that violence on television does lead to aggressive behaviour by children and teenagers who watch the programmes. This conclusion is based on laboratory experiments and field studies. Not all children become aggressive, of course, but the correlations between violence and aggression are positive. In magnitude, television violence is as strongly correlated with aggressive behaviour as any other behavioural variable that has been measured'.

HOW DOES TELEVISION EXERT ITS EFFECTS?

Four specific effects of television violence have been investigated. These are *arousal*, *disinhibition*, *imitation* and *desensitisation*. Some relevant findings are described in Box 14.6.

Box 14.6   The effects of television

Arousal: Arousal is a non-specific, physiological response, whose 'meaning' will be defined by the viewer in terms of the type of programme being watched (Zillman, 1978). Watching violence on television has been claimed to increase a viewer's overall level of emotional arousal and excitement (Berkowitz, 1993). However, there does not seem to be any strong overall relationship between perceiving a programme as violent and verbal or physiological reports of emotional arousal (Gadow and Sprafkin, 1993; Bryant and Zillman, 1994). Nevertheless, the more *realistic* the violence is perceived to be, the greater the reported arousal and involvement are likely to be.

Disinhibition: Disinhibition refers to the reduction of inhibitions about behaving aggressively oneself or coming to believe that aggression is a permitted or legitimate way of solving problems or attaining goals. Berkowitz's cue-arousal (aggressive cue) theory, discussed in Chapter 13, is relevant here.

Imitation: Perhaps the most direct link between watching television and the viewer's own behaviour is imitation. This, of course, is directly related to Bandura *et al.*'s studies of imitative aggression (see page 128). However, social learning theorists acknowledge the role of cognitive factors as mediating between stimulus and response (Bandura, 1994), and so how television violence is perceived and interpreted, and the importance of realism, are clearly important intervening variables for both children and adults.

Desensitisation: Desensitisation refers to the reduction in emotional response to television violence (an increased acceptance of violence in real life) as a result of repeated viewing of violence on the television. As with drug tolerance, it is argued that increasingly violent programmes are required to produce an emotional response (Gadow and Sprafkin, 1989). In one study implicating desensitisation, Drabman and Thomas (1974) showed 8-year-olds a violent or non-violent programme before witnessing a 'real' (but actually staged) fight between two other children. Those who saw the violent programme were much less likely than those who saw the non-violent programme to tell an adult that a fight was occurring.

RECONSIDERING MEDIA VIOLENCE

The debate about the relationship between media violence and aggression is far from being resolved. In Britain, the link between media violence and aggression was brought back into the spotlight following the murder of two-year-old James Bulger by two teenage boys in February, 1993. At their trial, Mr Justice Moreland said:

'It is not for me to pass judgement on their upbringing, but I suspect that exposure to violent video films may, in part, be an explanation' (cited in Cumberbatch, 1997).

The call for legislation controlling the supply of videos to children was supported by a number of psychologists, including Newson (1994), whose report entitled *Video Violence and the Protection of Children* was also endorsed by many psychiatrists and paediatricians. Cumberbatch (1997), however, has questioned the validity of the evidence on which Newson's report was based. He notes that whilst it might be true that the father of one of the murderers of James Bulger (Neil Venables) had rented the video *Child's Play 3* some weeks before the murder occurred (as one British tabloid claimed), James Venables was not living with his father at that time, disliked horror films, and was upset by violence in videos. Similarly, the massacre of 16 people in Hungerford in 1987 was claimed to have been inspired by the murderer seeing the character 'Rambo' in the film *First Blood*. In fact, there is no evidence to support this claim (Cumberbatch, 1997).

Cumberbatch has also criticised the conclusion of Comstock and Paik (1991) that, based on Huesmann and Eron's (1986) cross-national survey in six countries (Holland, Australia, USA, Israel, Poland and Finland), viewing television violence at an early age is a predictor of later aggression. Cumberbatch's criticisms are presented in Box 14.7.

Box 14.7   Cumberbatch's criticisms of the claim that viewing television violence at an early age is a predictor of later aggression

- The Dutch researchers, Wiegman *et al.* (1992), concluded that their results did not show any effects of television and refused to allow their findings to be included in Huesmann and Eron's edited book of the research study.
- The Australian research showed no significant correlation between early television violence viewing and later aggression.
- The American study found that when initial aggression was controlled for, the correlation between early television viewing and later aggression was significant only in girls.
- Israeli researchers found significant effects in the city samples but not in the Kibbutz samples.
- In Poland, the researchers agreed that a greater preference for violent viewing was predictive of later aggression, but that 'the effects are not large and must be treated cautiously'.
- The Finnish researchers appeared to misunderstand their own data. Rather than there being a positive correlation between viewing violent television and aggressive behaviour, the correlation is actually *negative*, indicating that the more television is watched the less aggressive children were later.

(Adapted from Cumberbatch, 1997.)

Cumberbatch (1997) cites several other studies (e.g. Belson, 1978; Hagell and Newburn, 1994) which cast doubt on the claims made about the connection between media violence and aggression in children. In his view:

'it is all too easy to scaremonger. However, we should remember that Britain is still a safe, highly regulated country. UK television has roughly half the amount of violence as most countries studied. It is ironic that the media seem largely to blame for the particularly British moral panic about our behaviour'.

The media and pro-social behaviour

According to Gunter and McAleer (1990),

'concern about the possible anti-social influences of television far outweighs the consideration given to any other area of children's involvement with television ... Television programmes contain many examples of good behaviour, of people acting kindly and with generosity. It is equally logical to assume that these portrayals provide models for children to copy'.

TELEVISION VIOLENCE AND CATHARSIS

One positive effect of television might be that witnessing others behaving aggressively helps viewers to get their own aggressive feelings 'out of their system' and hence be less likely to behave aggressively. The claim that television can act as a form of *vicarious catharsis* is based partly on the theories of aggression advanced by Freud and Lorenz (see Chapter 13, pages 123–125).

The evidence (e.g. Singer, 1989) does not, however, support the view that television is cathartic for everybody. Research suggests that if a discharge of hostile feelings can occur at all, it is probably restricted to people of a particular personality type or those who score highly on cognitive measures of fantasy, daydreaming and imagination. For some people, then, television violence can have positive effects and may provide a means by which aggressive feelings can be reduced (Gunter and McAleer, 1990).

TELEVISION AND PRO-SOCIAL BEHAVIOUR

If television can have harmful effects as a result of presenting anti-social behaviour then, presumably, it can have beneficial effects by promoting pro-social behaviour. According to Gunter and McAleer (1990), the evidence for the pro-social effects of television can be grouped into four types. These are shown in Box 14.8 (see opposite).

On the basis of their review of the literature, Gunter and McAleer concluded that

'televised examples of good behaviour can encourage children to behave in friendlier and more thoughtful ways to others'.

Box 14.8   The evidence for the pro-social effects of television

• **Laboratory studies with prepared television or filmed material**: Amongst other things, specially prepared materials have been shown to influence courage, the deferment of gratification, adherence to rules, charitable behaviour, friendliness, and affectionate behaviour.

• **Laboratory studies using broadcast materials specially produced for social skills teaching purposes**: Television productions designed to enhance the social maturity and responsibility of young viewers include *Sesame Street* and *Mister Rogers' Neighborhood*. A number of studies have shown that children who watch these programmes are able to identify and remember the co-operative and helping behaviours emphasised in certain segments of the shows. It seems that some programmes are better at encouraging pro-social behaviour in children than others, but the reasons for this are unclear.

• **Laboratory studies with programme materials from popular television series**: Specially manufactured television programmes or film clips have been shown to influence children's pro-social tendencies, at least when the pro-social behaviour portrayed in the material is very similar to that requested of the child. However, there is only some evidence that ordinary broadcast material can enhance a wide range of helping behaviours.

• **Field studies relating amount of viewing of pro-social television content to strength of pro-social behaviour tendencies**: Children who watch little television, but watch a lot of programmes with high levels of pro-social content, are more likely than other children to behave pro-socially. However, the correlations between viewing habits and pro-social behaviour are lower than those between viewing habits and anti-social behaviour. In part, this may be because pro-social behaviours are verbally mediated and often subtle, whereas anti-social behaviours are blatant and physical. Children learn better from simple, direct and active presentation, and so aggressive behaviours may be more readily learned. Also, the characters who display pro-social behaviour (typically female and non-white) and anti-social behaviour (typically male and white) may confound the relative influence of pro-social and anti-social behaviours with the types of character that portray them.

(From Gunter and McAleer, 1990.)

An alternative approach to what Greenfield (1984) calls *television literacy* involved teaching children to be 'informed consumers' of television. This includes distinguishing between social reality and the (at least sometimes) make-believe world of television, understanding the nature and purpose of advertisements, and interpreting and assessing sex-role and minority-group stereotyping.

In a study conducted by Huesmann *et al.* (1983), young children who were known to have a large amount of exposure to television were allocated to a control or experimental group. The experimental group received three training sessions which were designed to reduce the modelling of aggressive behaviour seen on television. The children were taught that television does not portray the world as it really is, that camera techniques and special effects give the illusion that characters are performing their highly aggressive and unrealistic feats, and that most people use other methods to solve the problems encountered by characters in television programmes. Compared with the control group, those in the experimental group showed less overall aggressive behaviour and lowered their identification with televised characters. These effects had persisted when the participants were followed up two years later.

COMPUTER GAMES AND PRO-SOCIAL BEHAVIOUR

According to Griffiths (1997), little is known about the long-term effects of playing violent computer games, but great concern has been raised that such games may have a more adverse effect on children than television because of the child's *active involvement*. Griffiths's review of the relevant research indicates that the effects of long-term exposure to computer games on subsequent aggressive behaviour are 'at best speculative'. As regards pro-social behaviour, computer games have received support from a number of researchers (e.g. Loftus and Loftus, 1983; Silvern, 1986). Some of the major claims about the pro-social effects of computer games are summarised in Box 14.9.

Box 14.9   The positive effects of computer games

- Computer games have become an integral part of modern language teaching in America because they are seen

  'as a motivating device, a means for providing comprehensible input and a catalyst for communicative practice and the negotiation of meaning' (Hubbard, 1991).

  However, whether a game is perceived as educational depends on factors such as the player's age, gender, proficiency level and educational background.
- Computer games give children access to 'state of the art' technology, a sense of confidence, and equips them with computer-related skills for the future (Surrey, 1982).
- Computer games may also promote social interaction. In a study on the impact of computers on family life, Mitchell (1983, cited in Griffiths, 1993) found that families generally viewed computer games as promoting interaction in a beneficial way through co-operation and competition.
- The aggressive content of some computer games may be cathartic (see page 130), in that they allow players to release their stress and aggression in a non-destructive way and have the effect of relaxing the players (Kestenbaum and Weinstein, 1984). Other benefits include the enhancement of cognitive skills, a sense of mastery, control and accomplishment, and a reduction in other youth problems due to 'addictive interest' in video games (Anderson and Ford, 1986).

(Adapted from Griffiths, 1997)

According to Griffiths (1997), there do appear to be some genuine applied aspects of computer game playing, although he notes that many of the assertions made in Box 14.9 were subjectively formulated and not based on empirical research findings.

And finally . . .

In a lecture given in 1994, the BBC newsreader Martyn Lewis claimed that television producers were failing to reflect the true state of the world through their tendency to ignore positive news (Lewis and Rowe, 1994). BBC managers attacked Lewis's views, charging that he was calling for news to be trivialised in order to make it more palatable, a charge Lewis vigorously denied.

Johnson and Davey (cited in Matthews, 1997) conducted a study in which three groups of participants were shown news bulletins with positive, negative or neutral blends of stories. After being shown the bulletins, those who saw the negative blend of stories were considerably more worried and depressed about their own lives (rather than the issues they had seen in the bulletin).

According to Davey (cited in Matthews, 1997),

'television producers need to think very carefully about the emotional impact news might have on their viewers'.

Davey sees slots like 'And finally . . .' on ITN's *News at Ten* as being beneficial:

'Having a light piece at the end is no bad thing. The trouble is [the broadcast] then gives a quick summary of all the news at the end, so it's not as effective as it could be'.

Reporting on solutions as well as problems, then, may be beneficial for all of us.

Conclusions

There has been much research into media influences on pro- and anti-social behaviour. On the basis of the evidence reviewed in this chapter, it seems reasonable to conclude that the media can exert an influence, although it would be dangerous to talk in simple cause-and-effect terms about the media's role.

SUMMARY

- Quantifying the amount of violence on television involves simple counting techniques. Samples of programmes are coded for incidents matching objective definitions of violence, as in Gerbner's American research. Gerbner showed an increase in the number of violent episodes per show since 1967, with children's weekend programmes (mainly cartoons) being four times more violent than prime-time television.
- Early British research was conducted by Halloran and Croll, and the BBC's Audience Research Department, both studies finding that, although common, violence was not as prevalent on British as on American television.
- Cumberbatch's study found that violence occupied just over 1 per cent of total television time. Generally, violent acts did not result in death, and blood and gore were hardly ever shown. The perpetrators were usually 'baddies' and violence was likely to be associated with law-breaking.
- Cumberbatch concluded that whilst social violence and concerns about it had increased between 1977 and 1987, this was not mirrored in television content, even in news broadcasts.
- The Sheffield University study found that violent acts account for 1 per cent of the content of the four main British terrestrial channels and less than 2 per cent on some satellite stations. Also, 1 per cent of programmes contained 19 per cent of all violent acts. According to Gunter and Harrison, these figures mean that violence is a tiny proportion of the total output.
- Violence, of course, also appears in films and videos. Despite the classification systems that operate for films shown at the cinema, and for videos, it is likely that a large percentage of 9–11-year-olds have watched 18-rated films.

- The BBC and ITC have their own programming guidance, ultimately regulated by the Broadcasting Act. The ITC can withdraw its licence from an offending company, whilst the BBC makes complaints from individuals or organisations public.
- Bandura's 'Bobo doll' experiments represented 'phase one' of research into the effects of media violence on children's behaviour. Using filmed (symbolic) models, these experiments showed that children can acquire new aggressive responses merely through exposure to a filmed or televised model.
- These findings implied that media portrayals of violence might be contributing to increased violence in society. However, Bandura also showed that learning does not equal performance. Nevertheless, the possibility of such effects ensured these experiments were taken seriously.
- Whilst American research suggests that people have been watching increasingly more television since the mid-1960s, the survey data may not be reliable. This was demonstrated by Anderson *et al.'s* study using time-lapse video recording equipment installed in people's homes, which showed that both children and adults spend less time actually **watching** the television than the time the set is switched on.
- According to Cumberbatch, **cartoons** contain a great deal of violence and yet are aimed mainly at children. However, viewers' **perceptions** of violent television content may not correspond with objective counts of violent incidents. Real-life incidents in news and documentaries are generally rated as being more violent than those shown in fictional settings.
- Whilst children and adults tend to give very similar judgements of the **amounts** of violence,

children's **ratings** of cartoons indicate that programmes which objectively contain a large number of violent acts may be subjectively perceived as hardly containing any. Thus, objective assessments of violence alone are not adequate.

- Research into the effects of media violence has used various methodological approaches. One consistent finding from **correlational studies** is that the overall exposure to television violence is related to self-reports of aggressive behaviour. Such data do not allow us to infer cause and effect, since those who watch violent programmes may **differ** in some way from those who do not.

- **Laboratory studies** are designed to detect causal links. However, most use small, unrepresentative samples, and the measures of television viewing and aggression are too far removed from normal everyday behaviour to make them relevant to the real world.

- **Field experiments** are much more ecologically valid. They involve controlled viewing over an extended period of time, mostly with children in group or institutional settings, such as the juvenile delinquents living in 'cottages' studied by Parke *et al.*

- Although such studies show quite consistently that children who watch violent television are more aggressive than those who do not, field experiments do not allow the same degree of control as is possible in the laboratory. Parke *et al.'s* delinquent boys were already living in **groups**, and they were hardly representative of adolescents in general.

- **Longitudinal panel studies** can tell us something about cause and effect, and also involve representative samples. They look at the **cumulative** influence of television (how relationships between television viewing and behaviour develop over time).

- Sims and Bailey reported several American and British studies linking heavy exposure to media violence and subsequent aggressive behaviour. Bailey's study of adolescent murderers and young sex offenders implicated both violent and pornographic videos, especially in the case of adolescents who abused while babysitting. However, not all studies have found such a link.

- **Natural experiments** involve a naturally occurring change, without any manipulation by the researcher. Williams' study of 'Notel' found that verbal and physical aggression in both male and female 6–11-year-olds increased during the two years following the introduction of television.

- Similarly, Charlton's ongoing natural experiment on St Helena is taking advantage of the rare existence of a group of children not previously exposed to television. Far from interfering with the development of social skills and mental capacities, results so far have shown that **pro-social behaviour** had actually **improved** slightly after 15 months of television.

- The American National Institute of Mental Health's review of 2500 laboratory experiments and field studies concluded that most researchers agree that television violence leads to aggressive behaviour in those exposed to it. It is as strongly correlated with aggression as any other behavioural variable that has been measured.

- The four specific effects of television violence that have been investigated are **arousal, disinhibition, imitation** and **desensitisation**.

- Although there does not seem to be any strong overall relationship between perceiving a programme as violent and measures of emotional arousal, more **realistic** violence is correlated with reported arousal and involvement.

- Berkowitz's cue-arousal/aggressive-cue theory is relevant to understanding disinhibition, and imitation was studied by Bandura *et al.* Social learning theorists like Bandura stress the importance of **cognitive factors**, such as the perception and interpretation of violence and how realistic it is, as intervening variables. As with drug tolerance, desensitisation involves the need for increasingly violent programmes to produce an emotional response.

- The call for legislation controlling the supply of videos following the murder of James Bulger was supported by several psychologists, including Newson. Cumberbatch, however, has questioned the validity of the evidence on which her report was based, such as the implication of *Child's Play*.

- Cumberbatch has also criticised the conclusions drawn from Huesmann and Eron's study of six countries. Given the findings of the individual studies, it seems very difficult to justify the overall conclusion that viewing television violence at an early age predicts later aggression. Several other studies cast doubt on the link between television and aggression and it is too easy to blame the media for social problems.

- Television may also have **positive** effects, such as the claim that it can act as a form of **vicarious catharsis**. However, if this is true at all, it is so only for individuals with a particular type of personality or who score high on fantasy, daydreaming and imagination.

- According to Gunter and McAleer, evidence for the **pro-social effects** of television derives from **laboratory studies** with **prepared television/ filmed material** or using **broadcast materials specially produced for teaching social skills** (such as *Sesame Street* and *Mister Rogers' Neighborhood*) or with **programme materials from popular TV series.**
- Evidence also comes from **field studies** relating amount of viewing of pro-social content to strength of pro-social behaviour. The correlations between viewing habits and pro-social behaviour are lower than those between viewing habits and anti-social behaviour. Children may learn the more direct, blatant and physical anti-social behaviours with greater ease than the more verbal and subtle pro-social behaviours. Their relative influence may also be compounded by who typically portrays them (white males and non-white females respectively).
- One approach to **television literacy** involved teaching children to be 'informed consumers' of television through distinguishing between social reality and television make-believe, understanding the nature and purpose of advertisements, and assessing sex-role, and minority-group stereotyping.
- According to Griffiths, little is known about the long-term effects of playing violent **computer games**, but the child's **active involvement** makes them potentially more harmful than television. Whilst there is little more than speculation regarding their effects on aggressive behaviour, several researchers have found evidence for the **pro-social effects** of computer games.
- Their benefits include providing motivation, a sense of confidence, mastery and control and computer-related skills for the future, acting as a catalyst for communication and social interaction, and the opportunity to release stress and aggression in a non-destructive way. Only some of these are based on empirical research findings.
- There is some evidence that news bulletins can induce anxiety and depression in viewers, making it necessary for producers to consider very carefully the emotional impact news might have on their audience. Light-hearted pieces at the end of a news broadcast, such as 'And finally...' on ITN's *News at Ten,* could have beneficial effects.

REFERENCES

ABRAHAMS, C. & STANLEY, E. (1992) *Social Psychology for Nurses*. London: Edward Arnold.

ABRAMS, D., WETHERELL, M., COCHRANE, S., HOGG, M.A. & TURNER, J.C. (1990) Knowing what to think by knowing who you are: Self-categorization and the nature of norm formation. *British Journal of Social Psychology*, 29, 97–119.

ABRAMSON, L.Y., SELIGMAN, M.E.P. & TEASDALE, J.D. (1978) Learned helplessness in humans: Critique and reformulation. *Journal of Abnormal Psychology*, 87, 49–74.

ADLER, A. (1927) *The Practice and Theory of Individual Psychology*. New York: Harcourt Brace Jovanovich.

ADORNO, T.W., FRENKEL-BRUNSWICK, E., LEVINSON, J.D. & SANFORD, R.N. (1950) *The Authoritarian Personality*. New York: Harper & Row.

ALLEN, V.L. & LEVINE, J.M. (1971) Social support and conformity: The role of independent assessment of reality. *Journal of Experimental Social Psychology*, 7, 48–58.

ALLPORT, G.W. (1954) *The Nature of Prejudice*. Reading, MA: Addison-Wesley.

AMATO, P.R. (1983) Helping behaviour in urban and rural environments: Field studies based on a taxonomic organisation of helping episodes. *Journal of Personality and Social Psychology*, 45, 571–586.

AMIR, Y. (1969) Contact hypothesis in ethnic relations. *Psychological Bulletin*, 71, 319–342.

AMIR, Y. (1994) The contact hypothesis in intergroup relations. In W.J. Lonner & R.S. Malpass (Eds.), *Psychology and Culture*. Boston: Allyn & Bacon.

ANCONA, L. & PAREYSON, R. (1968) Contributo allo studio della a aggressione: la dinimica della obbedienza distructiva. *Archivio di Psicologia Neurologia e Psichiatria*, 29, 340–372.

ANDERSON, C.A. & FORD, C.M. (1986) Affect of the game player: Short term effects of highly and mildly aggressive video games. *Personality and Social Psychology Bulletin*, 12, 390–402.

ANDERSON, D.R., LORCH, E.P., FIELD, D.E., COLLINS, P.A. & NATHAN, J.G. (1986) Television viewing at home: Age trends in visual attention and time with TV. *Child Development*, 57, 1024–1033.

ANDERSON, J. (1974) Bystander intervention in an assault. Paper presented at the meeting of the Southeastern Psychological Association, Hollywood, FL.

ARENDT, H. (1965) *Eichmann in Jerusalem: A Report on the Banality of Evil*. New York: Viking.

ARGYLE, M. (1983) *The Psychology of Interpersonal Behaviour* (4th edition). Harmondsworth: Penguin.

ARGYLE, M. & HENDERSON, M. (1984) The rules of friendship. *Journal of Social and Personal Relationships*, 1, 211–237.

ARKIN, R., COOPER, H. & KOLDITZ, T. (1980) A statistical review of the literature concerning the self-serving bias in interpersonal influence situations. *Journal of Personality and Social Psychology*, 48, 435–448.

ARMS, R.L., RUSSELL, G.W. & SANDILANDS, M.I. (1980) Effects of viewing aggressive sports on the hostility of spectators. In R.M. Suinn (Ed.), *Psychology in Sport: Methods and Applications*. Minneapolis: Burgess.

ARMSTRONG, S. (1997) 'Ello, 'ello: Where did all those bodies go? *The Sunday Times*, January 19, 4–5.

ARONSON, E. (1980) *The Social Animal* (3rd edition). San Francisco: W.H. Freeman.

ARONSON, E. (1988) *The Social Animal* (5th edition). New York: Freeman.

ARONSON, E. (1992) *The Social Animal* (6th edition). New York: Freeman.

ARONSON, E., BRIDGEMAN, D.L. & GEFFNER, R. (1978) The effects of a co-operative classroom structure on student behaviour and attitudes. In D. Bar-Tal & L. Saxe (Eds.), *Social Psychology of Education*. New York: Wiley.

ARONSON, E. & LINDER, D. (1965) Gain and loss of esteem as determinants of interpersonal attraction. *Journal of Experimental Social Psychology*, 1, 156–171.

ARONSON, E., WILLERMAN, B. & FLOYD, J. (1966) The effect of a pratfall on increasing attractiveness. *Psychonomic Science*, 4, 227–228.

ASCH, S.E. (1946) Forming impressions of personality. *Journal of Abnormal and Social Psychology*, 41, 258–290.

ASCH, S.E. (1951) Effect of group pressure upon the modification and distortion of judgements. In H. Guetzkow (Ed.), *Groups, Leadership and Men*. Pittsburgh, PA: Carnegie Press.

ASCH, S.E. (1952) *Social Psychology*. Englewood Cliffs, NJ: Prentice Hall.

ASCH, S.E. (1955) Opinions and social pressure. *Scientific American*, 193, 31–35.

ASCH, S.E. (1956) Studies of independence and submission to group pressure: 1: A minority of one against a unanimous majority. *Psychological Monographs*, 70, Whole No. 416.

ASHMORE, R. & DEL BOCA, F. (1976) Psychological approaches to understanding intergroup conflicts. In P. Katz (Ed.), *Towards the Elimination of Racism*. New York: Pergamon.

BAILEY, S. (1993) Fast forward to violence. *Criminal Justice Matters*, 3, 6–7

BALES, R.F. (1950) *Interactional Process Analysis: A Method for the Study of Small Groups*. Reading, MA: Addison Wesley.

BALES, R.F. & SLATER, P. (1955) Role differentiation in small decision-making groups. In T. Parsons & R.F. Bales (Eds.), *Family, Socialisation and Interaction Processes*. New York: Free Press.

BALL, S. & NUKI, P. (1996) Most under-11s watch violent videos. *The Sunday Times*, July 23, 1.

BANDURA, A. (1965) Influence of model's reinforcement contingencies on the acquisition of imitative responses. *Journal of Personality and Social Psychology*, 1, 589–595.

BANDURA, A. (1973) *Aggression: A Social Learning Analysis*. London: Prentice Hall.

BANDURA, A. (1994) Social cognitive theory of mass communication. In J. Bryant & D. Zillman (Eds.), *Media Effects: Advances in Theory and Research*. Hove: Erlbaum.

BANDURA, A., ROSS, D. & ROSS, S.A. (1961) Transmission of aggression through imitation of aggressive models. *Journal of Abnormal and Social Psychology*, 63, 575–582.

BANDURA, A., ROSS, D. & ROSS, S.A. (1963) Imitation of film-mediated aggressive models. *Journal of Abnormal and Social Psychology*, 63, 575–582.

BARKER, R., DEMBO, T. & LEWIN, K. (1941) Frustration and regression: An experiment with young children. *University of Iowa Studies in Child Welfare*, 18, 1–314.

BARON, R.A. (1977) *Human Aggression*. New York: Plenum.

BARON, R.A. (1983) The reduction of human aggression: An incompatible response strategy. In R.G. Geen & E. Donnerstein (Eds.), *Aggression: Theoretical and Empirical Reviews*. New York: Academic Press.

BARON, R.A. (1989) *Psychology: The Essential Science*. London: Allyn & Bacon.

BARON, R.A. & BYRNE, D.S. (1984) *Social Psychology: Understanding Human Interaction* (4th edition). London: Allyn & Bacon.

BARON, R.A. & BYRNE, D.S. (1994) *Social Psychology: Understanding Human Interaction* (7th edition). London: Allyn & Bacon.

BARON, R.A. & RICHARDSON, D.R. (1994) *Human Aggression* (2nd edition). New York: Plenum.

BATSON, C.D. & COKE, J.S. (1981) Empathy: A source of altruistic motivation for helping? In J.P. Rushton & R.M. Sorentino (Eds.), *Altruism and Behaviour: Social, Personality, and Development Prespectives*. Hillsdale, NJ: Erlbaum.

BAUMRIND, D. (1964) Some thoughts on the ethics of research: After reading Milgram's behavioural study of obedience. *American Psychologist*, 19, 421–423.

BELL, P.A. & BARON, R.A. (1974) Effects of heat, noise and provocation on retaliatory evaluative behaviour. *Bulletin of the Psychonomic Society*, 4, 479–481.

BELLUR, R. (1995) Interpersonal attraction revisited: Cross-cultural conceptions of love. *Psychology Review*, 1, 24–26.

BELSON, W.A. (1978) *Television Violence and the Adolescent Boy*. London: Teakfield.

BEM, D.J. (1967) Self-perception: An alternative interpretation of cognitive dissonance phenomena. *Psychological Review*, 74, 183–200.

BEM, D.J. (1972) Self-perception theory. In L. Berkowitz (Ed.), *Advances in Experimental Social Psychology* (Volume 6). New York: Academic Press.

BENEWICK, R. & HOLTON, R. (1987) The peaceful crowd: Crowd solidarity and the Pope's visit to Britain. In G. Gaskell & R. Benewick (Eds.), *The Crowd in Conteporary Britain*. London: Sage.

BENNETT, M. (1993) Introduction. In M. Bennett (Ed.), *The Child as Psychologist: An Introduction to the Development of Social Cognition*. Hemel Hempstead: Harvester Wheatsheaf.

BERKOWITZ, L. (1966) On not being able to aggress. *British Journal of Clinical and Social Psychology*, 5, 130–139.

BERKOWITZ, L. (1968) Impulse, aggression and the gun. *Psychology Today*, September, 18–22.

BERKOWITZ, L. (1978) Whatever happened to the frustration–aggression hypothesis? *American Behavioural Scientist*, 21, 691–708.

BERKOWITZ, L. (1983) Aversively stimulated aggression: Some parallels and differences in research with humans and animals. *American Psychologist* 38, 1135–1144.

BERKOWITZ, L. (1986) *A Survey of Social Psychology* (3rd edition). New York: Holt, Rinehart & Winston.

BERKOWITZ, L. (1989) The frustration–aggression hypothesis: an examination and reformation. *Psychological Bulletin*, 106, 59–73.

BERKOWITZ, L. (1990) On the formation and regulation of anger and aggression – a cognitive neoassociationistic analysis. *American Psychologist*, 45, 494–503.

BERKOWITZ, L. (1993) *Aggression: Its Causes, Consequences and Control*. New York: McGraw-Hill.

BERKOWITZ, L. (1995) A career on aggression. In G.G. Brannigan & M.R. Merrens (Eds.), *The Social Psychologists: Research Adventures*. New York: McGraw-Hill.

BERKOWITZ, L. & GEEN, R.G. (1966) Film violence and the cue properties of available targets. *Journal of Personality and Social Psychology*, 3, 525–530.

BERKOWITZ, L. & LePAGE, A. (1967) Weapons as aggression-eliciting stimuli. *Journal of Personality and Social Psychology*, 7, 202–207.

BERSCHEID, E., DION, K., HATFIELD, E. & WALSTER, G.W. (1971) Physical attractiveness and dating choice: A test of the matching hypothesis. *Journal of Experimental and Social Psychology*, 7, 173–189.

BERSCHEID, E. & WALSTER, E.M. (1974) Physical attractiveness. In L. Berkowitz (ed.), *Advances in Experimental Social Psychology*, Vol.7. New York: Academic Press.

BERSCHEID, E. & WALSTER, E.M. (1978) *Interpersonal Attraction* (2nd edition). Reading, MA: Addison-Wesley.

BICKMAN, L. (1971) The effects of another bystander's ability to help on bystander intervention in an emergency. *Journal of Experimental Social Psychology*, 7, 367–379.

BICKMAN, L. (1974) The social power of a uniform. *Journal of Applied Social Psychology*, 1, 47–61.

BIERHOFF, H.W. & KLEIN, R. (1988) Prosocial behaviour. In M. Hewstone, W. Stroebe, J.P. Codol & G.M. Stephenson (Eds.), *Introduction to Social Psychology*. Oxford: Blackwell.

BIRCH, B. (1985) *A Question of Race*. London: Macdonald and Co.

BLAU, P.M. (1964) *Exchange and Power in Social Life*. New York: Wiley.

BLIESZNER, R. & ADAMS, R. (1992) *Adult Friendships*. Newbury Park: Sage.

BLOOD, R.O. & WOLFE, D.M. (1969) *Husbands and Wives: The Dynamics of Married Lives*. New York: Free Press.

BOGDONOFF, M.D., KLEIN, R.F., ESTES, E.H., SHAW, D.M. & BACK, K. (1961) The modifying effect of conforming behaviour upon lipid responses accompanying CNS arousal. *Clinical Research*, 9, 135.

BOWER, G. & HILGARD, E. (1981) *Theories of Learning*. Englewood Cliffs, New Jersey: Prentice-Hall.

BRADBURY, T.N. & FINCHAM, F.D. (1990) Attributions in marriage: Review and critique. *Psychological Bulletin*, 107, 3–33.

BRADDOCK, J.H. (1985) School desegregation and black assimilation. *Journal of Social Issues*, 41, 9–29.

BREHM, J.W. (1966) *A Theory of Psychological Reactance*. New York: Academic Press.

BREHM, S.S. (1992) *Intimate Relationships* (2nd edition). New York: McGraw-Hill.

BREWER, M.B. & KRAMER, R.M. (1985) The psychology of intergroup attitudes and behaviour. *Annual Review of Psychology*, 36, 219–243.

BRIGHAM, J. (1986) *Social Psychology*. Boston: Little, Brown.

BRIGHAM, J. & WEISSBACH, T. (1972) *Racial Attitudes in America: Analyses and Findings of Social Psychology*. New York: Harper & Row.

BRIGHAM, J.W. & MALPASS, R.S. (1985) The role of experience and contact in the recognition of faces of own- and other-race persons. *Journal of Social Issues*, 41, 139–155.

BRISLIN, R. (1993) *Understanding Culture's Influence on Behaviour*. Orlando, FL: Harcourt Brace Jovanovich.

BRONFENBRENNER, U. (1960) Freudian theories of identification and their derivatives. *Child Development*, 31, 15–40.

BROOKS, J. & WATKINS, M. (1989) Recognition memory and the mere exposure effect. *Journal of Experimental Psychology: Learning, Memory and Cognition*, 15, 968–976.

BROOM, L. & SELZNICK, P. (1977) *Sociology* (6th edition). London: Harper & Row.

BROWN, H. (1985) *People, Groups and Society*. Milton Keynes: Open University Press.

BROWN, J.D. & SMART, S. (1991) The self and social conduct: Linking self-representations to prosocial behaviour. *Journal of Personality and Social Psychology*, 60, 368–375.

BROWN, R. (1954) Mass phenomena. In G. lindzey (Ed.), *Handbook of Social Psychology*. London: Addison-Wesley.

BROWN, R. (1965) *Social Psychology*. New York: The Free Press.

BROWN, R. (1986) *Social Psychology: The Second Edition*. New York: Free Press.

BROWN, R.J. (1988) Intergroup relations. In M. Hewstone, W. Stroebe, J.P. Codol & G.M. Stephenson (Eds.), *Introduction to Social Psychology*. Oxford: Blackwell.

BROWN, R.J. (1996) Intergroup relations. In M. Hewstone, W. Stroebe & G.M. Stephenson (Eds.), *Introduction to Social Psychology* (2nd edition). Oxford: Blackwell.

BROWN, R.J. & TURNER, J.C. (1981) Interpersonal and intergroup behaviour. In J.C. Turner & H. Giles (Eds.), *Intergroup Behaviour*. Oxford: Blackwell.

BRUCE, V., BURTON, A.M. & DENCH, N. (1994) What's distinctive about a distinctive face? *Quarterly Journal of Experimental Psychology*, 47A, 119–141.

BRUNER, J.S. & TAGIURI, R. (1954) The perception of people. In G. Lindzey (Ed.), *Handbook of Social Psychology* (Volume 2). London: Addison Wesley.

BRYANT, J. & ZILLMAN, D. (Eds.) (1994) *Media Effects: Advances in Theory and Research*. Hove: Erlbaum.

BUEHLER, C. & LEGGE, B.H. (1993) Mothers' receipt of social support and their psychological well being following marital separation. *Journal of Social and Personal Relationships*, 10, 21–38.

BURGER, F. (1982) The 46–hour-a-week habit. *The Boston Globe*, May 2.

BURR, W.R. (1970) Satisfaction with various aspects of marriage over the life cycle: A random middle class sample. *Journal of Marriage and the Family*, 32, 29–37.

BUSS, D.M. (1988) The evolutionary biology of love. In R.J. STERNBERG & M.L. BARNES (Eds.) *The Psychology of Love*. New Haven, CT: Yale University Press.

BUSS, D.M. (1989) Sex differences in human mate preferences: Evolutionary hypotheses tested in 37 cultures. *Behavioural and Brain Sciences*, 12, 1–49.

BUUNK, B.P. (1996) Affiliation, attraction and close relationships. In M. Hewstone, W. Stroebe & G.M. Stephenson (Eds.), *Introduction to Social Psychology* (2nd edition). Oxford: Blackwell.

BYRNE, D.S. (1971) *The Attraction Paradigm*. New York: Academic Press.

BYRNE, D.S. & MURNEN, S. (1988) Maintaining loving relationships. In R.J. Sternberg & M. Barnes (Eds.), *The Psychology of Loving*. New Haven, CT: Yale University Press.

CAMPBELL, D.T. (1967) Stereotypes and the perception of group differences. *American Psychologist*, 22, 817–829.

CANTRIL, H. (1941) *The Psychology of Social Movements*. New York: Wiley.

CARLSON, N.R. (1987) *Discovering Psychology*. London: Allyn & Bacon.

CARNEGIE, D. (1937) *How to Win Friends and Influence People*. New York: Simon & Schuster.

CHAIKIN, A.L. & DARLEY, J.M. (1973) Victim or perpetrator? Defensive attribution of responsibility and the need for order and justice. *Journal of Personality and Social Psychology*, 25, 268–275.

CHAPMAN, L.J. & CHAPMAN, J.P. (1969) Illusory correlation as an obstacle to the use of valid psychodiagnostic signs. *Journal of Abnormal Psychology*, 74, 271–280.

CHERRY, F. & BYRNE, D.S. (1976) Authoritarianism. In T. Blass (Ed.), *Personality Variables in Social Behaviour*. Hillsdale, NJ: Erlbaum.

CLAMP, A. & RUSSELL, J. (1998) *Comparative Psychology*. London: Hodder & Stoughton.

CLARK, K.B. & CLARK, M. (1947) Racial identification and preference in negro children. In T.M. Newcomb & E.L. Hartley (Eds.), *Readings in Social Psychology*. New York: Holt.

CLARK, R.D. & MAASS, A. (1988) The role of social categorization and perceived source credibility in minority influence. *European Journal of Social Psychology*, 18, 381–394.

CLARK, R.D. & WORD, L.E. (1974) Where is the apathetic bystander? Situational characteristics of the emergency. *Journal of Personality and Social Psychology*, 29, 279–287.

CLORE, G.L., BRAY, R.M., ITKIN, S.M. & MURPHY, P. (1978) Interracial attitudes and behaviour at a summer camp. *Journal of Personality and Social Psychology*, 36, 706–712.

CLORE, G.L. & BYRNE, D.S. (1974) A reinforcement-affect model of attraction. In T.L. Huston (Ed.), *Foundations of Interpersonal Attraction*. New York: Academic Press.

COCHRANE, R. (1983) *The Social Creation of Mental Illness*. London: Longman.

COCHRANE, R. (1996) Marriage and madness. *Psychology Review*, 3, 2–5.

COHEN, M. & DAVIS, N. (1981) *Medication Errors: Causes and Prevention*. Philadelphia: G.F. Stickley.

COLLETT, P. (1993) *Foreign Bodies*. London: Simon & Schuster.

COLMAN, A.M. (1987) *Facts, Fallacies and Frauds in Psychology*. London: Unwin Hyman.

COMSTOCK, G. & PAIK, H. (1991) *Television and the American Child*. New York: Academic Press.

COOK, E. (1997) Is marriage driving women mad? *Real Life. Independent on Sunday*, August 10, 1–2.

COOK, S.W. (1984) The 9154 social science statement and school desegregation. *American Psychologist*, 39, 819–832.

COOLICAN, H. (1997) Thinking about prejudice. *Psychology Review*, 4, 26–29.

COOPER, G. (1994) Napoleon island to end TV exile. *Independent on Sunday*, June 12, 7.

COOPER, H.M. (1979) Statistically combining independent studies: A meta-analysis of sex differences in conformity research. *Journal of Personality and Social Psychology*, 37, 131–146.

CORSARO, W.A. (1993) Interpretive reproduction in the 'scuola materna'. *European Journal of Psychology of Education*, 8, 357–374.

COSTANTINI, E. & CRAIK, K.H. (1980) Personality and politicians: California party leaders, 1960–1976. *Journal of Personality and Social Psychology*, 38, 641–661.

COUCH, C.J. (1968) Collective behaviour: An examination of some stereotypes. *Social Problems*, 15, 310–322.

CRAMER, D. (1994) Personal relationships. In D. Tantam & M. Birchwood (Eds.), *Seminars in Psychology and the Social Sciences*. London: Gaskell Press.

CRAMER, D. (1995) Special issue on personal relationships. *The Psychologist*, 8, 58–59.

CRAMER, P. & MECHEM, M.B. (1982) Violence in children's animated television. *Journal of Applied Developmental Psychology*, 3, 23–29.

CRIDER, A.B., GOETHALS, G.R., KAVANAUGH, R.D. & SOLOMON, P.R. (1989) *Psychology* (3rd edition). London: Scott, Foresman and Company.

CROCKER, J., THOMPSON, L., McGRAW, K. & INGERMAN, C. (1987) Downward comparison, prejudice, and evaluation of others: Effects of self-esteem and threat. *Journal of Personality and Social Psychology*, 52, 907–916.

CROOKS, R.L. & STEIN, J. (1991) *Psychology: Science, Behaviour and Life*. New York: Harcourt Brace Jovanovich.

CRUTCHFIELD, R.S. (1954) A new technique for measuring individual differences in conformity to group judgement. *Proceedings of the Invitational Conference on Testing Problems*, 69–74.

CRUTCHFIELD, R.S. (1955) Conformity and character. *American Psychologist*, 10, 191–198.

CUMBERBATCH, G. (1987) *The Portrayal of Violence on British Television*. London: BBC Publications.

CUMBERBATCH, G. (1997) Media violence: Science and common sense. *Psychology Review*, 3, 2–7.

CURPHEY, M. (1995) Witness pursued thief by taxi. *The Times*, June 8, 14.

CURTIS, R. & MILLER, K. (1988) Believing another likes or dislikes you: Behaviour making the beliefs come true. *Journal of Personality and Social Psychology*, 51, 284–290.

DARLEY, J.M. (1991) Altruism and prosocial behaviour research: Reflections and prospects. In M.S. Clark (Ed.), *Prosocial Behaviour, Review of Personality and Social Psychology*, 12. Newbury Park: CA: Sage.

DARLEY, J.M. & BATSON, C.D. (1973) From Jerusalem to Jericho: A study of situational and dispositional variables in helping behaviour. *Journal of Personality and Social Psychology*, 27, 100–108.

DARLEY, J.M. & HUFF, C.W. (1990) Heightened damage assessment as a result of the intentionality of the damage causing act. *British Journal of Social Psychology*, 29, 181–188.

DARLEY, J.M. & LATANÉ, B. (1968) Bystander intervention in emergencies: Diffusion of responsibility. *Journal of Personality and Social Psychology*, 8, 377–383.

DAVIES, J.C. (1969) The J-curve of rising and declining satisfactions as a cause of some great revolutions and a contained rebellion. In H.D. Graham & T.R. Gurr (Eds.), *The History of Violence in America: Historical and Comparative Perspectives*. New York: Praeger.

DAVIS, J.A. (1959) A formal interpretation of the theory of relative deprivation. *Sociometry*, 22, 280–296.

DAVISON, G.C. & NEALE, J.M. (1994) *Abnormal Psychology* (6th edition). New York: Wiley.

DAWKINS, R. (1976) *The Selfish Gene*. Oxford: Oxford University Press.

DE PAULO, B.M. & FISHER, J.D. (1981) Too tuned-out to take: The role of non-verbal sensitivity in help-seeking. *Personality and Social Psychology Bulletin*, 7, 201–205.

DEAUX, K. (1972) To err is humanizing: But sex makes a difference. *Representative Research in Social Psychology*, 5, 20–28.

DEAUX, K., DANE, F.C. & WRIGHTSMAN, L.S. (1993) *Social Psychology in the 90s*. Pacific Grove, CA: Brooks/Cole.

DERMER, M. & THIEL, D.L. (1975) When beauty may fail. *Journal of Personality and Social Psychology*, 31, 1168–1176.

DEUTSCH, F.M. & LAMBERTI, D.M. (1986) Does social approval increase helping? *Personality and Social Psychology Bulletin*, 12, 149–157.

DEUTSCH, M. & COLLINS, M.E. (1951) *Interracial Housing: A Psychological Evaluation of a Social Experiment*. Minneapolis, MN: University of Minnesota Press.

DEUTSH, M & GERARD, H.B. (1955) A study of normative and informational social influence upon individual judgement. *Journal of Abnormal and Social Psychology*, 51, 629–636.

DI GIACOMO, J.P. (1980) Intergroup alliances and rejections within a protest movement (analysis of social representations). *European Journal of Social Psychology*, 10, 329–344.

DIENER, E. (1979) Deindividuation, self-awareness and disinhibition. *Journal of Personality and Social Psychology*, 37, 1160–1171.

DIENER, E. (1980) Deindividuation: The absence of self-awareness and self-regulation in group members. In P.B. Paulus (Ed.), *Psychology of Group Influence*. Hillsdale, NJ: Erlbaum.

DIENER, E., FRASER, S.C., BEAMAN, A.L. & KELEM, R.T. (1976) Effects of deindividuation variables on stealing among Halloween trick-or-treaters. *Journal of Personality and Social Psychology*, 33, 178–183.

DION, K.K. (1972) Physical attractiveness and evaluation of children's transgressions. *Journal of Personality and Social Psychology*, 24, 207–213.

DION, K.K. & BERSCHEID, E. (1974) Physical attractiveness and peer perception among children. *Sociometry*, 37, 1–12.

DION, K.K., BERSCHEID, E. & WALSTER, E. (1972) What is beautiful is good. *Journal of Personality and Social Psychology*, 24, 285–290.

DION, K.K. & DION, K.L. (1995) On the love of beauty and the beauty of love: Two psychologists study attraction. In G.G. Brannigan & M.R. Merrens (Eds.), *The Social Psychologists: Research Adventures*. New York: McGraw-Hill.

DOLLARD, J., DOOB, L.W., MOWRER, O.H. & SEARS, R.R. (1939) *Frustration and Aggression*. New Haven, CT: Harvard University Press.

DONNERSTEIN, E. & BERKOWITZ, L. (1981) Victim reactions in aggressive erotic films as a factor in violence against women. *Journal of Personality and Social Psychology*, 41, 710–724.

DONNERSTEIN, E. & DONNERSTEIN, M. (1976) Research in the control of interracial aggression. In R.G. Geen & E.O'Neil (Eds.) *Perspectives on Aggression*. New York: Academic Press.

DONNERSTEIN, E., LINZ, D. & PENROD, S. (1987), *The Question of Pornography*. London: The Free Press.

DONNERSTEIN, E. & WILSON, W. (1976) Effects of noise and perceived control on ongoing and subsequent aggressive behaviour. *Journal of Personality and Social Psychology*, 34, 774–781.

DOTY, R.M., PETERSON, W.E. & WINTER, D.G. (1991) Threat and authoritarianism in the United States 1978–1987. *Journal of Personality and Social Psychology*, 61, 629–640.

DOVIDIO, J.F. (1995) With a little help from my friends. In G.G. Brannigan & M.R. Merrens (Eds.), *The Social Psychologists: Research Adventures*. New York: McGraw-Hill.

DOVIDIO, J.F., ALLEN, J.L. & SCHROEDER, D.A. (1990) Specificity of empathy-induced helping: Evidence for altruistic motivation. *Journal of Personality and Social Psychology*, 59, 249–260.

DOVIDIO, J.F., PILIAVIN, J.A., GAERTNER, S.L., SCHROEDER, D.A. & CLARK, R.D. (1991) The arousal: Cost-reward model and the process of intervention. In M.S. Clark (Ed.), *Prosocial Behaviour: Review of Personality and Social Psychology, 12*. Newbury Park, CA: Sage.

DOWD, M. (1984) Twenty years after the murder of Kitty Genovese, the question remains: Why? *The New York Times*, B1, B4.

DRABMAN, R.S. & THOMAS, M.H. (1974) Does media violence increase children's toleration of real-life aggression? *Developmental Psychology*, 10, 418–421.

DUCK, S. (Ed.) (1982) *Personal Relationships 4: Dissolving Personal Relationships*. London: Academic Press.

DUCK, S. (1988) *Relating to Others*. Milton Keynes: Open University Press.

DUCK, S. (1992) *Human Relationships* (2nd edition). London: Sage.

DUCK, S. (1995) Repelling the study of attraction. *The Psychologist*, 8, 60–63.

DURKHEIM, E. (1898) Representations individuelles et representations collectives. *Revue de Metaphysique et de Morale*, 6, 273–302.

DURKIN, K. (1995) *Developmental Social Psychology: From Infancy to Old Age*. Oxford: Blackwell.

EAGLY, A.H. & CROWLEY, M. (1986) Gender and helping behaviour: A meta-analytic review of the social psychological literature. *Psychological Bulletin*, 100, 232–308.

EAGLY, A.H. & STEFFEN, V.J. (1984) Gender stereotypes stem from the distribution of men and women into social roles. *Journal of Personality and Social Psychology*, 46, 735–754.

EISER, J.R. (1983) From attributions to behaviour. In M. Hewstone (Ed.), *Attribution Theory: Social and Functional Extensions*. Oxford: Blackwell.

ELLIOTT, J. (1977) The power and pathology of prejudice. In P. Zimbardo & F.L. Ruch (Eds.), *Psychology and Life* (9th edition). Glenview, IL: Scott, Forseman and Co.

ELLIOTT, J. (1990) In *Discovering Psychology. Program 20* (PBS Video Series). Washington, DC: Annenberg/CPB Program.

EMLER, N., OHANA, J. & DICKINSON, J. (1990) Children's representations of social relations. In G. Duveen & B.Lloyd (Eds.), *Social Representations and the Development of Knowledge*. Cambridge: Cambridge University Press.

ERIKSON, E.H. (1963) *Childhood and Society* (2nd edition). New York: Norton.

ERON, L.D. & HUESMANN, L.R. (1985) The role of television in the development of pro-social and anti-social behaviour. In D. Olweus, M. Radke-Yarrow, & J. Block (Eds.), *Development of Anti-Social and Pro-Social Behaviour*. Orlando, FL: Academic Press.

EYSENCK, H.J. (1954) *The Psychology of Politics*. London: Routledge & Kegan Paul.

FARR, R.M. & MOSCOVICI, S. (Eds.) (1984) *Social Representations*. Cambridge: Cambridge University Press.

FEATHER, N.T. & SIMON, J.G. (1971) Attribution of responsibility and valence of success and failure in relation to initial confidence and task performance. *Journal of Personality and Social Psychology*, 18, 173–188.

FELIPE, N.J. & SOMMER, R. (1966) Invasion of personal space. *Social Problems*, 14, 206–214.

FELMLEE, D.H. (1995) Fatal attractions: Affection and disaffection in intimate relationships. *Journal of Social and Personal Relationships*, 12, 295–311.

FESTINGER, L. (1954) A theory of social comparison processes. *Human Relations*, 7, 117–140.

FESTINGER, L., PEPITONE, A. & NEWCOMB, T. (1952) Some consequences of deindividuation in a group. *Journal of Abnormal and Social Psychology*, 47, 382–389.

FESTINGER, L., SCHACHTER, S. & BACK, K. (1950) *Social Pressures in Informal Groups: A Study of Human Factors in Housing*. Stanford, CA: Stanford University Press.

FIEDLER, F.E. (1964) A contingency model of leadership effectiveness. In J. Berkowitz (Ed.), *Group Processes*. New York: Academic Press.

FIEDLER, F.E. (1967) *A Theory of Leadership Effectiveness*. New York: McGraw-Hill.

FIEDLER, F.E. (1981) Leadership effectiveness. *American Behavioural Scientist*, 24, 619–632.

FIEDLER, F.E. & CHEMERS, M. (1984) *Improving Leadership Effectiveness: The Leader Match Concept*. New York: Wiley.

FLETCHER, G.J. & WARD, C. (1988) Attribution theory and processes: Cross-cultural perspectives. In M.Bond (Ed.), *The Cross-Cultural Challenge to Psychology*. Newbury Park, CA: Sage.

FISKE, S.T. & NEUBERG, S.L. (1990) A continuum of impression formation, from category-based to individuating processes: Influences of information and motivation on attention and interpretation. In L. Berkowitz (Ed.), *Advances in Experimental Social Psychology* (Volume 23). New York: Academic Press.

FISKE, S.T. & TAYLOR, S.E. (1991) *Social Cognition* (2nd edition). New York: McGraw-Hill.

FORD, C.S. & BEACH, F.A. (1951) *Patterns of Sexual Behaviour*. New York: Harper & Row.

FREAN, A. (1994) Researchers study TV's arrival on media-free island. *The Times*, June 6, 8.

FREAN, A. (1995) Getting a kick from TV violence. *The Times*, August 23, 31.

FREEDMAN, F. (1984) Effects of television violence on aggression. *Psychological Bulletin*, 96, 227–246.

FRENCH, J.R.P. & RAVEN, B.H. (1959) The bases of social power. In D. Cartwright (Ed.), *Studies in Social Power*. Ann Arbour, MI: Institute for Social Research, University of Michigan.

FREUD, S. (1920/1984) *Beyond the Pleasure Principle*. Pelican Freud Library (11). Harmondsworth: Penguin.

FREUD, S. (1921) *Group Psychology and the Analysis of the Ego*. (Standard Edition, Volume 18.) London: The Hogarth Press (1955).

FREUD, S. (1923/1984) *The Ego and the Id*. Pelican Freud Library (11). Harmondsworth: Penguin.

FRODI, A. (1975) The effect of exposure to weapons on aggressive behaviour from a cross-cultural perspective. *International Journal of Psychology*, 10, 283–292.

FROMM, E. (1941) *Escape From Freedom*. New York: Farrar & Rinehart.

FROMM, E. (1962) *The Art of Loving*. London: Unwin Books.

GADOW, J.D. & SPRAFKIN, J. (1989) Field experiments of television violence: Evidence for an environmental hazard? *Paediatrics*, 83, 399–405.

GADOW, J.D. & SPRAFKIN, J. (1993) Television violence and children. *Journal of Emotional and Behavioural Disorders*, 1, 54–63.

GAHAGAN, J. (1980) Social interaction. In J. RADFORD & E. GOVIER (Eds.) *A Textbook of Psychology*. London: Sheldon Books.

GAHAGAN, J. (1991) Understanding other people, understanding self. In J. Radford & E. Govier (Eds.), *A Textbook of Psychology* (2nd edition). London: Routledge.

GAMSON, W.B., FIREMAN, B. & RYTINA, S. (1982) *Encounters with Unjust Authority*. Hounwood, IL: Dorsey Press.

GEEN, R.G. & BERKOWITZ, L. (1966) Some conditions facilitating the occurrence of aggression after the observation of violence. *Journal of Personality*, 35, 666–676.

GEEN, R.G., STONNER, D. & SHOPE, G.L. (1975) The facilitation of aggression: A study in response inhibition and disinhibition. *Journal of Personality and Social Psychology*, 31, 721–726.

GERBNER, G. (1972) Violence in television drama: Trends and symbolic functions. In G.A. Comstock & E.A. Rubenstein (Eds.), *Television and Social Behaviour, Volume 1, Media Content and Control*. Washington, DC: US Government Printing Office.

GERBNER, G. & GROSS, L. (1976) Living with television: The violence profile. *Journal of Communication*, 26, 173–199.

GERBNER, G., GROSS, L., MORGAN, M. & SIGNORIELLI, N. (1980) The 'mainstreaming' of America: Violence profile No. II. *Journal of Communication*, 30, 10–29.

GERBNER, G., GROSS, L., SIGNORIELLI, N. & MORGAN, M. (1986) Television's mean world: Violence profile No. 14–15. Philadelphia: Annenberg School of Communications, University of Pennsylvania.

GERGEN, K.J. & GERGEN, M.M. (1981) *Social Psychology*. New York: Harcourt Brace Jovanovich.

GERGEN, K.J., GERGEN, M.M. & BARTON, W. (1973) Deviance in the dark. *Psychology Today*, 7, 129–130.

GIDDENS, A. (1993) *Sociology*. Cambridge: Polity Press.

GILBERT, D.T. (1995) Attraction and interpersonal perception. In A. Tesser (Ed.), *Advanced Social Psychology*. New York: McGraw-Hill.

GILBERT, G.M. (1951) Stereotype persistence and change among college students. *Journal of Abnormal and Social Psychology*, 46, 245–254.

GILBERT, S.J. (1981) Another look at the Milgram obedience studies: The role of the graduated series of shocks. *Personality and Social Psychology Bulletin*, 7, 690–695.

GILFORD, R. & BENGSTON, V. (1979) Measuring marital satisfaction in three generations: Positive and negative dimensions. *Journal of Marriage and the Family*, 41, 387–398.

GILOVICH, T. (1983) Biased evaluation and persistence in gambling. *Journal of Personality and Social Psychology*, 44, 1110–1126.

GOFFMAN, E. (1968) *Asylums – Essay on the Social Situation of Mental Patients and Other Inmates*. Harmondsworth: Penguin.

GOFFMAN, E. (1971) *The Presentation of Self in Everyday Life*. Harmondsworth: Penguin.

GOLDSTEIN, A.P., CARR, E.D., DAVIDSON, W.S. & WEHR, P. (1981) *In Response to Aggression: Methods of Control and Prosocial Alternatives*. New York: Pergamon.

GOODWIN, R. (1991) A re-examination of Rusbult's responses to dissatisfaction typology. *Journal of Social and Personal Relationships*, 8, 569–574.

GOODWIN, R. (1995) Personal relationships across cultures. *The Psychologist*, 8, 73–75.

GREENBERG, J., PSYZCZYNSKI, T. & SOLOMON, S. (1982) The self-serving attributional bias: Beyond self-presentation. *Journal of Experimental Social Psychology*, 18, 56–67.

GREENFIELD, P.M. (1984) *Mind and the Media: The Effects of Television, Video Games and Computers*. Cambridge, MA: Harvard University Press.

GRIFFITHS, M. (1993) Are computer games bad for children? *The Psychologist*, 6, 401–407.

GRIFFITHS, M. (1997) Video games and aggression. *The Psychologist*, 10, 397–401.

GROSS, R.D. (1994) *Key Studies in Psychology* (2nd edition). London: Hodder & Stoughton.

GROSS, R.D. (1996) *Psychology: The Science of Mind and Behaviour* (3rd edition). London: Hodder & Stoughton.

GROSS, R. & McILVEEN, R. (1997) *Cognitive Psychology*. London: Hodder & Stoughton.

GROSS, R. & McILVEEN, R. (1998) *Psychology: A New Introduction*. London: Hodder & Stoughton.

GRUSH, J.E. (1976) Attitude formation and mere exposure phenomena: A non-artifactual explanation of empirical findings. *Journal of Personality and Social Psychology*, 33, 281–290.

GUNTER, B. & McALEER, J.L. (1990) *Children and Television – The One-Eyed Monster?*. London: Routledge.

GUPTA, U. & SINGH, P. (1992) Exploratory study of love and liking and types of marriage. *Indian Journal of Applied Psychology*, 19, 92–97.

HAGELL, A. & NEWBURN, T. (1994) *Young Offenders and the Media*. London: Batsford.

HALL, E.T. (1959) *The Silent Language*. New York: Doubleday.

HALLORAN, J.D. & CROLL, P. (1972) Television programmes in Great Britain. In G.A. Comstock & E.A. Rubenstein (Eds.), *Television and Social Behaviour, Volume 1, Media Content and Control*. Washington, DC: US Government Printing Office.

HALPIN, A. & WINER, B. (1952) *The Leadership Behaviour of the Airplane Commander*. Columbus, OH: Ohio State University Research Foundation.

HAMILTON, D.L. & GIFFORD, R.K. (1976) Illusory correlation in interpersonal perception: A cognitive basis of stereotypic judgements. *Journal of Experimental Social Psychology*, 12, 392–407.

HAMILTON, V.L. (1978) Obedience and responsibility: A jury simulation. *Journal of Personality and Social Psychology*, 36, 126–146.

HAMILTON, W.D. (1964) The genetic evolution of social behaviour, I and II. *Journal of Theoretical Biology*, 7, 1–16, 17–52.

HARRÉ, R. (1983) *Personal Being*. Oxford: Blackwell.

HARVEY, J.H. & WEARY, G. (1984) Current issues in attribution theory and research. *Annual Review of Psychology*, 35, 427–459.

HATFIELD, E. & RAPSON, R. (1987) Passionate love/sexual desire: Can the same paradigm explain both? *Archives of Sexual Behaviour*, 16, 259–278.

HATFIELD, E. & SPRECHER, S. (1986) *Mirror, Mirror...The Importance of Looks in Everyday Life*. Albany, NY: State University of New York at Albany Press.

HATFIELD, E. & WALSTER, G.W. (1985) *A New Look at Love*. Lanham, MD: University Press of America.

HAYES, N. (1994) *Foundations of Psychology: An Introductory Text*. London: Routledge.

HAYES, N. (1997) Social representations: A European theory. *Psychology Review*, 4, 13–17.

HEAROLD, S. (1986) A synthesis of 1043 effects of television on social behaviour. In G. Comstock (Ed.), *Public Communication and Behaviour*. New York: Academic Press.

HEIDER, F. (1946) Attitudes and cognitive organisation. *Journal of Psychology*, 21, 107–112.

HEIDER, F. (1958) *The Psychology of Interpersonal Relations*. New York: Wiley.

HENDRICK, S.S., HENDRICK, C. & ADLER, N.L. (1988) Romantic relationships: Love, satisfaction and staying together. *Journal of Personality & Social Psychology*, 54, 980–988.

HENSLEY, W.E. (1981) The effects of attire, location, and sex on aiding behaviour: A similarity explanation. *Journal of Non-Verbal Behaviour*, 6, 3–11.

HEPWORTH, J.T. & WEST, S.G. (1988) Lynchings and the economy: A time series analysis of Hovland and Sears (1940). *Journal of Personality and Social Psychology*, 55, 239–247.

HEWSTONE, M. & BROWN, R.J. (1986) Contact is not enough: An intergroup perspective on the contact hypothesis. In M. Hewstone & R.J. Brown (Eds.), *Contact and Conflict in Inter-group Encounters*. Oxford: Blackwell.

HEWSTONE, M. & FINCHAM, F. (1996) Attribution theory and research: Basic issues and applications. In M. Hewstone, W. Stroebe & G.M. Stephenson (Eds.), *Introduction to Social Psychology* (2nd edition). Oxford: Blackwell.

HEWSTONE, M. & JASPARS, J.M.F. (1982) Explanations for racial discrimination: The effect of group discussion on intergroup attributions. *European Journal of Social Psychology*, 12, 1–16.

HEWSTONE, M., STROEBE, W. & STEPHENSON, G.M. (1996) *Introduction to Social Psychology* (2nd edition). Oxford: Blackwell.

HILL, C.Y., RUBIN, Z. & PEPLAU, A. (1976) Breakups before marriage: The end of 103 affairs. *Journal of Social Issues*, 32, 147–167.

HILTON, D.J. & SLUGOSKI, B.R. (1986) Knowledge-based causal attribution: The Abnormal Conditions Focus model. *Psychological Review*, 93, 75–88.

HINDE, R.A. (1974) *Biological Bases of Human Social Behaviour*. New York: McGraw-Hill.

HIRSCH, H. (1995) *Genocide and the Politics of Memory*. Chapel Hill, NC: The University of North Carolina Press.

HOBBES, T. (1651) *Leviathan*. London: Dent, 1914.

HOFLING, K.C., BROTZMAN, E., DALRYMPLE, S., GRAVES, N. & PIERCE, C.M. (1966) An experimental study in the nurse–physician relationships. *Journal of Nervous and Mental Disorders*, 143, 171–180.

HOGG, M.A. & ABRAMS, D. (1988) *Social Identifications: A Social Psychology of Intergroup Relations and Group Processes*. London: Routledge.

HOGG, M.A. & VAUGHAN, G.M. (1995) *Social Psychology: An Introduction*. Hemel Hempstead: Prentice Hall/Harvester Wheatsheaf.

HOLDAWAY, S. (1988) *Crime and Deviance*. London: Macmillan.

HOLLANDER, E.P. (1958) Conformity, status, and idiosyncrasy credit. *Psychological Review*, 65, 117–127.

HOLLANDER, E.P. (1985) Leadership and power., In G. Lindsay & E. Aronson (Eds.), *Handbook of Social Psychology* (3rd edition). New York: Random House.

HOLLIN, C. & HOWELLS, K. (1997) Controlling violent behaviour. *Psychology Review*, 3, 10–14.

HOMANS, G.C. (1974) *Social Behaviour: Its Elementary Forms* (2nd edition). New York: Harcourt Brace Jovanovich.

HORTON, P.B. & HUNT, C.L. (1976) *Sociology* (4th edition). New York: McGraw-Hill.

HOUSTON, J.P., HAMMEN, C., PADILLA, A. & BEE, H. (1991) *Introduction to Psychology* (3rd edition). London: Harcourt Brace Jovanovich.

HOVLAND, C.I. & SEARS, R.R. (1940) Minor studies in aggression, VI: Correlation of lynchings with economic indices. *Journal of Psychology*, 2, 301–310.

HOWARD, J.A., BLUMSTEIN, P. & SCHWARTZ, P. (1987) Social or evolutionary theories: Some observations on preferences in mate selection. *Journal of Personality and Social Psychology*, 53, 194–200.

HU, Y. & GOLDMAN, N. (1990) Mortality differentials by marital status: An international comparison. *Demography*, 27, 233–250.

HUBBARD, P. (1991) Evaluating computer games for language learning. *Simulation and Gaming*, 22, 220–223.

HUCZYNSKI, A. & BUCHANAN, D. (1991) *Organisational Behaviour: An Introductory Text* (2nd edition). Hemel Hempstead: Prentice-Hall.

HUESMANN, L.R. & ERON, L.D. (Eds.) (1986) *Television and the Aggresive Child: A Cross-National Comparison*. Hove: Erlbaum.

HUESMANN, L.R., ERON, L.D., KLEIN, R., BRICE, P. & FISCHER, P. (1983) Mitigating the imitation of aggressive behaviours by changing children's attitudes about media violence. *Journal of Personality and Social Psychology*, 44, 899–910.

HUMPHREYS, N. (Ed.) (1975) *Vital Statistics: A Memorial Volume of Selections from the Reports and Writings of William Farr*. Metuchen, NJ: Scarecrow Press.

HUMPHREYS, P.W. (1994) Obedience after Milgram. *Psychology Review*, 1, 2–5.

HUSTON, T. & KORTE, C. (1976) The responsive bystander: Why he helps. In T. Lickona (Ed.), *Moral Development and Behaviour*. New York: Holt, Rinehart & Winston.

HUSTON, T., RUGGERIO, M., CONNER, R. & GEIS, G. (1981) Bystander intervention into crime: A study based on naturally occurring episodes. *Social Psychology Quarterly*, 44, 14–23.

JAHODA, G. (1988) Critical notes and reflections on 'social representations'. *European Journal of Social Psychology*, 18, 195–209.

JELLISON, J.M. & OLIVER, D.F. (1983) Attitude similarity and attraction: An impression management approach. *Personality and Social Psychology Bulletin*, 9, 111–115.

JENSEN-CAMPBELL, L.A., GRAZIANO, W.G. & WEST, S.G. (1995) Dominance, prosocial orientation and females preferences: Do nice guys really finish last? *Journal of Personality and Social Psychology*, 68, 427–440.

JOHNSON, J.T. & JUDD, C.M. (1983) Overlooking the incongruent: Categorization biases in the identification of political statements. *Journal of Personality and Social Psychology*, 45, 978–996.

JOHNSON, R.D. & DOWNING, L.E. (1979) Deindividuation and valence of cues: Effects on prosocial and antisocial behaviour. *Journal of Personality and Social Psychology*, 37, 1532–1538.

JOHNSON, T.J., FEIGENBAUM, R. & WEIBY, M. (1964) Some determinants and consequences of the teacher's perception of causation. *Journal of Experimental Psychology*, 55, 237–246.

JONES, E.E. & DAVIS, K.E. (1965) From acts to dispositions: The attribution process in person perception. In L. Berkowitz (Ed.), *Advances in Experimental Social Psychology* (Volume 2). New York: Academic Press.

JONES, E.E., DAVIS, K.E. & GERGEN, K. (1961) Role playing variations and their informational value for person perception. *Journal of Abnormal and Social Psychology*, 63, 302–310.

JONES, E.E. & NISBETT, R.E. (1971) *The Actor and the Observer: Divergent Perceptions of the Causes of Behaviour*. Morristown, NJ: General Learning Press.

JUDD, C.M. & PARK, B. (1988) Out-group homogeneity: Judgements of variability at the individual and group levels. *Journal of Personality and Social Psychology*, 54, 778–788.

KARLINS, M., COFFMAN, T.L. & WALTERS, G. (1969) On the fading of social stereotypes: Studies in three generations of college students. *Journal of Personality and Social Psychology*, 13, 1–16.

KATZ, D. & BRALY, K. (1933) Racial stereotypes of one hundred college students. *Journal of Abnormal and Social Psychology*, 28, 280–290.

KAUFMAN, J. & ZIGLER, E. (1987) Do abused children become abused parents? *American Journal of Orthopsychiatry*, 57, 186–192.

KELLEY, H.H. (1967) Attribution theory in social psychology. In D. Levine (Ed.), *Nebraska Symposium on Motivation* (Volume 15). Lincoln, NE: Nebraska University Press.

KELLEY, H.H. (1972) Causal schemata and the attribution process. In E.E. Jones, D.E. Kanouse, H.H. Kelley, S. Valins & B. Weiner (Eds.), *Attribution: Perceiving the Causes of Behaviour*. Morristown, NJ: General Learning Press.

KELLEY, H.H. (1983) Perceived causal structures. In J.M.F. Jaspars, F.D. Fincham & M. Hewstone (Eds.), *Attribution Theory and Research: Conceptual, Developmental and Social Dimensions*. London: Academic Press.

KELMAN, H. & COHEN, S. (1979) Reduction of international conflict: An interactional approach. In W. Austin & S. Worchel (Eds.), *The Social Psychology of Intergroup Relations*. Monterey, CA: Brooks/Cole.

KELMAN, H. & LAWRENCE, L. (1972) Assignment of responsibility in the case of Lt. Calley: Preliminary report on a national survey. *Journal of Social Issues*, 28, 177–212.

KERCKHOFF, A.C. (1974) The social context of interpersonal attraction. In T.L. Huston (Ed.), *Foundations of Interpersonal Attraction*. New York: Academic Press.

KERCKHOFF, A.C. & DAVIS, K.E. (1962) Value consensus and need complementarity in mate selection. *American Sociological Review*, 27, 295–303.

KESSLER, R.C. & ESSEX, M. (1982) Marital status and depression: The importance of coping resources. *Social Forces*, 61, 484–507.

KESTENBAUM, G.I. & WEINSTEIN, L. (1985) Personality, psychopathology and developmental issues in males adolescent video game use. *Journal of the American Academy of Child Psychiatry*, 24, 325–337.

KILHAM, W. & MANN, L. (1974) Level of destructive obedience as a function of transmitter and executant roles in the Milgram obedience paradigm. *Journal of Personality and Social Psychology*, 29, 696–702.

KINGDON, J.W. (1967) Politicians' beliefs about voters. *American Political Science Review*, 61, 137–145.

KIRKPATRICK, S.A. & LOCKE, E.A. (1991) Leadership: Do traits matter? *Academy of Management Executives*, 5, 48–60.

KITZINGER, C. & COYLE, A. (1995) Lesbian and gay couples: Speaking of difference. *The Psychologist*, 8, 64–69.

KOLTZ, C. (1983) Scapegoating. *Psychology Today*, December, 68–69.

KREBS, D. & BLACKMAN, R. (1988) *Psychology: A First Encounter*. New York: Harcourt Brace Jovanovich.

KREMER, J.F. & STEPHENS, L. (1983) Attributions and arousal as mediators of mitigation's effect on retaliation. *Journal of Personality and Social Psychology*, 45, 335–343.

KULIK, J.A. & BROWN, R. (1979) Frustration, attribution of blame and aggression. *Journal of Experimental Social Psychology*, 15, 183–194.

KULIK, J.A. & MAHLER, H.I.M. (1989) Stress and affiliation in a hospital setting: Pre-operative roommate preferences. *Personality and Social Psychology Bulletin*, 15, 183–193.

LANG, K. & LANG, G.E. (1961) *Collective Dynamics*. New York: Thomas Y. Crowell Co.

LANGLOIS, J. & ROGGMAN, L. (1994) Attractive faces are only average. *Psychological Science*, 1, 115–121.

LANGLOIS, J., ROGGMAN, L., CASEY, R., RITTER, J., RIESER-DANNER, L. & JENKINS, Y. (1987) Infant preferences for attractive faces: Rudiments of a stereotype. *Developmental Psychology*, 22, 363–369.

LANGLOIS, J., ROGGMAN, L. & RISER-DANNER, L. (1990) Infants' differential social responses to attractive and unattractive faces. *Developmental Psychology*, 26, 153–159.

LARSEN, K.S. (1974) Conformity in the Asch experiment. *Journal of Social Psychology*, 94, 303–304.

LARSEN, K.S., TRIPLETT, J.S., BRANT, W.D. & LANGENBERG, D. (1979) Collaborator status, subject characteristics and conformity in the Asch paradigm. *Journal of Social Psychology*, 108, 259–263.

LATANÉ, B. & DARLEY, J.M. (1968) Group inhibitions of bystander intervention in emergencies. *Journal of Personality and Social Psychology*, 10, 215–221.

LATANÉ, B., NIDA, S. & WILLIAMS, D.W. (1981) The effects of group size on helping behaviour. In J.P. Rushton & R.M. Sorrentino (Eds.), *Altruism and Helping Behaviour*. Hillsdale, NJ: Erlbaum.

LATANÉ, B. & RODIN, J. (1969) A lady in distress: Inhibiting effects of friends and strangers on bystander intervention. *Journal of Experimental Social Psychology*, 5, 189–202.

LAU, R.R. & RUSSELL, D. (1980) Attributions in the sports pages. *Journal of Personality and Social Psychology*, 39, 29–38.

LE BON, G. (1879) *The Crowd: A Study of the Popular Mind*. London: Unwin.

LEA, M. & SPEARS, R. (1995) Love at first byte: Relationships conducted over electronic systems. In J.T. Wood & S. Duck (Eds.), *Understanding Relationship Processes 6: Understudied Relationships: Off the Beaten Track*. Thousand Oaks, CA: Sage.

LEA, S.E.G. (1984) *Instinct, Environment and Behaviour*. London: Methuen.

LEE, A. (1996) St. Helena study shows benefit of television. *The Times*, August 3, 7.

LEE, A.M. & HUMPHREY, N.D. (1943) *Race Riot*. New York: Holt, Rinehart & Winston.

LEE, L. (1984) Sequences in separation: A framework for investigating endings of the personal (romantic) relationship. *Journal of Social and Personal Relationships*, 1, 49–74.

LEFKOWITZ, M.M., ERON, L.D., WALDER, L.O. & HUESMANN, L.R. (1972) Television violence and child aggression: A follow-up study. In G.A. Comstock & E.A. Rubenstein (Eds.), *Television and Social Behaviour, Volume 3. Television and Adolescent Aggressiveness*. Washington, DC: US Government Printing Office.

LEVINGER, G. (1980) Toward the analysis of close relationships. *Journal of Experimental Social Psychology*, 16, 510–544.

LEVY, B. & LANGER, E. (1994) Ageing free from negative stereotypes: Successful memory in China and among the American deaf. *Journal of Personality and Social Psychology*, 66, 989–997.

LEWIN, K., LIPPITT, R. & WHITE, R. (1939) Patterns of aggressive behaviour in experimentally created 'social climates'. *Journal of Social Psychology*, 10, 271–299.

LEWIS, M. & ROWE, D. (1994) Good news. Bad news. *The Psychologist*, 7, 157–160.

LEYENS, J.P. & CODOL, J.P. (1988) Social cognition. In M. Hewstone, W. Stroebe, J.P. Codol & G.M. Stephenson (Eds.), *Introduction to Social Psychology*. Oxford: Blackwell.

LEYENS, J.P. & DARDENNE, B. (1996) Basic concepts and approaches in social cognition. In M. Hewstone, W. Stroebe & G.M. Stephenson (Eds.), *Introduction to Social Psychology* (2nd edition). Oxford: Blackwell.

LIEBERT, R.M. & BARON, R.A. (1972) Some immediate effects of televised violence on children's behaviour. *Developmental Psychology*, 6, 469–475.

LIEBERT, R.M. & SPRAFKIN, J. (1988) *The Early Window: Effects of Television on Children and Youth*. New York: Pergamon Press.

LIKERT, R. (1961) *New Patterns of Management*. New York: McGraw-Hill.

LINVILLE, P.W., FISCHER, G.W. & SALOVEY, P. (1989) Perceived distributions of the characteristics of in-group and out-group members: Empirical evidence and a computer simulation. *Journal of Personality and Social Psychology*, 57, 165–188.

LIPPMANN, W. (1922) *Public Opinion*. New York: Harcourt.

LLOYD, P., MAYES, A., MANSTEAD, A.S.R., MEUDELL, P.R. & WAGNER, H.L. (1984) *Introduction to Psychology – An Integrated Approach*. London: Fontana.

LOFTUS, G.A. & LOFTUS, E.F. (1983) *Mind at Play: The Psychology of Video Games*. New York: Basic Books.

LORENZ, K.Z. (1966) *On Aggression*. London: Methuen.

LOWE, G. (1994) The mating game. *The Psychologist*, 7, 225.

LYKKEN, D.T. & TELLEGREN, A. (1993) Is human mating adventitious or the result of lawful choice?: A twin study of mate selection. *Journal of Personality and Social Psychology*, 65, 56–68.

MAJOR, B. (1980) Information acquisition and attribution processes. *Journal of Personality and Social Psychology*, 39, 1010–1023.

MALLICK, S.K. & McCANDLESS, B.R. (1966) A study of catharsis of aggression. *Journal of Personality and Social Psychology*, 4, 591–596.

MANN, L. (1969) *Social Psychology*. New York: Wiley.

MANN, L. (1981) The baiting crowd in episodes of threatened suicide. *Journal of Personality and Social Psychology*, 41, 703–709.

MASLACH, C., STAPP, J. & SANTEE, R.T. (1985) Individuation: Conceptual analysis and assessment. *Journal of Personality and Social Psychology*, 49, 729–738.

MATTHEWS, R. (1997) Bad news poses health threat to TV audience. *The Sunday Telegraph*, March 30, 3.

MAYKOVICH, M.K. (1975) Correlates of racial prejudice. *Journal of Personality and Social Psychology*, 32, 1014–1020.

McARTHUR, L.A. (1972) The how and why of why: Some determinants and consequences of causal attribution. *Journal of Personality and Social Psychology*, 22, 171–193.

McCAULEY, C. & STITT, C.L. (1978) An individual and quantitative measure of stereotypes. *Journal of Personality and Social Psychology*, 36, 929–940.

McGHEE, P. (1969) Make or break. *Psychology Review*, 2, 27–30.

McGOVERN, L.P. (1976) Dispositional social anxiety and helping behaviour under three conditions of threat. *Journal of Personality*, 44, 84–97.

McGUIRE, W.J. (1969) The nature of attitudes and attitude change. In G. Lindzey & E. Aronson (Eds.), *Handbook of Social Psychology, Volume 3* (2nd edition). Reading, MA: Addison-Wesley.

McILROY, A.J. (1994) Screen test for children of St. Helena. *The Daily Telegraph*, September, 19, 9.

MEEUS, W.H.J & RAAIJMAKERS, Q.A.W. (1986) Administrative obedience: Carrying out orders to use psychological-administrative violence. *European Journal of Social Psychology*, 16, 311–324.

MEGARGEE, E.I. (1966) Uncontrolled and overcontrolled personality types in extreme antisocial aggression. *Psychological Monographs: General and Applied* (Whole No. 611).

MEGARGEE, E.I. & MENDELSOHN, G.A. (1962) A cross validation of twelve MMPI indices of hostility and control. *Journal of Abnormal and Social Psychology*, 65, 431–438.

MEREI, F. (1949) Group leadership and institutionalisation. *Human Relations*, 2, 18–30.

MEYER, J.P. & PEPPER, S. (1977) Need compatibility and marital adjustment in young married couples. *Journal of Personality and Social Psychology*, 35, 331–342.

MICHELINI, R.L. & SNODGRASS, S.R. (1980) Defendant characteristics and juridic decisions. *Journal of Research in Personality*, 14, 340–350.

MIDGLEY, C. (1998) TV violence has little impact on children, study finds. *The Times*, 12 January, 5.

MIELL, D. (1990) Issues in social psychology. In I. Roth (Ed.), *Introduction to Psychology* (Volume 2). Hove: Erlbaum/Open University.

MIKULA, G. (1994) Perspective-related defferences in interpretations of injustice by victims and victimizers: A test with close relationships. In M.J. Lerner & G. Mikula (Eds.), *Injustice in Close Relationships: Entitlement and the Affectional Bond*. New York: Plenum.

MILAVSKY, J.R., KESSLER, R.C., STIPP, H. & RUBENS, W.S. (1982) *Television and Aggression: A Panel Study*. New York: Academic Press.

MILGRAM, S. (1963) Behavioural study of obedience. *Journal of Abnormal and Social Psychology*, 67, 391–398.

MILGRAM, S. (1964) Issues in the study of obedience: A reply to Baumrind. *American Psychologist*, 19, 848–852.

MILGRAM, S. (1965) Liberating effects of group pressure. *Journal of Personality and Social Psychology*, 1, 127–134.

MILGRAM, S. (1974) *Obedience to Authority*. New York: Harper & Row.

MILGRAM, S. (1992) *The Individual in a Social World* (2nd edition). New York: McGraw-Hill.

MILGRAM, S. & TOCH, H. (1969) Collective behaviour: Crowds and social movements. In G. Lindzey & E. Aronson (Eds.), *Handbook of Social Psychology* (Volume 4). Reading, MA: Addison-Wesley.

MILLER, D.T. & ROSS, M. (1975) Self-serving biases in the attribution of causality: Fact or fiction? *Psychological Bulletin*, 82, 213–225.

MILLER, J.G. (1984) Culture and the development of everyday social explanation. *Journal of Personality and Social Psychology*, 46, 961–978.

MILLER, N.E. (1941) The frustration–aggression hypothesis. *Psychological Review*, 48, 337–342

MILLER, N.E. & DOLLARD, J. (1941) *Social Learning and Imitation*. New Haven, CT: Yale University Press.

MILLS, J. & CLARK, M.S. (1980) Exchange in communal relationships. Unpublished manuscript.

MILNER, D. (1996) Children and racism: Beyond the value of the dolls. In W.P. Robinson (Ed.), *Social Groups and Identities*. Oxford: Butterworth/Heineman.

MILNER, D. (1997) Racism and childhood identity. *The Psychologist*, 10, 123–125.

MINARD, R.D. (1952) Race relations in the Pocohontas coalfield. *Journal of Social Issues*, 8, 29–44.

MITA, T.H., DERMER, M. & KNIGHT, J. (1977) Reversed facial images and the mere exposure hypothesis. *Journal of Personality and Social Psychology*, 35, 597–601.

MOGHADDAM, F.M., TAYLOR, D.M. & WRIGHT, S.C. (1993) *Social Psychology in Cross-cultural Perspective*. New York: W.H. Freeman & Co.

MORELAND, R.L. & ZAJONC, R.B. (1982) Exposure effects in person perception: Familiarity, similarity, and attraction. *Journal of Experimental Social Psychology*, 18, 395–415.

MORLAND, J. (1970) A comparison of race awareness in northern and southern children. In M. Goldschmid (Ed.), *Black Americans and White Racism*. Monterey, CA: Brooks/Cole.

MOSCOVICI, S. (1961) *La Psychoanalyse: Son Image et Son Public*. Paris: Presses Universitaires de France.

MOSCOVICI, S. (1976) *La Psychoanalyse: Son Image et Son Public* (2nd edition). Paris: Presses Universitaires de France.

MOSCOVICI, S. (1981) On social representations. In J.P. Forgas (Ed.), *Social Cognition: Perspectives on Everyday Understanding*. London: Academic Press.

MOSCOVICI, S. (1984) The phenomenon of social representations. In R.M. Farr & S. Moscovici (Eds.), *Social Representations*. Cambridge: Cambridge University Press.

MOSCOVICI, S. & FAUCHEUX, C. (1972) Social influence, conforming bias and the study of active minorities. In L. Berkowitz (Ed.), *Advances in Experimental Social Psychology* (Volume 6). New York: Academic Press.

MOSCOVICI, S. & HEWSTONE, M. (1983) Social representations and social explanations: From the 'naive' to the 'amateur' scientist. In M. Hewstone (Ed.), *Attribution Theory: Social and Functional Extensions*. Oxford: Blackwell.

MOSCOVICI, S. & LAGE, E. (1976) Studies in social influence III: Majority versus minority influence in a group. *European Journal of Social Psychology*, 6, 149–174.

MOYER, K.E. (1976) *The Psychobiology of Aggression*. New York: Harper & Row.

MULLEN, B. (1983) Operationalising the effect of the group on the individual: A self-attentive perspective. *Journal of Experimental Social Psychology*, 19, 295–322.

MULLEN, B. & JOHNSON, C. (1990) Distinctiveness-based illusory correlations and stereotyping: A meta-analytic integration. *British Journal of Social Psychology*, 29, 11–28.

MUMMENDEY, A. (1996) Aggressive behaviour. In M. Hewstone, W. Stroebe & G.M. Stephenson (Eds.), *Introduction to Social Psychology* (2nd edition). Oxford: Blackwell.

MUMMENDEY, A. & OTTEN, S. (1989) Perspective specific differences in the segmentation and evaluation of aggressive interaction sequences. *European Journal of Social Psychology*, 19, 23–40.

MURSTEIN, B.I. (1972) Physical attractiveness and marital choice. *Journal of Personality and Social Psychology*, 22, 8–12.

MURSTEIN, B.I. (1976) The stimulus-value-role theory of marital choice. In H. Grunebaum & J. Christ (Eds.), *Contemporary Marriage: Structures, Dynamics and Therapy*. Boston: Little, Brown.

MURSTEIN, B.I. (1987) A clarification and extension of the SVR theory of dyadic parting. *Journal of Marriage and the Family*, 49, 929–933.

MURSTEIN, B.I. & MacDONALD, M.G. (1983) The relation of 'exchange orientation' and 'commitment' scales to marriage adjustment. *International Journal of Psychology*, 18, 297–311.

MURSTEIN, B.I., MacDONALD, M.G. & CERETO, M. (1977) A theory of the effect of exchange orientation on marriage and friendship. *Journal of Marriage and the Family*, 39, 543–548.

NAHEMOW, L. & LAWTON, M.P. (1975) Similarity and propinquity in a friendship formation. *Journal of Personality and Social Psychology*, 32, 205–213.

NAPOLITAN, D.A. & GOETHALS, G.R. (1979) The attribution of friendliness. *Journal of Experimental Social Psychology*, 15, 105–113.

NATIONAL INSTITUTE OF MENTAL HEALTH (1982) *Television and Behaviour: Ten Years of Scientific Progress and Implications for the Eighties* (Volume 1). Washington, DC: US Government Printing Office.

NEMETH, C. & WACHTLER, J. (1973) Consistency and modification of judgement. *Journal of Experimental Social Psychology*, 9, 65–79.

NEWCOMB, T.M. (1943) *Personality and Social Change*. New York: Holt, Rinehart & Winston.

NEWCOMB, T.M. (1953) An approach to the study of communication. *Psychological Review*, 60, 393–404.

NEWCOMB, T.M. (1961) *The Acquaintanceship Proces*. New York: Holt, Rinehart & Winston.

NEWCOMB, T.M. (1978) The acquaintance process: Looking mainly backwards. *Journal of Personality and Social Psychology*, 36, 1075–1083.

NEWSON, E. (1994) Video violence and the protection of children. *Psychology Review*, 1, 2–6.

NIAS, D.B.K. (1979) Marital choice: Matching or complementation? In M. Cook & G. Wilson (Eds.), *Love and Attraction*. New York: Pergamon Press.

NICHOLSON, J. (1977) *Habits*. London: Macmillan

NISBETT, R.E. & BORGIDA, E. (1975) Attribution and the psychology of prediction. *Journal of Personality and Social Psychology*, 32, 923–943.

NUTTIN, J.M. (1987) Affective consequences of mere ownership: The name-letter effect in twelve European languages. *European Journal of Social Psychology*, 17, 381–402.

NYDEGGER, R.V. (1975) Information processing complexity and leadership status. *Journal of Experimental Social Psychology*, 11, 317–328.

OAKES, P.J., HASLAM, S.A. & TURNER, J.C. (1994) *Stereotyping and Social Reality*. Oxford: Blackwell.

O'NEILL, S. (1996) A little kindness goes a long way. *The Daily Telegraph*, August 31, 1.

OPTON, E.M. (1973) 'It never happened and besides they deserved it.' In W.E. Henry & N. Sanford (Eds.), *Sanctions for Evil*. San Francisco: Jossey-Bass.

ORNE, M.T. & HOLLAND, C.C. (1968) On the ecological validity of laboratory deceptions. *International Journal of Psychiatry*, 6, 282–293.

ORUM, A.L. (1972) *Black Students in Protest: A Study of the Origins of the Black Student Movement*. Washington, DC: American Sociological Association.

OWUSU-BEMPAH, J. & HOWITT, D. (1994) Racism and the psychological textbook. *The Psychologist*, 7, 163–166.

PANTIN, H.M. & CARVER, C.S. (1982) Induced competence and the bystander effect. *Journal of Applied Social Psychology*, 12, 100–111.

PAPASTAMOU, S. (1979) Strategies d'influence minoritaires et majoritaires. Unpublished doctoral dissertation. Paris: Ecole des Hautes Etudes en Sciences Sociales.

PARKE, R.D., BERKOWITZ, L., LEYENS, J.P., WEST, S.G. & SEBASTIAN, R.J. (1977) Some effects of violent and non-violent movies on the behaviour of juvenile delinquents. In L. Berkowitz (Ed.), *Advances in Experimental Social Psychology* (Volume 10). New York: Academic Press.

PATTERSON, G. (1986) Performance models for anti-social boys. *American Psychologist*, 41, 432–444.

PENNINGTON, D.C. (1986) *Essential Social Psychology*. London: Edward Arnold.

PENROD, S. (1983) *Social Psychology*. Englewood Cliffs, NJ: Prentice-Hall.

PERRET, D.J., MAY, K.A. & YOSHIKAWA, S. (1994) Facial shape and judgements of female attractiveness. *Nature*, 368, 239–242.

PERRIN, S. & SPENCER, C. (1980) The Asch effect – A child of its time? *Bulletin of the British Psychological Society*, 33, 405–407.

PERRIN, S. & SPENCER, C. (1981) Independence or conformity in the Asch experiment as a reflection of cultural and situational factors. *British Journal of Social Psychology*, 20, 205–209.

PETTIGREW, T.F. (1958) Personality and sociocultural factors in intergroup attitudes: A cross-national comparison. *Journal of Conflict Resolution*, 2, 29–42.

PHILLIPS, D.P. (1986) National experiments on the effects of mass media violence on fatal aggression: Strengths and weaknesses of a new approach. In L. Berkowitz (Ed.), *Advances in Experimental Social Psychology* (Volume 19). New York: Academic Press.

PILIAVIN, I.M., RODIN, J. & PILIAVIN, J.A. (1969) Good samaritanism: An underground phenomenon? *Journal of Personality and Social Psychology*, 13, 289–299.

PILIAVIN, J.A., DOVIDIO, J.F., GAERTNER, S.L. & CLARK, R.D. (1981) *Emergency Intervention*. New York: Academic Press.

PILIAVIN, J.A. & PILIAVIN, I.M. (1972) Effects of blood on reactions to a victim. *Journal of Personality and Social Psychology*, 23, 353–362.

PINEO, P.C. (1961) Disenchantment in the later years of marriage. *Journal of Marriage and Family Living*, 23, 3–11.

PRENTICE-DUNN, S. & ROGERS, R.W. (1982) Effects of public and private self-awareness on deindividuation and aggression. *Journal of Personality and Social Psychology*, 43, 503–513.

PRENTICE-DUNN, S. & ROGERS, R.W. (1983) Deindividuation in aggression. In R.G. Geen & E.I. Donnerstein (Eds.), *Aggression: Theoretical and Empirical Reviews* (Volume 2). New York: Academic Press.

PRICE, R.A. & VANDENBERG, S.G. (1979) Matching for physical attractiveness in married couples. *Personality and Social Psychology Bulletin*, 5, 398–400.

PRINGLE, M.L. KELLMER (1986) *The Needs of Children* (3rd edition). London: Hutchinson.

PUSHKIN, I. & VENESS, T. (1973) The development of racial awareness and prejudice in children. In P. Watson (Ed.), *Psychology and Race*. Harmondsworth: Penguin.

QUATTRONE, G.A. (1982) Overattribution and unit formation: When behaviour engulfs the person. *Journal of Personality and Social Psychology*, 42, 593–607.

QUATTRONE, G.A. (1986) On the perception of a group's variability. In S. Worchel & W. Austin (Eds.), *The Psychology of Intergroup Relations* (Volume 2). New York: Nelson-Hall.

RADECKI, T. (1989) On picking good television entertainment. *NCTV News*, 10, 5.

RAPER, A.F. (1933) *The Tragedy of Lynching*. Chapel Hill, NC: University of North Carolina Press.

RATHUS, S.A. (1991) *Psychology* (4th edition). New York: Holt Rinehart & Winston.

RAZRAN, G. (1950) Ethnic dislikes and stereotypes: A laboratory study. *Journal of Abnormal and Social Psychology*, 45, 7–27.

REBER, A.S. (1985) *The Penguin Dictionary of Psychology*. Harmondsworth: Penguin.

REGAN, D.T. & TOTTEN, J. (1975) Empathy and attribution: Turning observers into actors. *Journal of Personality and Social Psychology*, 32, 850–856.

REICH, B. & ADCOCK, C. (1976) *Values, Attitudes and Behaviour Change*. London: Methuen.

REICHER, S.D. (1984) The St. Paul's riot: An explanation of the limits of crowd action in terms of a social identity model. *European Journal of Social Psychology*, 14, 1–21.

RICE, R.W. (1978) Construct validity of the esteem for least preferred coworker (LPC) scale. *Psychological Bulletin*, 85, 1199–1237.

ROHLFING, M. (1995) 'Doesn't anybody stay in one place any more?': An exploration of the understudied phenomenon of long-distance relationships. In J.T. Wood & S. Duck (Eds.), *Understanding Relationship Processes 6: Understanding Relationships: Off the Beaten Track*. Thousand Oaks, CA: Sage.

ROKEACH, M. (1948) Generalised mental rigidity as a factor in ethnocentrism. *Journal of Abnormal and Social Psychology*, 43, 254–278.

ROKEACH, M. (1960) *The Open and Closed Mind*. New York: Basic Books.

ROSE, P. & PLATZER, H. (1993) Confronting prejudice. *Nursing Times*, 89, 52–54.

ROSENBAUM, M.E. (1986) The repulsion hypothesis: On the non-development of relationships. *Journal of Personality and Social Psychology*, 51, 1156–1166.

ROSENTHAL, A.M. (1964) *Thirty-Eight Witnesses*. New York: McGraw-Hill.

ROSENTHAL, R. & ROSNOW, R.L. (1966) *The Volunteer Subject*. New York: Wiley.

ROSS, L. (1977) The intuitive psychologist and his shortcomings. In L. Berkowitz (Ed.), *Advances in Experimental Social Psychology* (Volume 10). New York: Academic Pres.

ROSS, M. & FLETCHER, G.J.O. (1985) Attribution and social perception. In G. Lindzey & E. Aronson (Eds.), *Handbook of Social Psychology, Volume 2* (3rd edition). New York: Random House.

ROWAN, J. (1978) *The Structured Crowd*. London: Davis Poynter.

RUBENSTEIN, C. (1983) The modern art of courtly love. *Psychology Today*, June, 39–49.

RUBIN, Z. (1973) *Liking and Loving*. New York: Holt, Rinehart & Winston.

RUBIN, Z. & McNEIL, E.B. (1983) *The Psychology of Being Human* (3rd edition). London: Harper & Row.

RUNCIMAN, W.G. (1966) *Relative Deprivation and Social Justice*. London: Routledge & Kegan Paul.

RUSBULT, C. (1987) Responses to dissatisfaction in close relationships: The exit–voice–loyalty–neglect model. In D. Perlman & S. Duck (Eds.), *Intimate Relationships: Development, Dynamics and Deterioration*. London: Sage.

SANBONMATSU, D.M., SHAVITT, S., SHERMAN, S.J. & ROSKO-EWOLDSEN, D.R. (1987) Illusory correlation in the perception of performance by self or a salient other. *Journal of Experimental Social Psychology*, 23, 518–543.

SANDE, G.N., GOETHALS, G.R. & RADLOFF, C.E. (1988) Perceiving one's own traits and others': The multifaceted self. *Journal of Personality and Social Psychology*, 54, 13–20.

SANTEE, R. & MASLACH, C. (1982) To agree or not to agree: Personal dissent amid social pressure to conform. *Journal of Personality and Social Psychology*, 42, 690–700.

SARTRE, J.P. (1948) *Anti-Semite and Jew*. New York: Shocken.

SAYLES, S.M. (1966) Supervisory style and productivity: Reward and theory. *Personnel Psychology*, 19, 275–286.

155

SCHACHTER, S. (1951) Deviation, rejection and communication. *Journal of Abnormal and Social Psychology*, 46, 190–207.

SCHACHTER, S. (1959) *The Psychology of Affiliation: Experimental Studies of the Sources of Gregariousness.* Stanford, CA: Stanford University Press.

SCHACHTER, S. (1964) The interaction of cognitive and physiological determinants of emotional state. In L. Berkowitz (Ed.), *Advances in Experimental Social Psychology* (Volume 1). New York: Academic Pres.

SCHIFFMAN, R. & WICKLUND, R.A. (1992) The minimal group paradigm and its minimal psychology. *Theory and Psychology*, 2, 29–50.

SCHNEIDER, B.H. (1991) A comparison of skill-building and desensitisation strategies for intervention with aggressive children. *Aggressive Behaviour*, 17, 301–311.

SCHROEDER, D.A., PENNER, L.A., DOVIDIO, J.F. & PILIAVIN, J.A. (1995) *The Psychology of Helping and Altruism: Problems and Puzzles.* New York: McGraw-Hill.

SEARS, D.O. & McCONAHAY, J.B. (1969) Participation in the Los Angeles riot. *Social Problems*, 17, 3–20.

SEARS, D.O., PEPLAU, L.A. & TAYLOR, S.E. (1991) *Social Psychology* (7th edition). Englewood Cliffs, NJ: Prentice-Hall.

SEGAL, M.W. (1974) Alphabet and attraction: An unobtrusive measure of the effect of propinquity in the field setting. *Journal of Personality and Social Psychology*, 30, 654–657.

SELLERI, P., CARUGATI, F. & SCAPPINI, E. (1995) What marks should I give? A model of the organisation of teachers' judgements of their pupils. *European Journal of Psychology of Education*, 10, 25–40.

SHARPE, M. (1994) 30 just watched as drunk yobs did *this* to Sgt. Gary. *The Sun*, April 30, 7.

SHAW, M.E. (1981) *Group Dynamics: The Psychology of Small Group Behaviour.* New York: McGraw-Hill.

SHAW, M.E., ROTHSCHILD, G.H. & STRICKLUND, J.F. (1957) Decision processes in communication nets. *Journal of Abnormal and Social Psychology*, 54, 323–330.

SHELLOW, R. & ROEMER, D.V. (1966) No heaven for 'Hell's Angels'. *Trans-action*, July–August, 12–19.

SHERIDAN, C.L. & KING, R.G. (1972) Obedience to authority with an authentic victim. *Proceedings of the 80th Annual Convention, American Psychological Association, Part 1*, 7, 165–166.

SHERIF, M. (1935) A study of social factors in perception. *Archives of Psychology*, 27, Whole No. 187.

SHERIF, M. (1936) *The Psychology of Social Norms.* New York: Harper & Row.

SHERIF, M. (1966) *Group Conflict and Co-operation: Their Social Psychology.* London: Routledge & Kegan Paul.

SHERIF, M., HARVEY, O.J., WHITE, B.J., HOOD, W.R. & SHERIF, C.W. (1961) *Intergroup Conflict and Co-operation: The Robber's Cave Experiment.* Norman, OK: University of Oklahoma Press.

SHIBUTANI, T. (1966) *Improvised News: A Sociological Study of Rumour.* Indianapolis: Bobbs-Merrill Co.

SHOTLAND, R.L. & HEINOLD, W.D. (1985) Bystander response to arterial bleeding: Helping skills, the decision-making process, and differentiating the helping response. *Journal of Personality and Social Psychology*, 49, 347–356.

SHOTLAND, R.L. & STRAW, M.K. (1976) Bystander response to an assault: When a man attacks a woman. *Journal of Personality and Social Psychology*, 34, 990–999.

SIANN, G. (1985) *Accounting for Aggression – Perspectives on Aggression and Violence.* London: Allen & Unwin.

SIGALL, H. & LANDY, D. (1973) Radiating beauty: Effects of having a physically attractive partner on person perception. *Journal of Personality and Social Psychology*, 28, 218–224.

SILVERMAN, I. (1971) Physical attractiveness and courtship. *Sexual Behaviour*, September, 22–25.

SILVERN, S.B. (1986) Classroom use of video games. *Education Research Quarterly*, 10, 10–16.

SIMS, A.C.P. & GRAY, P. (1993) *The Media, Violence and Vulnerable Viewers.* Document presented to the Broadcasting Group, House of Lords.

SINGER, D. (1989) Children, adolescents, and television – 1989. *Paediatrics*, 83, 445–446.

SINGER, J.E., BRUSH, C.A. & LIBLIN, J.C. (1965) Some aspects of deindividuation: Identification and conformity. *Journal of Experimental Social Psychology*, 1, 356–378.

SISTRUNK, F. & McDAVID, J.W. (1971) Sex variable in conforming behaviour. *Journal of Personality and Social Psychology*, 2, 200–207.

SLAVIN, R.E. (1985) Cooperative learning: Applying contact theory in desegregated schools. *Journal of Social Issues*, 41, 45–62.

SLAVIN, R. & MADDEN, N. (1979) School practices that improve race relations. *American Edcuation Research Journal*, 16, 169–180.

SMELSER, N.J. (1963) *Theory of Collective Behaviour.* New York: The Free Press.

SMITH, P.B. (1995) Social influence processes. In M. Argyle & A.M. Colman (Eds.), *Social Psychology.* London: Longman.

SMITH, P.B. & BOND, M.H. (1993) *Social Psychology Across Cultures: Analysis and Perspectives.* Hemel Hempstead: Harvester Wheatsheaf.

SMITH, P.B. & PETERSON, M.F. (1988) *Leadership, Organisations and Culture.* London: Sage.

SOBER, E. (1992) The evolution of altruism: Correlation, cost and benefit. *Biology and Philosophy*, 7, 177–188.

SOLOMON, M. (1987) Standard issue. *Psychology Today*, December, 30–31.

SOMMER, R. (1969) *Personal Space: The Behavioural Basis of Design.* Englewood Cliffs, NJ: Prentice-Hall.

SORRENTINO, R.M. & FIELD, N. (1986) Emergent leadership over time: The functional value of positive motivation. *Journal of Personality and Social Psychology*, 50, 1091–1099.

SPANIER, G.B. & LEWIS, R.A. (1980) Marital quality: A review of the seventies. *Journal of Marriage and the Family*, 42, 825–840.

SPERLING, H.G. (1946) An experimental study of some psychological factors in judgement. Master's thesis, New School for Social Research.

SPERRY, R.W. (1982) Some effects of disconnecting the cerebral hemispheres. *Science*, 217, 1223–1226.

SPROTT, W.J.H. (1958) *Human Groups.* Harmondsworth: Penguin.

STEPHAN, C.W. & LANGLOIS, J. (1984) Baby beautiful: Adult attributions of infant competence as a function of infant attractiveness. *Child Development*, 55, 576–585.

STEPHAN, W.G. & ROSENFIELD, D. (1978) Effects of desegregation on racial attitudes. *Journal of Personality and Social Psychology*, 36, 795–804.

STERNBERG, R.J. (1986) A triangular theory of love. *Psychological Review*, 93, 119–135.

STERNBERG, R.J. (1988) Triangulating love. In R.J. Sternberg & M.L. Barnes (Eds.), *The Psychology of Love.* New Haven, CT: Yale University Press.

STOGDILL, R.M. (1974) *Handbook of Leadership.* New York: Free Press.

STORMS, M.D. (1973) Videotape and the attribution process: Reversing actors' and observers' points of view. *Journal of Personality and Social Psychology*, 27, 165–175.

STOUFFER, S.A., SUCHMAN, E.A., DeVINNEY, L.C., STARR, S.A. & WILLIAMS, R.M. (1949) *The American Soldier: Adjustment During Army Life* (Volume 1). Princeton, NJ: Princeton University Press.

STRAUS, M., GELLES, R. & STEINMETZ, S. (1980) *Behind Closed Doors: Violence in the American Family.* Garden City, NY: Anchor Press.

SUMNER, W.G. (1906) *Folkways.* Boston: Ginn.

SURREY, D. (1982) 'It's like good training for life'. *Natural History*, 91, 71–83.

TAJFEL, H. (1969) Social and cultural factors in perception. In G. Lindzey & E. Aronson (Eds.), *Handbook of Social Psychology* (Volume 3). Reading, MA: Addison-Wesley.

TAJFEL, H. (Ed.) (1978) *Differentiation Between Social Groups: Studies in the Social Psychology of Intergroup Relations.* London: Academic Press.

TAJFEL, H. & BILLIG, M. (1974) Familiarity and categorization in inter-group behaviour. *Journal of Experimental Social Psychology*, 10, 159–170.

TAJFEL, H., BILLIG, M.G. & BUNDY, R.P. (1971) Social categorization and intergroup behaviour. *European Journal of Social Psychology*, 1, 149–178.

TAJFEL, H. & TURNER, J.C. (1986) The social identity theory of intergroup behaviour. In S. Worchel & W. Austin (Eds.), *Psychology of Intergoup Relations.* Chicago: Nelson-Hall.

TANFORD, S. & PENROD, S. (1984) Social influence model: A formal investigation of research on majority and minority influence proceses. *Psychological Bulletin*, 95, 189–225.

TAVRIS, C. (1993) The mismeasure of woman. *Feminism and Psychology*, 3, 149–168.

TAYLOR, D.M. & PORTER, L.E. (1994) A multicultural view of stereotyping. In W.J. Lonner & R.S. Malpass (Eds.), *Psychology and Culture.* Boston: Allyn & Bacon.

TAYLOR, S.E., PEPLAU, L.A. & SEARS, D.O. (1994) *Social Psychology* (8th edition). Englewood Cliffs, NJ: Prentice-Hall.

TETLOCK, P.E. & LEVI, A. (1982), Attribution bias: On the inconclusiveness of the cognition–motivation debate. *Journal of Experimental Social Psychology*, 18, 68–88.

THE DAILY SPORT (1995) Sex pest battler bashed. May 5, 7.

THIBAUT, J.W. & KELLEY, H.H. (1959) *The Social Psychology of Groups*. New York: Wiley.

TOCH, H. (1980) *Violent Men* (revised edition). Cambridge, MA: Schenkman.

TRIVERS, R.L. (1971) The evolution of reciprocal altruism. *Quarterly Review of Biology*, 46, 35–57.

TROWLER, P. (1988) *Investigating the Media*. London: Unwin Hyman Limited.

TURNER, J.C. (1991) *Social Influence*. Milton Keynes: Open University Press.

TURNER, R.H. (1964) Collective behaviour. In R.E.L. Faris (Ed.), *Handbook of Modern Sociology*. Chicago: Rand McNally.

TURNER, R.H. & KILLIAN, L.M. (1957) *Collective Behaviour*. Englewood Cliffs, NJ: Prentice-Hall.

TURNER, R.H. & KILLIAN, L.M. (1972) *Collective Behaviour* (revised edition). Englewood Cliffs, NJ: Prentice-Hall.

TYERMAN, A. & SPENCER, C. (1983) A critical test of the Sherifs' Robber's Cave experiment: Intergroup competition and co-operation between groups of well-acquainted individuals. *Small Group Behaviour*, 14, 515–531.

VAN AVERMAET, E. (1996) Social influence in small groups. In M. Hewstone, W. Stroebe & G.M. Stephenson (Eds.), *Introduction to Social Psychology* (2nd edition). Oxford: Blackwell.

VANNEMAN, R.D. & PETTIGREW, T.F. (1972) Race and relative deprivation in the urban United States. *Race*, 13, 461–486.

VITELLI, R. (1988) The crisis issue reassessed: An empirical analysis. *Basic and Applied Social Psychology*, 9, 301–309.

VIVIAN, J. & BROWN, R. (1995) Prejudice and intergroup conflict. In M. Argyle & A.M. Colman (Eds.), *Social Psychology*. London: Longman.

VIVIAN, J., BROWN, R.J. & HEWSTONE, M. (1994) Changing attitudes through intergroup contact: The effects of membership salience. Unpublished manuscript, Universities of Kent and Wales, Cardiff.

WADE, C. & TAVRIS, C. (1993) *Psychology* (3rd edition). New York: HarperCollins.

WALSTER, E.M. (1966) The assignment of responsibility for an accident. *Journal of Personality and Social Psychology*, 5, 508–516.

WALSTER, E.M., ARONSON, E. & ABRAHAMS, D. (1966) On increasing the persuasiveness of a low prestige communicator. *Journal of Experimental Social Psychology*, 2, 325–342.

WARD, S.H. & BRAUN, J. (1972) Self-esteem and racial preference in Black children. *American Journal of Orthopsychiatry*, 42(4), 644–647.

WARK, P. & BALL, S. (1996) Death of innocence. *The Sunday Times*, June 23, 12.

WATSON, R.J. (1973) Investigation into deindividuation using a cross-cultural survey technique. *Journal of Personality & Social Psychology*, 25, 342–345.

WEARY, G. & ARKIN, R.M. (1981) Attributional self-presentation. In J.H. Harvey, W.J. Ickes & R.F. Kidd (Eds.), *New Directions in Attributional Research* (Voulme 3). Hillsdale, NJ: Erlbaum.

WEATHERLEY, D. (1961) Anti-semitism and expression of fantasy aggression. *Journal of Abnormal and Social Psychology*, 62, 454–457.

WEGNER, D.M., BENEL, D.C. & RILEY, E.N. (1976) Changes in perceived inter-trait correlations as a function of experience with persons. Paper presented at the meeting of the SouthWestern Psychological Association, Alberquerque (April).

WEGNER, D.M. & VALLACHER, R.R. (1976) *Implicit Psychology: An Introduction to Social Cognition*. Oxford: Oxford University Press.

WEINER, B. (1986) *An Attributional Theory of Motivation and Emotion*. New York: Springer-Verlag.

WEINER, B. (1992) *Human Motivation: Metaphors, Theories and Research*. Newbury Park, CA: Sage.

WEINER, M.J. & WRIGHT, F.E. (1973) Effects of undergoing arbitrary discrimination upon subsequent attitudes toward a minority group. *Journal of Applied Social Psychology*, 3, 94–102.

WELLS, G.L. & HARVEY, J.H. (1977) Do people use consensus information in making causal attributions? *Journal of Personality and Social Psychology*, 35, 279–293.

WELLS, P.A., WILLMOTH, T. & RUSSELL, R.J.H. (1995) Does fortune favour the bald?: Psychological correlates of hair loss in males. *British Journal of Psychology*, 86, 337–344.

WETHERELL, M. (1982) Cross-cultural studies of minimal groups: Implications for the social identity theory of intergroup relations. In H. Tajfel (Ed.), *Social Identity and Intergroup Relations*. Cambridge: Cambridge University Pres.

WHITE, G.L. (1980) Physical attractiveness and courtship progress. *Journal of Personality and Social Psychology*, 39, 660–668.

WHYTE, W.W. (1956) *The Organization Man*. New York: Simon and Schuster.

WIEGMAN, O., KUTTSCHREUTER, M & BARDA, B. (1992) A longitudinal study of the effects of television viewing on aggressiveness and prosocial behaviours. *British Journal of Social Psychology*, 31, 147–164.

WILDER, D.A. (1977) Perceptions of groups, size of opposition and influence. *Journal of Experimental Social Psychology*, 13, 253–268.

WILDER, D.A. (1984) Intergroup contact: The typical member and the exception to the rule. *Journal of Experimental Social Psychology*, 20, 177–194.

WILLIAMS, K.B. & WILLIAMS, K.D. (1983) Social inhibition and asking for help: The effects of number, strength and immediacy of potential help givers. *Journal of Personality and Social Psychology*, 44, 67–77.

WILLIAMS, T.M. (Ed.) (1986) *The Impact of Television: A National Experiment in Three Communities*. New York: Academic Press.

WILLIS, R.H. (1963) Two dimensions of conformity–nonconformity. *Sociometry*, 26, 499–513.

WILNER, D.M., WALKLEY, R. & COOK, S.W. (1955) *Human Relations in Interracial Housing: A Study of the Contact Hypothesis*. Minneapolis: University of Minnesota Press.

WILSON, E.O. (1978) *On Human Nature*. Cambridge, MA: Harvard University Press.

WINCH, R.F. (1958) *Mate Selections: A Study of Complementary Needs*. New York: Harper.

WINEBERG, H. (1994) Marital reconciliation in the United States: Which couples are successful? *Journal of Marriage and the Family*, 56, 80–88.

WOLPE, J. (1958) *Psychotherapy by Reciprocal Inhibition*. Stanford, CA: Stanford University Press.

WOOD, J.T. & DUCK, S. (1995) *Understanding Relationship Processes 6: Understudied Relationships: Off the Beaten Track*. Thousand Oaks, CA: Sage.

WOOD, W., LUNDGREN, S., OUELLETTE, J.A., BUSCEME, S. & BLACKSTONE, T. (1994) Minority influence: A meta-analytic review of social influence processes. *Psychological Bulletin*, 115, 323–345.

WORCHEL, S., COOPER, J. & GOETHALS, G.R. (1988) *Understanding Social Psychology* (4th edition). Chicago: The Dorsey Press.

WYER, R.S. (1966) Effects of incentive to perform well, group attraction and group acceptance on conformity in a judgement task. *Journal of Personality and Social Psychology*, 4, 21–27.

YOUNG, K. (1946) *Handbook of Social Psychology*. London: Kegan Paul.

ZAJONC, R.B. (1968) Attitudinal effects of mere exposure. *Journal of Personality and Social Psychology*, Monograph Supplement 9, Part 2, 1–27.

ZEBROWITZ, L.A. (1990) *Social Perception*. Milton Keynes: Open University Press.

ZILLMAN, D. (1978) Attribution and misattribution of excitatory reactions. In J.H. Harvey, W. Ickes & R.F. Kidd (Eds.), *New Directions in Attribution Research* (Volume 2). New York: Erlbaum.

ZILLMAN, D. (1982) Transfer of excitation in emotional behaviour. In J.T. Cacioppo & R.E. Petty (Eds.), *Social Psychophysiology: A Sourcebook*. New York: Guilford Press.

ZILLMAN, D. & BRYANT, J. (1974) Effect of residual excitation on the emotional response to provocation and delayed aggressive behaviour. *Journal of Personality and Social Psychology*, 30, 782–791.

ZILLMAN, D. & BRYANT, J. (1982) Effects of massive exposure to pornography. In M.N. Malamuth & E. Donnerstein (Eds.), *Pornography and Sexual Aggression*. New York: Academic Press.

ZIMBARDO, P.G. (1969) The human choice: Individuation, reason, and order versus deindividuation, impluse, and chaos. In W.J. Arnold & D. Levine (Eds.), *Nebraska Symposium on Motivation*. Lincoln: University of Nebraska Press.

ZIMBARDO, P.G., BANKS, W.C., CRAIG, H. & JAFFE, D. (1973) A Pirandellian prison: The mind is a formidable jailor. *New York Times Magazine*, April 8th, 38–60.

ZIMBARDO, P.G. & LEIPPE, M. (1991) *The Psychology of Attitude Change and Social Influence*. New York: McGraw-Hill.

ZIMBARDO, P.G. & WEBER, A.L. (1994) *Psychology*. New York: HarperCollins.

INDEX

Page numbers which appear in **bold** refer to definitions and main explanations of particular concepts.

PICTURE CREDITS

The authors and publisher would like to thank the following for their permission to reproduce illustrative material in this book:

Action Images for Figure 3.4 (p.27); **Academic Press, Inc.** for Figure 12.4 (p.117); **Addison Wesley Educational Publishers, Inc.** for Figure 9.4 (p.83) from *Psychology* by P.G. Zimbardo and A.L. Weber. Copyright © 1994 by P.G. Zimbardo and A.L. Weber; **AKG Photo** for Figure 10.2 (p.97); **American Psychological Association** for Figure 11.3 (p.105) and 12.3 (p.114); **Associated Press** for Figure 3.2 (p.25, right) and Figure 12.5 (p.119); **Alfred Bandura, Stanford University** for Figure 13.3 (p.128); **BFI Stills** for Figure 14.1 (p.137); **Phil Callaghan/The Sun** for Figure 12.1 (p.111); **Camera Press Ltd** for Figure 3.1 (p.25, left) and 11.1 (p.101); **Concord Video and Film Council** for Figure 4.1 (p.33); **Corbis Bettman** for Figure 11.2 (p.104); **FLPA © T. Whittaker** for Figure 13.1 (p.124, top); **The Helen Dwight Reid Educational Foundation** for Figure 5.3 (p.44) from *The Journal of Psychology*, 21, 107–22. Published by Heldref Publications, 1319 Eighteenth St, NW, Washington DC 20036–1802. Copyright © 1946; **John Brown Publishing** for Figure 1.2 (p.8, top) and Figure 2.1 (p.13); **Little, Brown & Co.** for Figure 6.2 (p.54); **Macmillan** for Figure 5.2 (p.43) **McGraw-Hill** for Figures 7.1, 7.2 (p.62) and 7.3 (p.63) based on S. Brehm, *Intimate Relationships*, © 1992 and Figure 12.2 (p.113) from Schroeder, *et al.*, *The Psychology of Helping and Altruism*, © 1995; **Alexandra Milgram/Penn State Media Sales** for Figure 9.2 (p.81) and 9.3 (p.82) from the film *Obedience* by Stanley Milgram: **National Film Archive/Ronald Grant Collection** for Figure 13.1 (p.124, bottom); **Private Eye** for Figure 4.2 (p.34), 8.1 (p.69); **Philip Allan Publishers** for Figure 7.4 (p.66); **Pinter & Martin Ltd./HarperCollins Publishers, Inc.** for Figure 9.1 (p.80); **The British Psychological Society** for Figure 5.4 (p.45) first published in *The Psychologist*, the bulletin of the British Psychological Society, 1995, 8(2), p.77. Copyright © The British Psychological Society; **Rex Features/Mike Daines** for Figure 6.3 (p.56); **Stanford University Press** for Figure 5.1 (p.42); Telegraph Colour Library for the figure in Box 14.9 (p.144); **Tony Stone Images/Chip Henderson** for Figure 4.3 (p.36).

The authors and publisher would also like to thank the following for permission to reproduce text extracts:

Blackwell Publishers for Box 2.7 (p.18) from Durkin, K. (1995); *Developmental Social Psychology, From Infancy to Old Age*; **Mark Griffiths** for Box 14.9 (p.144) from *The Psychologist*, 9, 401–407; **Henry Holt & Company, Inc.** for Box 11.4 (p.102), from *Race Riot* by A.M. Lee and N.D. Humphrey, Copyright © 1943 by A.M. Lee and N.D. Humphrey; **Philip Allan Publishers** for Box 13.5 (p.131), from Hollins, C. & Howells, K. (1997) Controlling violent behaviour. *Psychology Review*, 3(3): *Times Newspapers Limited* for Box 14.2 (p.136); **Parliamentary Office of Science and Technology** for Box 14.3 (p.137) from Briefing Note 44; **Routledge** for Box 14.8 (p.143), from Gunter B. and McAleer J.L. (1990) *Children and Television – The One-Eyed Monster?*

Every effort has been made to obtain necessary permission with reference to copyright material. The publishers apologise if inadvertently any sources remain unacknowledged and will be glad to make the necessary arrangements at the earliest opportunity.

Index compiled by Indexing Specialists, Hove, Sussex.